Surfing on the Sea of Faith

The Ethics and Religion of Don Cupitt

Nigel Leaves

Surfing on the Sea of Faith: The Life & Writings of Don Cupitt

Published in 2005 by Polebridge Press, P.O. Box 6144, Santa Rosa, California 95406.

Library of Congress Cataloging-in-Publication Data

Leaves, Nigel, 1958-
    Surfing on the sea of faith : the ethics and religion of Don Cupitt / by Nigel Leaves.
        p. cm.
    Based on the author's thesis (Ph. D.)--Murdoch University, 2001.
    Includes bibliographical references (p.) and index.
    ISBN 0-944344-63-1
    1. Cupitt, Don 2. Church of England--Clergy--Biography. 3. Anglican Communion--England--Clergy--Biography. I. Title.

BX5199.C87L43 2003
230'.3'092--dc22

                                                                2003066354

Surfing on the Sea of Faith

Don Cupitt and family 1989

Don Cupitt and daughter Sally 1971

Don Cupitt and son John 1967

Contents

Preface

Cupitt's detractors ask: "What practical use is non-realism?" "Can it counteract the evil and the inhumanity that is perpetrated in this world?" "What is the faith of the future now that you have deconstructed and reformed Christianity?" "After throwing us into the Void, show us how to get out of it?"

In this Second Volume I will argue that Cupitt's thirty years of writing does not lead to despair and the abandonment of all values. I will show that after many years of finding fault with Christianity he has now turned his attention to reconstructing a viable contemporary faith that is in harmony with both the postmodern world and the original message of Jesus. Moreover, there are many people in Networks such as Sea of Faith who are similarly engaged in creating a faith for the future. Rather than wallow in the Void there is much creative theology and ethical thinking being done by ordinary people.

My thanks once again go to Robert Funk and all at Polebridge Press for their help in the production of this Volume, especially Tom Hall. To those in both the Perth branch of the Sea of Faith Network and those who attended the Sea of Faith in Australia 1st National Conference I am indebted for your ideas and stimulation as we debate new ways of being religious. Likewise, it was wonderful to have Don and Susan Cupitt with us at Wollaston College as we wrestled with his first drafts of *Life, Life*. My wife Julie and my son Sebastian have again been instrumental in helping me get this Volume finished on time. Whilst Sebastian has helped refresh his father by insisting that he take a break for backyard cricket or a round of golf, Julie has kept the coffee mug refilled and gently pressurized me to complete the project.

I dedicate this book to my mother and to the memory of my father, Reginald Arthur Leaves, who died several years ago, but always hoped that I would write a book "some day." His belief in my ability has been realized with the publication of those two books on Don Cupitt.

Nigel Leaves
John Wollaston Theological College
Perth, Western Australia

Introduction

This is the second volume of an analysis and evaluation of the writings of one of the most prolific and original religious experimenters of the postmodern age — Don Cupitt. In Volume 1, *Odyssey on the Sea of Faith*, I mapped out the route Cupitt followed in his rejection of belief in an objective God. I plotted the seven stages of Cupitt's development from his emphasis on negative theology to his latest position, "empty radical humanism." His central concern since 1980 has been to urge people (including his friend the radical Anglican Bishop John Shelby Spong) to "take leave" of belief in that "last sliver of objectivity": the feeling that in religion there is, there must be, something Real "out there" and quite independent of our language.[1] Cupitt has argued that this world is "outsideless," and we are dependent on nothing greater than ourselves. Everything — including ethics, religion, and even God — is pure human invention: "a human creation." Once people rid themselves of that final speck of metaphysical objectivity, he proposes, then the Platonically rooted disciplinary cultures of dependency under which they have groaned for so long (the church, the state, the military, etc.) will be renounced and new ways of living religiously can be created. The questions that Cupitt has raised are both fundamental and challenging: "How, now that the old certainties (including an objective God) have gone, can life be made meaningful for people?" "Can Christianity be reinterpreted in the light of this new situation?" "What kind of religion will be able to create a future for a way of living centered in *this* world?"

In *Odyssey on the Sea of Faith* I characterized Cupitt's response to these questions as an attempt to explore how we might create new ethics and new religion in the Second Axial Age. The phrase "Axial Age" is

1

taken from the German philosopher Karl Jaspers, who used it to describe a period of radical cultural and religious change. The First Axial Age (800–200 B.C.E.) responded to the eternal philosophical questions — "What are we, and what is our world?" — with the ontological dualisms of body and soul, heaven and earth; and mastery of the passions as the path to individual salvation. *This* world was seen as a preparation for a better world elsewhere; and by following the path of faith outlined by a Great Teacher (Jesus, Muhammad, etc.) and defined by one of what we now term the "World Religions," we would find our reward in the here-after. But that all came to an end with the anti-realism of the philosopher Friedrich Nietzsche and the late-modern turn to *this* world in art, culture and science. We are now living in the midst of a Second Axial Age, a groundswell of cultural change that began with the clamor for universal education, the rise of the media and the demythologizing of God. Truth does not come as revelation to special teachers or prophets, but grows out of a constantly evolving public consensus: there are only *our* truths and *anyone* may access them. The world is now *our* world and our language comprehensively describes, differentiates and theorizes it. Thinking is no longer governed by timeless absolutes (realism) but is brought down into time and the flux of human exchange (anti-realism). God is no longer seen as an objective Being, and all god-talk becomes symbolic reflections of our highest ideals and aspirations. Thus new religion and new ethics become anti-realist, post-dogmatic, and post-Christian. To survive in these circumstances, Christianity must transform itself by growing out of the ecclesiastical form with which we are most familiar, and into its final Kingdom form.

In *Odyssey on the Sea of Faith* I argued that the fifteen years since Scott Cowdell's study of Cupitt in *Atheist Priest* have witnessed a sharply increased public interest in exploring new anti-realist ethics and religion. Cupitt himself has pointed the way towards loose networks and democratic associations that are not constrained by demands for orthodoxy. In particular, he views the Sea of Faith Networks as providing settings in which people can and *do* find an opportunity to discuss these sorts of issues *openly*. Cupitt's ideas have been debated not only by the "disaffected Christian intellectuals" or "lapsed churchgoers" predicted by Cowdell, but by humanists, members of diverse religious traditions, and some who have little or no connection with organized religion.

From the previous book's analysis of Cupitt's theological development emerged three central topics: ethics, religion, and the Sea of Faith Networks. These constitute the areas of engagement in this volume. The first two issues, ethics and religion, are the most important, for they have been the central concerns of Cupitt's ongoing thirty-year project. The Sea of Faith Networks, although of lesser theoretical significance, deserve recognition for their practical importance as a sort of unplanned realization of part of his ideas and hopes. The Networks are still evolving, and despite a limited membership — perhaps no more than twenty-five hundred worldwide — they are linked with such theologically progressive groups and networks as the Westar Institute in the United States and SnowStar in Canada. All these networks might reasonably be viewed as part of a loosely interconnected but growing movement that seeks to find a means of expression for religion that is post-dogmatic and welcomes the death of traditional theism.

As I noted in *Odyssey on the Sea of Faith*, Cupitt has variously described the postmodern condition as "living in the Void," embracing "nihilism," "pure fleeting transience," and "Be-ing." Following Richard Rorty, he urges upon us the "very late-twentieth-century lesson" not to "get stuck for life with a single final vocabulary."[2] Recently, the change in *his* language has been from "the nihilistic Void" to an exploration of "Be-ing," yet the vital concern is still the same: how can one live after God? That is, what kind of ethics and religion are possible without belief in an objective, realist God? In short, Cupitt has all along been wrestling with how people might *themselves* create religious and ethical ways of living.

This book is divided into three sections. In the first section I will analyse five phases of Cupitt's ethics. Phase 1, "moral asceticism," covers the early years of Cupitt's development and coincides with his espousal of non-realism. The non-realist view of God derives mainly from the philosopher Immanuel Kant, and sees God as a guiding spiritual ideal. In the old language, God is not the Efficient Cause of all, but remains the Final Cause or ideal goal; he doesn't push, but may have great pulling power. Your God is an object of the same kind as your dream, your hope, your guiding star, and "the pearl of great price." Thus God can be defined as "the ideal which inspires continual discontent and moral aspiration." If God is a regulative ideal that distinguishes what ought to be from what is, then Christian ethics supplies guiding ideals that regulate how we should live. Cupitt identifies four ethical principles from the life of Jesus — "truth," "disinterestedness," "creativity," and "love." By adopting these moral principles, the believer will be inwardly changed and guided through the fires of nihilism to create new social ethics. The Christian faith is thus transformed into a project for a new humanity in a world that has "come of age."

Phase 2, "the new christian ethics," appears in 1988 with the book bearing that title. Cupitt describes how it is possible to create Christian ethics in the light of non-realism and the linguistic naturalism of post-modernism. His central argument is that *all of us* should enrich and revalue the world by redescribing and cherishing *our own* corner of it. Adopting his "language constructs reality" thesis, he argues that language is steeped in evaluations and we need to make the world "bright" (differentiated, intelligible, and beautiful) by the way that we use language. Language is more than the simple labelling of things; as the later Wittgenstein argued, language shapes our perception of the world. Words don't simply describe or copy reality; they both fashion what we see and incorporate our evaluation of the perceived world: "I like it" or "I hate it." The two ideas undergirding this argument are Nietzsche's proposed revaluation of values and the view that Christian ethics is simply ethics produced by Christian communities. Moreover, like all socially constructed ethics, Christian ethics is provisional and needs to be continually revisited and redefined. Cupitt advocates piecemeal ethical conversation that criticizes and reforms the valuations inherent in every society's language and way of life. It is only by our daily interaction through and in language that public value and public ethics are created.

Cupitt's adoption of philosophical anti-realism leads into Phase 3, "transactional ethics." If, as anti-realism affirms, new uses of language precede new definitions, so it is in ethics as well. If words establish their currency by the way they are used, so the value of a particular thing or behavior is determined by how we find ourselves speaking about it. Ethics consists of verbal judgments, and the valuations annexed to words are transactional: they are traded daily in much the same way as stocks and shares are traded on the Stock Market. Consider how in the past certain animals (snakes and dogs, for example) or racial minorities were given a *bad* name, and then were revalued as we debated the way we spoke about them. Even within a supposed monoculture opposing communities will seek to change the current "high" or "low" status given to one thing or another. The only way to change the value ascribed to something is to change the way language is used: we must enter the debate and put forward arguments for an adjustment to the current valuation. Since we bring about such change only through language, ethics is forever fluctuating, human, untidy, and democratic. In postmodernity our overall valuation of life is no longer a permanent formula imposed from "outside" or by "higher authorities," but evolves through consensus. Indeed, all valuations are socially constructed fictions adopted by people to help them live in harmony with each other, and they persist until by general agreement they become outdated or unworkable.

Phase 4, "solar ethics," is perhaps Cupitt's best known yet least understood concept. It involves an analogy between the sun and the expressivist humanist ethical way of being that he promotes from 1994 onwards. Thus "we should live as the sun does... it simply expends itself gloriously, and in so doing gives life to us all." The sun also epitomizes an integrated "be-ing" of both dying and living. The sun gives "life" to plants and so to all living things on our planet, yet at the same time it is dying because "the process by which it lives and the process by which it dies are one and the same." The sun is thus a moral example of how we should live — giving out warmth and love to others. We should not be anxious or cautious, but burn brightly in reckless and extravagant self-expression. Cupitt looks to artists and entertainers as those who show what it means to be solar by putting on a good performance. Perhaps the nearest one may come to experience this expressivist, solar self-exteriorization is in the Canadian "human circus" productions by the aptly named *Cirque du Soleil* (Circus of the Sun). Through dance, acrobatics, music and a made-up language (that everyone understands) the cast evokes a joyous affirmation of life in which entertainers and those being entertained are caught up in a delirious adventure. They experience a remarkable bond as they participate in an extraordinary performance that celebrates human life. In effect, it is a solar liturgy that most of the audience find more in tune with their spirituality than, for example, the Christian Eucharist; it could appropriately be described as a postmodern, "death of God" form of worship. In the words of the official program: "I am creature of neither fantasy nor reality, neither incantation nor dream. *I am neither man nor woman, god nor demon, song nor story. I am no one. I am legion.*" Solar ethics is about living *beyond* all distinctions and *living-and-dying* for others *now* as we pour ourselves into the flux of existence.

Cupitt's insistence on the ephemeral nature of the solar performance has led to challenges from his critics that this results in extreme individualism and a bohemian existence. Phase 5 corrects that mistaken impression by affirming "humanitarian social ethics" in conjunction with solar personal ethics. He points to the fact that in postmodernity people show little or no hesitation to help their fellow human beings in distress in conflicts around the world. Indeed, he reiterates the accepted view that "for postmodern humanitarianism, thoroughgoing anti-discrimination is axiomatic." Co-humanity thus becomes the key feature of the moral equation, for we now reject discrimination as a basis for difference of moral treatment. People no longer accept the notion that gender or race or creed can render one person more deserving than another. This is nowhere better shown than in the figure of the selfless professional — the *unperson* — represented by the "United Nations peace-keeper," the "aid-worker" or the "client-centered professional" who keeps his/her own personal beliefs in check while helping other human beings of whatever ethnic or religious background. Cupitt mentions the case of Muslim Kosovars who in 1999 were defended by "Western" Christians against their Serbian Orthodox (Christian) attackers. In acts of compassion people "acknowledge the nihil" (they *do not even ask* whether the needy person objectively *merits* assistance), and so Cupitt can assert that in its humanitarianism secular postmodernity has nobly combined humanism with nihilism. Indeed, it has adopted what one might term a post-nihilistic ethic. In the figures of the selfless professional and the solar performer, Cupitt offers a viable postmodern alternative to those critics such as Adrian Hastings who view him (and other "death of God" theologians) as having "very little to say to a world in greater and greater distress."[3]

The five phases of Cupitt's ethics reveal how his radical writings, far from fleeing postmodernity, embrace it. The postmodern condition is often caricatured as an era in which people are left criterionless, value-free, seemingly adrift and incapable of making moral judgments. If, following the French postmodernist philosopher Jacques Derrida, we have "to start from where *we* are" in confronting axiological and metaphysical nihilism, we must confront Dostoyevsky's warning that "If there is no God, then everything is permitted."[4] Moreover, what kind of ethical life is possible now that "ethics replaces metaphysics as a contemporary 'dancing partner' for the Cinderella of theology"?[5]

Cupitt notes that having been described as a "postmodern moralist who rejects talk of absolute values," he has been assumed to deny values altogether. I will show that Cupitt's agenda does not lead to this popular assessment of postmodern ethics. Neither should it be thought that his ethics lead to some sort of "apolitical aestheticism." I will counter critics such as Allan Megill who allege that the postmodern/post-structuralist agenda has no cutting edge in matters political and ethical.[6] Nor are Cupitt's ethics a return to a form of existentialism or individualism; indeed, I will contend, they are consistent with his "active non-realism" and are a postmodern alternative to traditional Christian ethics. For while Cupitt's anti-realism starts from the premise that *we* are responsible for inventing/creating ethics, he adds the important caveat that we do not create out of nothing, because valuations *already* exist within the culture and are encoded in language. We never find ourselves in a moral void: we always stand within a moral tradition, and are constantly debating how we might want to develop it.

In arriving at this position Cupitt essentially discards three current models of ethics that might have been viable alternatives to solar personal ethics and social humanitarianism. I will analyze why instead of formulations represented by three respected ethicists — Alasdair MacIntyre (realist ethics), Iris Murdoch (non-realist theology, but realist ethics) and Richard Holloway (ethical non-realism, but residually realist theology) — he favors ethical expressivism.[7] I will argue that the criticisms of Cupitt's ethics from such critical realists as Joseph Runzo are misplaced and ill-considered. I will also examine Cupitt's characteristic self-criticism by way of showing that he is now confident that his approach to ethics (solar living) can provide a way of be-ing *after* God. I will further argue that Cupitt straddles the "fault line" in postmodern ethics by embracing both "différance" and "ecstasy." Moreover, since he is much more positive about *this* world than most people seem to recognize, it will be my major preoccupation to show that he seeks to affirm a way of living that is both for "others" and for "oneself." He defies the criticisms of Graham Ward and Gavin Hyman that he is a late-modernist and not a full-blown postmodernist because of his alleged refusal of alterity and otherness.[8] Indeed the whole thrust of his solar ethics and humanitarianism is to offer a way of embracing the postmodern "other" in selfless living-and-dying that effaces "us" and "them."

The second section of this book is concerned with Cupitt's attitude towards religion in general, and in specific what kind of Christianity is possible *after* God. In particular, his work poses these questions: Is it now time to take leave of organised Christianity, most notably by abandoning church membership? Is Christianity reformable? What does it mean to say that we are post-Christian? Can Christianity exist without belief in an objective God? What will be the religion of the future for those of us who inhabit the nihilistic void?

Just as Cupitt's ethics have gone through various phases, so Cupitt's ideas about religion have changed as a result of his "circling obsessively" around the question of what the religion of the future might be. Cupitt has gone from being a radical Anglican apologist to post-Christian. It is a fascinating and still continuing journey. I shall identify four different ideas about "the essence of religion" that Cupitt has adopted in the space of twenty years.

The first idea is that of "the religious requirement," which was originally promulgated in *Taking Leave of God*. This was linked to his desire for religion to be autonomous. Just as Kant had taught autonomy in ethics by insisting on the capacity of rational beings to be self-legislating and to decide for themselves (that is, without reference to divine authority) on the right course of action, so too religion should exhibit a similar autonomy. By understanding religion as "spirituality" and insisting that humans are "spiritual beings," Cupitt is able to argue that we are conscious of our own ability to love spiritual values for their own sakes, disinterestedly. This is the religious requirement that does not rely on any external validation. Precisely because religion is a human creation, religious practices must be chosen and followed for "their own sakes." Like such other creative human activities as music and art, religion does not *have* to be about anything other than itself.

Cupitt's famous maxim in *Taking Leave of God* that the new religion would be a form of Christian Buddhism — "the content; the spirituality and the values, are Christian; the form is Buddhist" — opens up the way for his second idea: that religion requires a "discipline of the void." Cupitt advocates a religious discipline to cope with the seeming nihilism of his age and "to wrest it back from Nietzsche," so "all that remains is the creative choice to get out of the void."[9] The new situation that "God is dead" can lead either to a feeling of terror or to the sense of "freedom." With the recognition that there is nothing from beyond that can give life meaning and purpose, and we must do that for ourselves, religion becomes a human construct. Thus the task of the Christian is turned upside down: we must face the void or the nihil and *embrace* it. We need to be saved not so much from sin as from meaninglessness, worthlessness, and nihilism. Indeed, we must now do what God used to do for us. The discipline of the void is linked to Cupitt's endorsement of non-realism, and his central theological concern becomes the *imitatio dei*. Non-realism requires us to be like God, who in traditional theology confronts the nihil, posits his world, orders and values it, loves and redeems it all — and does so out of gratuitous generosity and pleasure in self-expression. Non-realism sees this traditional theology as a myth about how we should conquer nihilism by building, ordering, and giving value to the ever-changing worlds we create from experience.

The discipline of the void is a spiritual discipline that requires us to accept what might be called the Buddhist sense of the "nothingness" and "emptiness" of life: everything lacks a permanent, stable essence of its own and everything is a product of time and chance. We have to make friends with the void and accept "the insubstantiality, the relativity, the transience and the lack of any hard centre in the sign itself." Indeed, "the void is universal slipping-away" and is "just movement and change." This is the new religious object to which we have to learn to say "Yes."[10] This is our religious discipline — to confront the void!

The discipline of the void was replaced in the mid-1990s by his third idea of religion — "religious humanism." His central concern was to work through the issues of whether religion can survive once it is accepted as a wholly human creation and understood to exist in a humanistic, *this*-worldly dimension. He argues that although Christian scholars are often reluctant to admit it, this has been happening within Christianity for centuries. He points to such fourteenth and fifteenth century North European painters as Rogier van der Weyden, who were visibly turning late medieval Christianity into a new religious humanism that rejoices in the affirmation of *this* world, rather than waiting for a heavenly world after death. In a painting like *The Magdalen Reading* (c. 1435; in the National Gallery, London) van der Weyden shows the old harsh religion of the early Middle Ages being visibly transformed, even as one looks at it, into a more compassionate Christian humanism. Likewise, such Christian doctrines as that of the incarnation can be understood in a non-realist way: "God" becomes "Man," with the old transcendent sacred dispersed into humanity. The divine comes down into the human world. One can see this happening in the fact that the whole of our postmodern experience is a kind of secularized religion. We have *already* largely secularized Christian doctrine into common life. Theology is turned into anthropology and the doctrine of Christ becomes the doctrine of us. All that which was originally said of God becomes a sort of template for the construction of our new religion. We become ourselves by the living of our lives, by pouring forth into expression and passing away. Cupitt wants to keep much of the old theology, but by giving it new humanistic interpretations generate from it a human religion.

In the late 1990s religious humanism was combined with Cupitt's latest idea of religion — "post-Christianity." After the year 1500, he argued, Christianity began to change. It had once supplied the cosmological basis of a whole civilization with an outlook that was broadly "platonic" and was bolstered by an all-encompassing belief system. Doctrines provided an inner programming or guidance system by which Christians could live a religious life in a corrupt and evil world. Salvation was mediated by the Church and deferred until after death. Today's new outlook, which Cupitt calls Kingdom Christianity, is underpinned by ethics, and accordingly religion becomes a radically *here-and-now* phenomenon. This new situation has caused great unease and upheaval, especially with the Church shrinking (at the rate of 2% per annum) and people searching for a "future faith" (post-Christianity) that is oriented towards the "Kingdom." In short, Cupitt advocates a shift from ecclesiastical theology — by nature mediated, hierarchical, authoritarian and disciplinary — towards a Kingdom theology that is immediate, non-hierarchical and egalitarian. It doesn't care about distinguishing "us" from "them," "the sound" from "the unsound;" it just *is*, it calls itself up, it is happy with life. The Church, he urges, must take on board the idea of the Kingdom to serve as its conscience. The Kingdom is what Jesus promised, but the Church was what we got, and the Church is not quite as good as the Kingdom. It constantly idolizes itself and postpones the Kingdom. It prefers the hierarchy, the mystery, the authority and power. Cupitt's reformation of Christianity is not like Dietrich's Bonhoeffer's claim of "religionless Christianity," but rather, to borrow the title of Lloyd Geering's latest book, it is *Christianity without God*. It is not the case of living religiously *as if* God does not exist, but living in the knowledge that God as an objective Being **does not** exist. This is post-Christianity.

Cupitt's post-Christianity is not a deviation from the ideas of the Galilean founder of the tradition; rather it is in greater harmony with the emerging consensus about the message of the historical Jesus. Latterly, Cupitt has shown a renewed interest in discovering the original message of Jesus, a topic he first explored in 1977 with Peter Armstrong in the television series: *Who was Jesus?* He has now become a D. F. Strauss Fellow of the most innovative and groundbreaking group of scholars in the theological world — the Jesus Seminar in the United States. Like them, Cupitt has insisted on separating Jesus "from the mythical matrix in which he was framed."[11] For Cupitt the historical Jesus was like a post-Christian who teaches no system and is anti-dogmatic. Cupitt's understanding of Jesus has four major components. First, he considers that Jesus' emphasis on eschatology fits into our postmodern world; for we too must "live *as if* at the end of the world" — indeed we are at the end of many deeply entrenched beliefs such as life after death, progress, *our* political ideology — and thereby pass from realism into an acceptance of our own humanly constructed and provisional world views (anti-realism). Second, Jesus' message was directed against religious objectification. As an opponent of hierarchy and rank, he was not a supporter of established religion. Third, Jesus locates God "in the heart" and has no doctrine of inherent or "original" human sinfulness. Religion is dissolved into ethical living and God is privatized and hidden. Fourth, Jesus is concerned with religion in the "here-and-now"; we must choose blessedness *at this moment*. These four components coalesce to provide a vision that will enable us to reform

Christianity and move forward into a kingdom religion based on ethical commitment to life and to one's neighbour *now*.

The third section of this book is concerned with the Sea of Faith Networks. The disparaging comment of Stephen Clark that "someone, somewhere, likes this sort of thing" is rebutted by the evidence that a number of people *are* engaged in debating Cupitt (and other radical writers) about how to create religious faith without God.[12] The growth of these Networks has been due not only to Cupitt, but also to the equally challenging writings of those who have wittingly or unwittingly followed his oft-repeated injunction to others to "outdate him" by unleashing their own creative powers and carrying the discussion across new theological frontiers. This has included two groups of writers.

The first is represented by such scholars as Lloyd Geering, Graham Shaw, David A. Hart, and Anthony Freeman. Geering, whom some have imprecisely labelled "the Cupitt of New Zealand," in fact began writing at least a decade *before* Cupitt and quite independently of him, and arrived in *Faith's New Age* at almost the same conclusions as those Cupitt came to suggest in *Taking Leave of God*. Perhaps we should refer to Cupitt as "the Geering of the United Kingdom." In some ways he has been even more of a pioneer than Cupitt, for he has been developing his own global vision of what the religion of the future might be since the 1970s. The second group consists of non-specialist members of the Networks who have stretched the boundaries of faith and its expression. The existence of the Networks and this considerable body of work indicates that Cupitt's radical exploration of religious faith as a human creation amounts to far more than the maunderings of an eccentric English philosopher of religion. Jude Bullock, a member of the Sea of Faith (U.K.), outlines how new forms of religious expression are already being explored:

> The religious person is the one who is prepared to fathom the depths of existence and chuck himself whole-heartedly into creating meaning, starting from an overwhelming love for the world and all that therein is. The quaint picture that secular society has of the sentimental inadequate, pottering off for a weekly fix of fear and hope, clinging absurdly to the irrational, is the symbol of the dying of just one form of religion. The Sea of Faith, liberation theology, creation theology, the diverse forms of new spirituality (often drawn from ancient sources) and the theological professionals in universities (if they are honest), are all symptoms of something new and refreshing coming to be.[13]

In conclusion, I will show in this book how Cupitt's approach to ethics and religion can offer something constructive to those struggling with theological questions in postmodernity — a world aptly described by D. Vaden House as "living without God or his doubles." In an era when people are less inclined to look to a divine being for help, and have rejected moral absolutes with the subsequent loss of unitary Meaning, we see the growing acceptance of pluralism and *our* ever-changing socially constructed worldviews. For Cupitt, the Christian task is to conquer nihilism — that is, "to overcome the fear that because the extra-historical absolutes are now gone, life is meaningless or worthless."[14]

By joining with others in loose associations and networks like the Sea of Faith in order to create a new ethics and a new religion, Cupitt has made his radicalism far more positive than most people give him credit for. Although some — and even Cupitt himself — often remark that he is by temperament an iconoclast, "a subtractor, removing the eyesores," it will be my central purpose to show that he is ultimately a theological visionary who attempts to persuade people of the need to create meaning and values for themselves, *and* for others. He puts it succinctly: "the ethics of life has to find some way of responding to the encompassing threats to life."[15] He knows whereof he speaks: as was shown in *Odyssey on the Sea of Faith*, the double blow of being diagnosed with an aneurysm following his father's death from the same medical condition was not the only case of being *in extremis*. The log of Cupitt's journey is more than the scribblings of an off-beat academic from the closeted comfort of a room overlooking Parker's Piece in Cambridge. Even after the "death of God," Cupitt affirms, people can *still* embrace with confidence the contingent world as we know it. This is the religious voyage for the post-Christian: a journey into life.

Chapter 1

Cupitt's five phases

In 1888 — the last year of his sane life — Friedrich Nietzsche wrote *The Twilight of the Idols*. It was dubbed 'a grand declaration of war' on all the established ideas of his time. One particular idea that he fought against was what he considered to be the inconsistency of some nineteenth century English writers, especially George Eliot (Marian Evans), who while acknowledging the death of God still wanted to retain Christian morality. Eliot's life has some uncanny parallels with that of Cupitt.

Eliot had lost her belief in God many years before she translated two of the most influential attacks on traditional Christianity: D.F. Strauss' *The Life of Jesus Critically Examined* and Ludwig Feuerbach's *The Essence of Christianity*. After a deeply religious childhood, she moved toward a rationalism and secularism that replaced the Calvinism of her strict upbringing. Her humanitarian impulses, her avowed humanism, her earnestness as to individual duty and discipline were all calculated replacements for a religious life that she could no longer experience. She wanted a version of Christianity that reflected her own kind of moral Christ. She sought not to find a church, but rather to become an individual who was her own church. In a letter to her distraught father, Eliot claimed to "admire and cherish much of what I believe to be the moral teaching of Jesus himself," although she herself lived contrary to accepted Victorian Christian moral principles, notably as the live-in partner of George Henry Lewes, whose legal wife resided elsewhere. She found in reason, logic, and dutiful living a replacement for a God she could no longer believe in. Nietzsche, on the other hand, argued that Christianity was a complete system, and if you got rid of belief in God the whole edifice would come tumbling down. In his view it was not only inconsistent but impossible for Eliot (and others) to cling to any kind of Christian morality after having taken leave of God.[1]

Although he has never asserted it in print, Cupitt has occasionally confided in person that his lifetime project was to be the Nietzsche of religious thought. Indeed, Mason Olds describes him as "being unable to get the monkey of Nietzsche's thought off his back." It is ironic that Nietzsche would be the first to protest against Cupitt's desire to retain, in however modified form, *any* kind of Christian ethics, and understandable that Cupitt's critics echo Nietzsche's chastisement of Eliot. Robin Gill, for example, declares that "whilst it is important to view Christian ethics as a perspective that is indeed creative, it is still consciously carried out in a context of God's creation."[2] So how can Cupitt advocate Christian ethics without God? Will not the whole system break into pieces? If God is removed will not the anarchy predicted by Dostoevsky prevail?

Cupitt is adamant that God's death does not result in moral chaos. In this chapter I will identify and describe the five phases that Cupitt's "Christian ethics without God" has passed through. These phases mirror his religious "movement" from the religious requirement to post-Christianity (see chapter 3). The first phase in Cupitt's ethics extends up to 1987 and may be categorized as "moral asceticism."

Phase 1: Moral asceticism (1975–1987)

Apart from *Crisis of Moral Authority* (1972), Cupitt's early forays into ethics are found in articles or talks that are printed as Appendices, or in a compilation of his writings: see for example *The Leap of Reason* (1976) and *Explorations in Theology* 6 (1979). In the 1970s Cupitt emphasises that Christians must follow the figure of Jesus as a sort of Nietzschean revaluer of all values. To be "a follower of Jesus is to be his contemporary at the end of the world" which means that Christian ethics is to undertake a "critique of all teachings and all world views."[3] Moreover, Jesus is seen as the one who bore witness to the history-transcending religious ideals that can shape our lives. These religious ideals and values go beyond the pluralistic and relativistic world that we now inhabit.[4]

In 1976 Cupitt identifies three moral principles from the teaching and life of Jesus. These are "utter purity of heart, disinterestedness, and commitment to the way of love." In *The World to Come* (1982) he adds "creativity," and these four moral principles are combined with a self-discipline that is "purgative" and "non-egoistic." Following the radicals of the 1960s, Cupitt adopts the battle cry of a new reformation for "a faith come of age." In the spirit of Jesus's teaching we can work for a better world by disregarding self-interest and the will to power. Jesus initiated a new Kingdom of love that was "a covenant-brotherhood (sic) based on the principle of unconditional value-conferring altruism." The Kingdom of God is the guiding ideal that symbolises the twin goals of ethical striving: a better world and a better self. This makes the Christian faith "a project for a new humanity in a new world," which he characterizes as being both "a spirituality, a way of inner transformation for each believer" and "a social ethic."[5]

For the early Cupitt, then, the Christian life called for a kind of moral self-discipline or asceticism that helps people face the "new" situation that confronts them. In traditional Christianity the individual had to be saved from falling into sinful ways. Sins (usually "of the flesh and the devil") were the enemy. But with the "death of God" we need to be saved not from sin but from nihilism — not so much anxiety over "outsidelessness" as the fear that nothing has value and life is meaningless.

Cupitt points to the high incidence of depression and the lack of social cohesion within British society. Here he may have touched the raw nerve of life in the inner cities of Britain in the 1980s during the Conservative administration of the "iron lady," Margaret Thatcher. With a government hell-bent on curbing the strength of the Trades Union Movement (most notably those associated with the coal mining industry) and the resultant increase in unemployment, many people feared that they were expendable pawns in a political/economic war-zone.

Surely the motion pictures *Brassed Off* and *The Full Monty* (produced in 1997, but retrospectively set in the 1980s) reflect the mood of the times. Both films take place in regional centers where people's lost sense of worth and value is symbolized by lack of job opportunities and the resulting effects of low income, broken relationships, depression, attempted suicide and despair. However, each of the films gives a different perspective on how to cope with this debilitating situation. In *Brassed Off*, the confrontation between the coal miners and the British Tory Government symbolises depression, a theme that contrasts with *The Full Monty*'s zest for life and constructing ("solar") values in the face of correct morality (i.e., "ordinary" men should not take off all their clothes in public). In *The Ticklish Subject* Slavoj Zizek interprets both these films as illustrating an "acceptance of the loss" of employment etc. However, this misses the central message of *The Full Monty*, which I interpret, following Cupitt's later ethical standpoint (see Phase 4), as expressivist. Denied their normal life-long employment in the Sheffield steel works, the unemployed men activate their longing for wholeness by generating a new symbolic expressionism. Despite their allegedly inadequate bodies, they can be beautiful (even the "fat" Dave can be appreciated by the opposite sex), and by "stripping" they rescue themselves from depression and despair (nihilism). Through their discovery of moments of joy in times of affliction, the film actually adopts the central theme of Cupitt's *After All*. To be sure, *Brassed Off* also appropriates that theme by having the brass band achieve success in the national contest, but it is much more resigned to accepting whatever befalls miners who still hanker after the "good old days." The film is much more stoical and conventionally heroic. These two films poignantly dramatize Cupitt's underlying concern. How can ethics adapt to the new nihilistic situation — the nagging sense of purposelessness and worthlessness — and offer something constructive in the postmodern world?

Cowdell interprets Cupitt's thoughts on the issue as the sort of "passive nihilism" that scared even Nietzsche. By this he means that for Cupitt there is no will to power, but rather "when the self and the world become completely deconstructed, egoism is uprooted (and) there is no longer anything *there* that is anxious for itself or that might attempt to assert itself by domination or by projecting and imposing its own ordered self-expression upon the world."[6] In other words, Cupitt is trying to "make Christian" the seeming hopelessness of his age and to wrest it back from Nietzsche so that there *can* be a creative choice to get out of the void. Indeed, we now have to do what "God" used to do for us.

What most of Cupitt's critics and commentators seem to have missed (and what this section seeks to readdress) is that his ethics always goes hand in hand with his espousal of non-realism. If he wishes to live *after* God yet still affirm the continuing relevance of that symbol in confronting nihilism, then he has to turn to ethics to provide the way. Cupitt's central theological concern is the *imitatio dei*. Non-realism insists that *we* become like the God outlined in traditional theology who creates the cosmos *ex nihilo* and confers order and value on it. God sustains and redeems it simply because of his love for it. Non-realism sees this traditional theology as a myth about how *we* should conquer nihilism by building, ordering, and giving value to our world(s). God is a guiding spiritual ideal. Your God is a phenomenon of the same kind as your dream, your hope, your guiding star, and "the pearl of great price." If God is a regulating ideal that distinguishes what ought to be from what is, then Christian ethics is a set of guiding ideals that regulate how we should live. Contrary to popular opinion, Cupitt (during this phase) does not simply "take leave of God," but rather swaps supernaturalism (God as an objective Being) for idealism (God as the moral ideal) — in short, realism for non-realism. Even Cowdell fails to mention the very important link between Cupitt's ethics and non-realism. Moreover, no one has noted that even *before* the non-realist publications of the 1980s, Cupitt was already arguing that "God" is the regulating, *history-transcending ideal* that points to the way things ought to be. Instead of looking back to the Creation as *the* age to which people must return, Christian ethics must look forward to the Kingdom, believing in God as "the ideal that inspires continual discontent and moral aspiration." Indeed, in 1979 he wrote that we "know God in the moral life in so far as (we) live by an absolute ideal which continually judges and inspires (us), which is indeed unfulfillable and transcendent, and for that very reason inexhaustibly powerful."[7]

Whence does he derive this idea of God as an ideal? It has three sources. First, in 1977 Cupitt conducted a reading experiment on *Purity of Heart* by the Danish theologian, Søren Kierkegaard. Instead of reading him as an "orthodox western Christian" he re-read the book as "an exercise in religious subjectivity" and concluded that "for Kierkegaard God is not an active personal Being, but simply an ideal." Second, Cupitt acknowledges a debt to the 1960s "death of God" and "secular Christian" theologian, Paul Van Buren, who said that the idea of God would work just as well and have the same effect upon people if God was not a personal being, but an ideal. Statements of Christian theology are not about a metaphysical "God" but about a strong conviction that that "love" is the way. Third, Cupitt notes that the world religion scholar Ninian Smart once suggested that everything people say about God might equally be said about faith in God. It is not so much God as it is *faith* in God that comforts us, that "moves mountains" and provides aid in time of trouble. Faith in God has something of the same potency that God used to have. Thus, "God is like the one who is dead but is still venerated: the dead person is constantly, silently present with us, acting as a reference-point and a standard to be lived up to." Indeed it is quite common for people to act in a certain way because of the memory of an inspirational loved one who is no longer alive. Very often they say: "I did it for X" because they hold in the highest regard X's life and the impact it made up their own. For Cupitt all these ideas coalesced into the premise that Christianity is a moral code or guiding ideal, showing the way to live. Thus, for example, as outlined in a book like *Only Human* (1985), the Christian is one who has a "purity of heart or integrity of will" and "the objects of faith" are guiding spiritual ideals that we live by.

The implications of his non-realist ethics become fleshed out in his writings in the mid-1980s. This is nowhere better seen than in *The Long Legged Fly* (1987). Cupitt outlines five styles of moral arguments that have traditionally been classified as "foundational" and used to support morality from "outside" or "from above:"

1. The appeal to Nature: "We should act according to Nature."
2. The appeal to rational consistency and universalizability.
3. The utilitarian appeal to consequences.
4. The appeal to tradition and the revealed will of God.
5. The appeal to individual self-realization.[8]

Cupitt dismisses all "appeals" to "foundations" or external criteria of "the right" on the grounds that no "external" vantage point from which to judge moral actions exists. We have no extra-linguistic reference for language or any grounding of the ethical in how things are or in what people claim to be "the nature of things." Morality belongs within language and, following Ludwig Wittgenstein, Cupitt sees it as built into our constantly evolving language-games. Morality or ethics is "rooted in history and the ever-changing social life of human beings." It clearly reflects its particular historical period and changes as historical events or developments occur, thus rendering certain attitudes obsolete and altering the way that language is used. The obvious example is the gradual acceptance in recent years of homosexuality. In the 1930s it was widely viewed as a perversion; in the 1950s it was commonly considered an illness; in the 1990s a person's sexuality was understood to be innate and morally neutral.

Cupitt's argument in *The Long-Legged Fly* is a complex one setting in dialectical opposition the writings of the Continental philosophers, Jacques Lacan and Gilles Deleuze. He makes the former a symbol of a fixed and dominant culture because "the subject submits to the law of the signifier" and it is "society or language which constitutes him/her as a *subject*" allowing him/her little freedom to think and act.[9] For Cupitt this reversion to realism makes morality — as it was in Plato — a bridle constraining freedom. But Platonism has vanished with the advent of postmodernism, and all meanings (including ethical meanings) are "a dance of difference in the void." Ethics is constantly changing: there are no fixed positions any longer. While he concedes that some cultural conditioning is inevitable, he follows Jesus and Nietzsche in recognizing that the task is to begin a perpetual scrutiny of received evaluations and the creation of new ones. Still, that does not lead him into the arms of a radical Utopian like Deleuze who represents a "theology of desire," allowing us to do whatever "turns us on." Cupitt is not about to countenance the distortion of postmodernism to mean that we can do whatever we want to because "it feels good." It is noteworthy that the radical theologian, viewing the Deleuzian notion of *delire* (wild, ecstatic interpretation) as *too* radical, observes that "the rhetoric of thoroughgoing utopianism leaves us at a loss. We do not know how we could even begin to put it into practice."[10] Cupitt's radical affirmation of human desire does not lead him into either hedonism or revolutionary utopianism.

Both the Lacanian "Symbolic Order" as well as the Deleuzian "body without organs" and "desiring machines" of *Anti-Oedipus* and *Mille Plateaux* leave Cupitt perplexed. He forges an ethical strategy for living between extremes, insisting that today everyone is a postmodern ironist or constructivist who realises that judgments are unavoidably made on the shifting ground of our own socially constructed cultural world-views. Cowdell correctly points out that Cupitt has since 1979 abjured "any grounding in the nature of things," and that the only basis for the ethical he will now allow is enhancement of the "life-energy." Since Cupitt is putting forward a form of biological naturalism where value is "what avails for life," the ethical becomes "that which makes us most alive."[11] Here he is indebted to John Ruskin's early statement of "biological naturalism."[12] As I showed in *Odyssey on the Sea of Faith* this emphasis on enhancing life, along with his fascination with "biological life" and how we can balance the constraints of culture and freedom of life, have been (and remain) constant themes. What we have here in 1987 is an earlier version of his 1998 attempt to locate a "position" between autonomy and heteronomy. Just as in 1998 he rejects the autonomous individual (the Enlightenment project failed) and is aware of the postmodern emphasis on heteronomy (the claim of another over the self), so already in 1987 he wanted to find an ethic that balances individual freedom and cultural constraint. How can we say a religious "Yes" to biological life and our own mortality without being dominated by our cultural baggage? How can we live for others without being sucked dry by cultural pressures and, failing to fulfill our own life-desires, resign ourselves to vicarious living? How can we enhance our "life-energy" without squandering it in "a flight of daydreams," nomadism, or hippie culture that ignores the needs of others and disregards social ethics?

Cupitt answers these questions by adopting a "middle" position between total freedom of desire and bending to pressures of the culture. He proposes a self-discipline or "theology of the cessation of desire." This is similar to what Buddhism and ascetical religion have traditionally taught. Cupitt avoids the Western predilection for extreme individualism by repudiating total abandonment to selfish concerns and, as in Buddhism, by enjoining the surrender of egoistic illusions. Everything is impermanent and things consist in their own shifting relations with everything else. There must be a social component to how one lives.

So he affirms *both* "human drives" *and* "the constraints of culture," with one working out the legitimacy of this or that position by a dialectical process. Between the two asymptotes represented by Lacan and Deleuze, Cupitt enables one to live within one's own limitations. The "purgative," "disinterested" and "non-egoistic" way is compatible with postmodernism in that it enables us to rein in our desires without being constrained by cultural forces. Similarly, it does not lead us to fall into the trap of vicarious living. Using the four principles identified from the life of Jesus — utter purity of heart, disinterestedness, a commitment to the way of love and creativity — Cupitt advocates a moral asceticism that enhances our lives, yet at the same time enhances the lives of others. Our lives become fulfilled as we direct our *surplus* life energies into creative activity and ethical struggle for the emancipation of all humanity. Cupitt is moving from an emphasis on individualistic spirituality to a greater affirmation of the world of public meaning and discourse. The non-realist understanding of the doctrine of the incarnation is that God has become human, the two-worlds dualism has become replaced by this world only, and we have to create a new co-human world in which everything happens on the surface. As Cowdell explains: "Very cleverly, Cupitt has succeeded in combining here his affirmation of the religious primacy of the manifest and contingent, his critique of religious and philosophical realism, his liking for Buddhism and the *via negativa*, and his grounding of ethics in whatever enhances the life energy (against the 'wowserism' of much so-called 'Christian morality'), while nevertheless, leaving the way open for a very conventional moral position with all its virtues of self-discipline intact — and all of this carried out while immersed in the epistemologically corrosive acid of post-modernism!"[13] Nevertheless, this self-discipline or moral asceticism gives way in 1988 to "the new Christian ethics."

Phase 2: New Christian Ethics (1988–1991)

Cupitt boldly announces in 1988 that "no subject is more important to us than ethics," and Stephen Williams claims that in *The New Christian Ethics* "more than in any other, Cupitt reveals his heart."[14] While it is foolhardy to try to locate Cupitt's "heart" in any *one* of his books because of the fluidity of his project, Williams pinpoints the increasing importance of ethics to Cupitt now that he has dismissed an objective God.

Cupitt's original title for *The New Christian Ethics* — "Adding to the World" — is a clue to the central theme of the book. Christians are "adding to the world" by giving themselves to a humanistic ethic of offering their lives in the service of causes that create new value. Cupitt is expanding the thesis of *The Long-Legged Fly*: that ethics enrich or enhance the value of life for both the individual and the public world that we inhabit and in which we create meaning. Indeed, as Cowdell accurately remarks, *The Long-Legged Fly* is "the prolegomena to a Christian ethics."[15]

Cupitt is at pains to point out that the "non-historical absolutes" (i.e. the metaphysical Western tradition associated with the philosophy from Plato to Kant) have now been swept aside. The values that are to be found in any culture are those created by the people of that culture, and are especially enshrined in their religions. Religions function as "frames" imposing a structure on the "life-world." However, in the case of Christianity it was not creative ethics that were promoted, but complete submission to a wrathful realist God. In a rare autobiographical moment he outlines how traditional Christian ethics affected him:

> Historically, there just was no Christian ethics. You were too much afraid of attracting God's jealous wrath if you achieved anything. The idea instead was to work to rule and to concentrate on cleansing yourself. . . . You sought to make yourself as passively-conforming and perfectly inoffensive as possible. There was no *ethic*, because the whole grand system of psychological terrorism had no other purpose than to procure total submission to the power of God and the church. . . . I can personally testify that the old terroristic, corrupt, cosmic-protection-racket Christianity was flourishing in the 1950s, because I was raised in it.[16]

Mason Olds correctly notes that the "new" in Cupitt's title emphasises his disenchantment with the "old" ethics that needs replacing. This "old" ethics has three "aspects": (a) the earliest Christian ethic, (b) the Platonic dualist ethic, and (c) the Christian version of the Platonic ethic.[17] The earliest Christian ethic was an interim construct to deal with the eschatological crisis caused by the belief of the first Christians that Jesus would return soon. Now that this belief has been shown to be false, that ethic is no longer applicable. The Platonic ethic, in both its secular and Christian forms, was an avoidance of the concerns of this world, since the "real" world was elsewhere. Christianity exploited this Platonic system for the benefit of its own "power-structure" and the resulting ethic was "radically anti-life." This is the "cosmic-protection-racket" that Cupitt faced in his early undergraduate years and which he labelled "doctrinal realism" (see *Life Lines*).

The "new" ethics is for "the world as it appears to be" which, following Nietzsche's perspectivism in *The Will to Power*, is the world of interpretations. There is no moral world order "out there" and we do not discover, but rather create or invent value. Supernaturalism is dissolved into naturalism. Cupitt, in an important endnote, acknowledges his debt to Wittgenstein, emphasising that everyone is born into a culture that *already* contains historically evolved moral language-games.[18] Thus he can see the error of his ways, throwing off the "Kierkegaardian path" of *Taking Leave of God*, which too much emphasised Western religious individualism, and he can prioritize the social over the individual. Values are *already* there in the culture; they are like codes that we have to unravel and interpret. It is up to everyone to critique and reassess these values, and to create new ones if the existing ones are unacceptable. But the only way that we can do that is through language. Adopting his "language constructs reality" thesis he argues that language is steeped in evaluations and we have to make the world differentiated, intelligible and beautiful by the way that we use language. Language is more than the simple labelling of things but; indeed, as we know from Wittgenstein, it shapes our perception of the world. Words don't just copy reality: they create or mould what we see (and this also involves our evaluation of what we see — "I like it" or "I hate it"). As the South African black consciousness leader, Steve Biko, is reported to have said to the white liberal journalist, Donald Woods, in the film *Cry Freedom*: "Change the way that people think and the world is *never the same*." Thoughts are unspoken words; and so we all "add to" (i.e. enrich and revalue) the world by how we redescribe and cherish our corner of it.

At this point the obvious objection is heard from Cupitt's critics: How is this to be done without falling into what Joseph Runzo disparagingly calls "a parochial homocentrism?"[19] Williams likewise asks whether

Cupitt's "route" will really make the world a better place. Cupitt is not perturbed by such comments. For him they are the objections of (critical) realists who vainly yearn for "outside" criteria just when he is about to announce a new shibboleth: "the world is outsideless." Indeed most critics attempt to combat Cupitt in a "religious space and time" from which he has already taken leave. Williams himself admits that Cupitt is trying to create new Christian ethics *after* God, yet surprisingly commits the same error as others in trying to defeat Cupitt by simply affirming that Christian ethics must be "rooted in objectivity."[20]

It is perhaps Mason Olds who has understood Cupitt's ethical agenda best when he points to Cupitt's "basic value principle." This proposes that "there is only one moral imperative left: Create value! Value is Grace! So . . . the ethical question becomes: 'How then can we find the *strength* to create; how is productive, value-realizing action possible?'"[21] Olds correctly notes that this imperative is general and vague and that Cupitt is "not concerned with the specific 'do's' and 'don't's' embodied in most moral rules." Rather he argues — as he did in *The Long-Legged Fly* — that like artists, social activists, and humanitarians we have to discover for ourselves the life impulse that drives us to creative action and leads us to enhance life for others. We might be driven to political action to redress social inequalities. We might value those who are marginalized by society and place a higher value on their worth. We might enhance the level of concern that people accord to ecological issues. The list is endless. Cupitt allows a huge amount of freedom for people to pour themselves into social action and social relations and thereby change, revalue, and add to their fragment of the world. Nevertheless Olds points to what he perceives to be significant problems with advancing so vague a value imperative. While he agrees with Jean-François Lyotard that no shared metanarrative can any longer guide people's actions, and that we must use our powers of persuasion to convince others of the necessity to act in certain ways for the greater benefit of all, he nonetheless urges Cupitt to demonstrate how the value imperative plays out in the market-place. In other words, he wants Cupitt to supply "a text in applied ethics which relates the value imperative to specific cases."[22]

Inexplicably, Olds seems to have forgotten that for Cupitt ethics is a way of living that adds value to the world. His value imperative is deliberately vague because he argues (at this phase) that if, in a large society of people, everyone cares for and enriches a different bit or aspect of the world, then together they create a rich tapestry. Obviously he cannot be prescriptive because, as the old saying reminds us, "it takes all sorts to make a world"; yet it is very important to note that Cupitt still wants to adopt the humanistic values *already extant* in society. In a hint of what is to develop seven years later into solar ethics, Cupitt advises that since each of us is, like him, "merely the sum of my social relations, my life-task is not to save my soul but to lose it. I need to forget about myself and to pour out my life into the human world."[23] This is often overlooked by commentators (and he himself takes many years to draw out the implications of his social humanitarian ethics), but Cupitt is keen to affirm "the humanism of the human world" and avoid excessive individualism. After all, he urges, we are *all* human beings who should relate to one another by living-and-dying for others. This is the non-realist understanding of the Christian story of the incarnation and resurrection.

As for the justification of Christian ethics, Cupitt argues that it is eminently rational for us, each starting in his or her own corner of the world, to try to create value and make life worth living by loving and valuing each bit of the world and each aspect of life as highly as is self-consistently possible. It is rational to be an enthusiast and to create value: it is rational to make life worth living. Thus ethics is to be justified not as a bridle, but as a way to happiness.

Williams pours scorn on that attempt to engage in a moral struggle for human liberation without any specific ethical norms. Cowdell, however, comes to Cupitt's defence by observing that his radical Christian activism can redraw unjust social and linguistic boundaries as, for example, by the use of inclusive language in the revaluing of women.[24]

But there is more to it than simply the redrawing of a few unjust boundaries! What Williams and even Cowdell seem to miss (or choose to ignore) is the observation that anti-realism has ethical implications that are just as pertinent as those of realist ethics. By 1989 Cupitt is influenced by philosophical anti-realism, the impact of which is to "unmask" what has hitherto been identified as "real" and unchanging. Anti-realism in ethics is the theory that moral values are human inventions and hence social constructions. By insisting on moral value as a human invention, we maximize human freedom with the benefit that we are not constrained morally by anything apart from ourselves and other human beings. We are also able to determine that the major tyrannies that have afflicted the world are of human origin. Sexism, fascism, and racism might have clothed themselves in realism by purporting to be the Truth about how things are (for example, sexism is based on the realist assumption that nature has revealed that men are 'superior' to women); nevertheless, anti-realism reveals these tyrannies as the culturally or historically linked creations of the human mind. Culture (social construction) precedes nature (how things are), as William Schweiker explains:

> the voice of anti-realism in ethics is important. When feminist theorists show the social construction of gender, when African American theologians and ethicists chart the development of racism, then tyrannous appeals to "the real" are unmasked. The emperor has no clothes! Antirealism in ethics has been in the service of liberation.[25]

It cannot be stated any more forcefully that Cupitt's new Christian ethics are a consequence of his anti-realism and, more significantly, that they can be accommodated within *the Christian tradition when it is understood in an anti-realist way*. That is why Gill's bewilderment at Cupitt's position being "a mirror image of (his) own thesis" makes sense; but Gill does not mention Cupitt's anti-realism, nor can he envisage an anti-realist understanding of Christianity.[26] The "mirror-image" is the correct description of Cupitt as an exponent of the anti-tradition in which the question of ethics becomes central *after* the demise of God. Unlike some anti-realists who might wish to abandon Christianity, Cupitt does not. It is in this context that one should note the incredulity of his critics who wonder how Cupitt can discard an objective God, yet remain within the Christian Church and espouse Christian ethics. Cupitt stands between his critics. On the one side those like Williams and Runzo argue that without an objective God Christianity is internally inconsistent. On the other side are rationalists, humanists, and secularists who argue that Christianity is simply irrational and Christian ethics has been made redundant by secular humanism. Cupitt partly accepts the insights of this latter group, declaring that Christianity is indeed a human creation. However, that very insight reveals that as such Christianity remains very important even though philosophical and historical criticism has demolished all our received religious beliefs. Having been created by us, Christianity deserves our attention.

As a consequence, despite the rebuff of both sets of detractors, Cupitt's ethical agenda returns to a community and culture that embodies certain values — the Christian Church. As he outlines in *Radicals and the Future of the Church* (1989), he is still wedded to the Church. His postmodern anti-realist ethical agenda is that collectively people create and redeem their world by structuring it and filling it with value. With the death of God, Christians put Christian doctrine into practice by "playing

God." In postmodernity people have come to the realization that indeed they are *already* playing God, and theologians need to address this situation. David Edwards expresses surprise that one should declare Cupitt's ethics "specifically 'Christian.'"[27] Again, this misses the point that what makes Cupitt's ethics Christian is its identification with a particular value-supporting organization that interprets what enhances life from a specific point of view. This is Christianity interpreted from a non-realistic perspective. The life of Jesus and the Christian doctrine of the incarnation are understood to mean that love is the highest way. Eternal life is to die with Christ by expending ourselves in human acts of generosity. We do not seek to save our souls (there is no soul), but to lose them by pouring our lives into the human world. Christian ethics is ethics produced by Christians; similarly, some feminist theologians have reinvented God as "goddess" and liberation theologians have remade Jesus into an armed revolutionary. *Everything* is a human creation and a social construct. We invented our ideas of God and ethics and continually update them to fit our ongoing re-evaluation of our world(s).

Perhaps, as Kierkegaard suggested, it is easier to understand the narrative backwards rather than forwards. If so, then Cupitt's *What Is a Story?* may be seen as a piece of the jigsaw puzzle that was missing for Edwards when he was writing in 1989. The Christian stories are those that help people create value, especially the "conviction that our life is worth living."[28] As I have argued, Cupitt's concern is: "How can one avoid meaninglessness and nihilistic despair?" The "new" Christian ethics is created as Christians interpret and re-interpret their myths and stories to accommodate them to the world as it appears to them today. Obviously this is Christianity understood in a non-realist/anti-realist way and freed from the old Platonic world-view. And Cupitt avoids the Kantian or non-cognitivist trap of reducing the religious to the moral. Instead, religions operate just as any other sub-culture, attempting to influence the moral decisions that will be made within societies. As will be shown later in this book religion is *still* needed by Cupitt. There is no Enlightenment separation of the religious and the secular but, as Cowdell argues, Cupitt embraces the postmodern awareness (influenced by Durkheim and Weber) that "religion and society are closely interwoven in a *Gestalt*."[29] Thus Williams' advice that Cupitt would be "safer with individualism," rather than rely on a congregation who are similarly disillusioned with realism, is to misread Cupitt's agenda.[30] Williams is also scathing in his assessment of the likelihood that such Christian humanist congregations could ever be formed, let alone succeed better than realist congregations.

It is obvious that he has never considered that Unitarian Universalists constitute such congregations.

So, values are already there in communities and everyone is involved — even those who are interpreting that tradition in an anti-realist way. Indeed, ethics is the Trojan horse that Cupitt uses to destabilize realist Christianity. Cupitt remains within the Christian church actively subverting the existing values by following the example of Jesus in raising up those who are worthless and whom "the world regards as trash."[31] This is the revaluation of values. Cupitt is devoted to Jesus as a symbol of "all who suffer forsakenness and die with him," which means that there "isn't any cosmic endorsement" and "historical forces are actively destroying value." In such a time "we can side with each other." Cupitt's ethical agenda makes him plunge headlong into creating new Christian values in a seemingly valueless postmodern world. He has unified his philosophy of life with his philosophy of language. He wrestles with what this means for ethical living without recourse to an objective God. It takes him five years to resolve exactly *how* expressivist non-realist ethics might be embraced. In the meantime his anti-realism insists that all ethics must be "transactional" with "currency establishing value."

Phase 3: Transactional ethics (1992–1994)

Cupitt's anti-realism affirms that in language "meaning is always *first* currency, and only *then* a definition" i.e. new words first establish their currency by being needed, and coming to be used in a certain way, and only after this meaning has become established is it then codified by a lexicographer and put in a dictionary. Cupitt links what happens in language to what happens in ethics. If there are no "outside" valuers or valuations — Platonic, Divine, Foundational, or otherwise — then the worth or value of something is simply its current market value. Cupitt hinted at this as early as 1989 in *Radicals and the Future of the Church* when he compared the meaning of a word to the price of a commodity in a market. It is a relative and ever changing entity that is the resultant of a large number of small human interactions. Like the prevailing price of stocks and shares, or tins of food on the supermarket shelf, the value is set by the way people esteem it at a particular moment in time. Thus the social market is what in Christian theology was known as the Last Judgment. We may disagree with the current verdict of the market, and seek to change it. But we can no longer apply some transcendent absolute standard to draw the old metaphysical distinction between a thing's current market value, and its alleged real, eternal value. If we consider that someone or something is overrated or underrated, then we must join the discussion and submit our own arguments for a change in the current valuation.

In 1992 Cupitt re-emphasises his position in a paper presented at a conference on postmodernism and religion with his concept of "transactional values." Here he states that "the strength of the currency is only a communally generated fiction sustained by our own belief in it" and so "moral values (are) shifting transactional market phenomena, like prices."[32] Cupitt links morality to language and the postmodern decentering of the self. Morality is "*moody*, a matter of *ethos*, something shifting, human, untidy, democratic and transactional, like language" . . . "We must move away from the self in the direction of how people, things, and aspects of the world and our life are valued in the language."[33] He explores this further in *After All* (1994), where his thesis is that since all words carry some overtones of value then value and meaning evolve simultaneously. Cupitt says that his ethical theory becomes "objective" in three senses:

1. The whole life-world in all its aspects is valued.
2. The "Ground of value is that we are living beings with a highly sensitive interest in life. Our evaluative response to things is not secondary or dispensable, but on the contrary is primitive . . . valuation comes first."
3. Values are objectively decided upon by a consensus that we continually confirm and re-negotiate.

In this way Cupitt fends off any critical charges of subjectivism; altering the valuations annexed to words as they are used day-by-day *does* bring about moral change, and indeed the same process works to effect political change. Cupitt favours democratic, transactional politics — and he challenges his critics to name a virtuous theocracy extant today. In both ethics and politics, then, relativity is creativity and, following postmodernism, the world is just *play*. We must accept universal pure contingency, go with the flow, and trust the processes of life spontaneously to generate form and meaning. There are no Absolutes, but only a democratically evolving consensus. The purpose of entering into ethical (and political) debate is to "give something a better name." By the very way language works, "the Word has the power to destroy as well as to create."[34] That the worth of anything is the esteem in which it is currently held is revealed in the way people speak about it. To redeem something is give it a better name; to try to change the way people talk about it. It is especially necessary to attack derogatory words — for example words used to reinforce the marginalization of women and sexual or racial minorities. If each person revalues his/her own bit of the world, the common world of all is enriched.

To be sure, this transactional, democratic notion of meaning and value has not met with universal agreement; as Cupitt freely admits, the reverse is the case:

> Now you see what I mean by outsidelessness. I mean radical immanence. People hate it. They think up abusive names for it: it is capitalism, it is materialism, it is "trendy" liberalism, it is nihilism, it represents the end of all real and abiding values. The confused tirade of abuse that people direct against it reveals their crippling fear of Being. But the Revelation of Being is a vision of things . . . as humming, brimming, glowing with life and value. Everything is immanent, transactional, secondary — and yet, extraordinarily *radiant*. Hence the idea of *solar living*, and of a religious life that is entirely content with all this, just this, out-sidelessly.[35]

The concept of "outsidelessness" is, of course, the central theme of Cupitt's arguments and position. It also links the themes of this chapter so far — nihilism, radical immanence, transactional values, and what emerges in 1995 as solar living. Cupitt unifies his ethics of life with his philosophy of language by coming to a supposed "final position" which he expresses as "energetic Spinozism, solar ethics, poetical theology." People live to communicate, to express themselves ethically: they emerge from themselves into symbolism and are solar!

Phase 4: Solar "personal" ethics (1995 onwards)
The theory

Cupitt's postulation of solar ethics as putting on a "good show" through our self-expression dates back to chapter 8 of *The Time Being* (1992). Despite the attraction of Buddhism as a religion that has existed without belief in God, he is uncomfortable with its propensity to seek escape from this world; for he is persuaded that the spiritual life must incorporate both an active as well as a passive component. He thus prepares the ground for his "active non-realism," which is released in 1995 as "solar ethics."

The slim book so entitled (Cupitt's shortest at only seventy-one pages) is both theoretical and practical. By the time of its writing in 1995, the United Kingdom and New Zealand Sea of Faith Networks have begun, and Cupitt dedicates the book to their members. This is a highly significant move. In this work Cupitt is crossing the rubicon from academia to the populace, and thereby offering a *modus vivendi* to the many who, like him, are disaffected with traditional Christian teaching. It also introduces Cupitt to a wider public and stands as a significant response to Cowdell's challenge seven years earlier: Was Cupitt's religion perhaps "too high-and-dry, too intellectual or in other ways too demanding for 'ordinary people'?"[36] It is interesting to note that university theologians who tend to dismiss Cupitt's writings as academically lightweight at the same time criticize him for being too intellectually demanding for people in the street!

Just as the stance of *The New Christian Ethics* opposed any supernatural or heteronomous accounts of morality, so in *Solar Ethics* Cupitt is careful to avoid making room for any systematizing or legislating power. From the outset ethics is more an expression of the way one lives than an involvement with the moral question, "Who instructs/legislates that I should live in a particular way?" Cupitt uses the word ethics not in the sense of a moral code or a "position" in moral philosophy, but in the old-fashioned sense of a way of living or an approach to life that will lead to the highest possible degree of happiness. In short, "an ethic is a doctrine of the good life: it teaches a way of life by following which we can attain the highest Good, beatitude."[37]

David Hart correctly observes that in *After All* (1994) Cupitt presents us with a visual image to "enable an imaginative participation in the project envisioned." "[W]e should live as the sun does ... it simply expends itself gloriously, and in so doing gives life to us all." In *Solar Ethics* we find a practical description of *how* we should live each day in a human-centered and outsideless world. Like the sun we must put on a "good show" in outpouring self-expression. The sun symbolizes an integrated "be-ing" of both life and death. The sun gives "life" to plants and so to all living things on our planet, yet at the same time it is dying — the sun is pure act! And thus it presents a moral example of how we should live — giving life to others by our "uninhibited self-publication." We should not be anxious or cautious, but burn brightly in reckless extravagance. As noted earlier, Cupitt points to artists and entertainers as those who express what it means to be solar and put on a good show.

If we accept solar living and see the world as "outsideless," then many things follow. We admit that the public realm is the only real world and we are giving our *one and only* life-performance. There is no other world in which we can rectify our mistakes or make amends for the life that we have lived. There is no fixed moral code or moral order "out there." We must go forth into self-expression with our whole being. If we hold back, then we are trapped by an ideal we think we should live by or up to. We must love life (*all* life) and pour out our hearts in selfless living, dying for others in this world. We create our common world by generating expressions and symbolic exchanges. It is important to note, Cupitt says, that solar ethics should not be confused with a return to existentialism. This would lead to his former myopic individualism and the error he committed in *Taking Leave of God* by relying too heavily upon Kierkegaard. Although solar ethics is "personal," in the sense that a person commits him/herself to self-realization by symbolic self-expression and transience, this way of living has social implications. Cupitt's postmodern assertion that human beings co-arise with the world and are embedded in the world of intersubjectivity means that solar ethics has radically communal consequences. Adrian Hastings offers a typical misrepresentation of Cupitt's ethical agenda as "privatisation" when he announces that Cupitt's denial of objectivity makes Christianity ineffectual in the public forum. He argues that if you don't have a divine object as a referent, then religion is redundant because, lacking an external Law-giver to distinguish right from wrong, it can pass no judgment on the evils perpetrated by governments. Solar ethics is therefore inadequate; it cannot "denounce genocide as diabolical, any more than it can condemn a crocodile for snatching a woman washing clothes at the river bank."[38]

Leaving aside the obvious retort that orthodox Christianity would be hard pressed to pronounce moral judgment on the inclinations of a crocodile, Cupitt's solar ethics is very much about how people communicate with each other, how they treat others in this world; and what kind of world is to be created now and in the future. The person who endorses solar ethics is continually being prophetic by living and dying simultaneously, not as an ethical individualist like the Christian existentialist Kierkegaard or the atheist Sartre, but as a *social activist*. We should relate ourselves not to the moment-by-moment ethical choice, but to the whole of life in which we lose ourselves. "We find happiness by plunging ourselves into and identifying ourselves with the outpouring flux of existence — of which we are indeed just parts — so that we are lost in life, burning, rapt."[39]

Cupitt's solar ethics is based on the anti-realist premise that value is given to us by language — we are, as it were, born into already existing ethical codes which are continually changing just as *our* world is in a state of flux. He is extremely explicit:

There is, one might say, a starting point for moral discourse in the pleasure we take just in experience — still more, in experience *articulated and so shared*. Experience gives us a world already language-formed, and therefore already valued, bright, *common*. We are always world-building, always (at least implicitly) with others, and always valuing. . . . It is simply a mistake to imagine oneself sitting mournfully alone in a world without value, and wondering how the absent good is to be found and brought into this world. From a solar point of view, there is and can be nowhere else for the good to be but already here and waiting to be affirmed.[40]

Solar ethics is not the privatisation of religion, nor is it to quote Hastings "a sort of therapeutic spiritual game." On the contrary, it is a way of living that embraces not only the world of common experience, but as postmodernity especially affirms, those who are the excluded 'other' that still remains a part of the whole. Cupitt is very concerned about what human beings are going to make of themselves and their world in the future. Thus solar ethics can respond to the rise of religious fundamentalism, and the recent acts of inhumanity against ordinary people in the United States, as well as tourists, Hindus and Muslims in Bali. Except for a belief in martyrdom or an endorsement of acts of inhumanity in the name of a higher God, how could one justify the slaughter of the innocent? Those who adopt solar living could *not* "expend themselves gloriously in giving life to others" by piloting flying bombs into the Twin Towers and killing thousands of people from many nations, or indiscriminately slaughtering hundreds of locals and holidaymakers in a nightclub. If there were no idea of another world, few if any could be urged into strapping on a vest packed with explosives. If we have no second chance, if death is the end, if we have no notion of God rewarding us in Paradise, then we have to get on with living well with *everyone* in the here-and-now. Solar ethics is a corrective to those who use traditional religion to devalue their own and other people's lives. Instead of diminishing the worth of human life because all wrongs will be corrected in an afterlife, religion would have the opposite effect. It would revalue *this* life by restating our commitment to going on a "moral spending-spree," burning not buildings but ourselves in selfless living and loving. We've got to live all the time by dying all the time. The unity of life and death is the crucial concept in solar ethics.

So what are the major influences that have helped to shape this new understanding of ethics? Cupitt mentions three main sources: Georges Bataille, Thomas Traherne and Benedict Spinoza, together with George Berkeley's image of a fountain.

Of particular importance is the writer Georges Bataille (1897–1962). In *The Last Philosophy* and *After All* Cupitt acknowledges Bataille's influence on two counts. Firstly, he admits that Bataille's idea of the sun was instrumental for his thinking:

> Solar living is Georges Bataille's term for what I have else-where called "Glory." Bataille teaches that we should live as the sun does. Its life, the process by which it lives, and the process by which it dies all exactly coincide. It believes nothing, it hasn't a care, it just pours itself out. Its heedless life-giving generosity is its glory. Glory is a state of being wholly and unreservedly given to one's own life.[41]

Cupitt has used different expressions to describe this way to happiness, this giving of oneself one hundred per cent to life so that one's self-outpouring coincides with the outpouring and passing away of everything. Initially he used the word "Glory," but gradually it is replaced by phrases such as "ecstatic immanence," "being solar," "solar living," "solar loving" and "solar ethics." It is also vital to note that this entails not simply the "inner experience" of individualism or existentialism but Cupitt's emphasis on communicative religion as "public expression." He endorses Bataille's insistence on the public nature of the sacred: it is not an ideal state set apart from what happens to people in the world, but includes those things from which traditionally Christianity has tried to escape — darkness, otherness, ambivalence, and perversity. The sacred is our life-world, warts and all.

Bataille's social philosophy offers a way of living that comes *after* God yet still can deal with the absorption of the self into "an intersubjective and polycentric social world."[42] The sacred for Bataille is characterized by sacrifice and expenditure of oneself in the creation of unauthoritarian communities in the wake of the death of God. This theme is crucial for Cupitt. Though some critics of Bataille have argued that he moved from community to individualism with the publication of his trilogy *La Somme Atheologique* and its supposed emphasis on "inner experience," the present consensus of opinion is that his primary need was to "re-invent a sense of community embodied in a new conception of the sacred that responds to our contemporary needs."[43] In his youth Bataille converted to Roman Catholicism as a protest against his parents' lack of religious faith. However, after training for the priesthood, he rejected traditional Christianity because of the harm that it had inflicted on a woman he loved. His project is similar to that of Cupitt's in that both find Christianity (in its usual form) not religious enough. One must go beyond Christianity to a "hyper-Christianity" that can "give meaning to the experience of life as it (is) really lived." This is what Bataille means by an "atheology."[44]

For both him and Cupitt the significant point is to define a way of living that will help us to say a wholehearted 'Amen' to our own lives. The death of God has left a terrible emptiness, and we are revealed to be fragile and perishable. Bataille places life at the level of the "impossible." To be sure, we can return to the "possible" by reintroducing God or some notion of salvation (a future Paradise). As responsible moral agents, however, we must not deny or try to avoid the impossible: we must admit that with God dead we face others and ourselves in the void. Like the animals that we are, we should love life and not moan about temporality, contingency and finitude. Like Cupitt, Bataille is not searching for the "why" of existence — that is rejected as a disease of Reason — but espouses plunging headlong into the violence, excess and disturbance of life. Cupitt would concur with Bataille's assessment that "Christianity's impoverishment . . . lies in its will (through asceticism) to escape a state in which fragility or non-substance is painful."[45]

Bataille has been appropriated by postmodernist writers as the philosopher of excess and "virulent nihilism" — a nightmarish vision of scatology, dissipation, eroticism, and death. However, Bataille uses each of these themes in the service of a tenet that needs to be undermined — that of "the homogeneity of the world." This, as Mark C. Taylor argues, is the dream of Western philosophy, science, and technology; and Bataille is "attempt(ing) to expose an altarity that can never be domesticated."[46] This is the nightmare that needs to be replaced by a "science of heterology." It is only by communication with the "other" that the master-slave relationship (foreshadowed by Nietzsche) comes to an end: the known has to embrace the unknown, and "by taking the step beyond, the transgressor glimpses the altarity of the sacred."[47] This has been made possible by the death of the Christian God, a deity that had promoted separation and an infinite qualitative difference between oneself and the "Other." To communicate is to give oneself in sacrificial expenditure, burning with absolute loss. Taylor makes the crucial point that for Bataille, sacrifice is not only *le coup* (the gift) but also, following Marcel Mauss, *le coup de don* — the gift (which expects no return).[48]

Bataille's later works have had such an influence on Cupitt that he has a recurrent dream. He is in a spacecraft heading towards the sun. He can look out of the rocket and see the white heat as he plunges towards it. Yet, he is not afraid, but feels happy at being utterly consumed and welcomes the impending destruction. It is now that Cupitt departs from Bataille by backing away from any interpretation of the image of the sun as "surrealist." Using Nick Land's *The Thirst for Annihilation*, Cupitt rejects Bataille's "less than friendly" ideas about the sun. The "curse of the sun" is to fall into "virulent nihilism," and "the thirst for annihilation is the same as the sun."[49] Cupitt dismisses both Bataille's atheological interpretation and that of those who see the sun as a subconscious metaphor for union with God. He much prefers his own positive interpretation: the dream of the sun was a dream of ecstatic immanence: "fully expressed, and therefore utterly consumed, one passes joyfully away into the flux of things."[50]

The metaphor of the rocket speeding towards the sun is repeated in *The Last Philosophy*. This is linked to his key theme of revaluing traditional "metaphysical evil" — temporality, contingency and one's own mortality. Solar loving is ardent and heedless.

> Thus, one should hope to go up like a rocket and burn out at the summit of one's flight, falling unnoticed to earth in the darkness. Solar loving . . . idolizes neither its object nor its own abjection. It is not planning to achieve immortality . . . solar loving is . . . easy, going. It burns ardently, it gives, it passes away. Its peculiar joy is . . . "ecstatic immanence." It is immersed in and unreservedly given over to its own utter transience.[51]

"Ecstatic immanence" becomes a catchword for Cupitt; and neatly sums up his "expressivist" approach to ethics and religion. Here is his "end of metaphysics" and a closure of the old dualisms that are a direct result of Western philosophy (and science) holding on to Plato and realism. Indeed, these cancellations are synonymous.

Another clue to unlocking Cupitt's *Solar Ethics* can be found in a "ghostly title" to *The Last Philosophy*, "Felicific Philosophy." This rather obscure designation is a reference to the works of the 17th Century

Anglican priest-poet, Thomas Traherne. A radical Christian, Traherne is remembered as the "poet of felicity." By this is meant that a person has a "double awareness, of enjoying the phenomenal world and of belonging to a spiritual life."[52] One is conscious not only of the happiness of this world *but actually the beauty of enjoying it as well.* This is the "ecstatic immanence" that Cupitt equates with solar ethics, and it is a spirituality so rapt with the happiness of life that one cannot help but communicate it to others. As Traherne writes about felicity:

> When we have it (felicity), we are so full, that we know not what to do with it: we are in danger of bursting, till we can com-municate all to some fit and amiable recipient, and more delight in Communication than we did in Reception.... It is a Principle so strong, that Fire does not burn with a more certain Violence.[53]

Even though Traherne's mysticism was centered on a realist God, Cupitt can still use his central idea of a life lived in a state of ecstatic happiness. In his *Christian Ethicks*, Traherne is not interested in conscience, external Lawgivers, or exhorting others to avoid what the Anglican Prayer Book calls "wickedness and vice," but rather on *how to live* a good life by being felicity's lover. This accords nicely with Cupitt's aim, for he can quite neatly demythologize felicity to mean being so rapt in the present moment that one says a whole-hearted "Yes to Life," and recognize that we are "citizens of this world *only*, without any remaining trace of the old idea of dual citizenship."[54]

Cupitt also describes solar ethics as an energetic version of Spinoza's naturalism. The attraction to Spinoza could result from his dubious distinction of being declared a heretic by both Jewish and Christian reli-gions. However, the reference to the Jewish-Christian theologian/philoso-pher is something of a red herring, because Cupitt is using him as a foil to emphasize his own advocacy of ethics that are *this* worldly. He understands Spinoza's system not as pantheism, but as religious naturalism with a non-realist or non-objectifying view of God. He is directing attention to Spinoza's insistence that "religion and morality make no sense unless human beings can make free choices."[55] Mason Olds accurately outlines Cupitt's debt to Spinoza's idea of "conatus" as the life impulse within human beings that strives to continue its own existence. As I showed ear-lier in discussing *The Long-Legged Fly*, that life impulse is manifested in people's struggles to express themselves against the constraints of culture: in that case the concept was exemplified by pitting Deleuze versus Lacan.

Cupitt affirmed "Spinoza's thought (that) no negative constraint is placed on the life impulse; its full self-expression is affirmed."[56]

Cupitt always refuses to embrace totally the thoughts of another philosopher. He uses Spinoza for his own ends, picking out what suits his cause and rejecting the rest. Olds shows that although Cupitt does not believe that today we can agree completely with Spinoza's theory of morality, he does think that the Dutch philosopher was heading in the right direction in two important respects: he emphasised the importance of the body and the natural world, and by rejecting the traditional platonic dualism provided an escape from the nature/culture distinction with its corollary that morality bridles human nature.[57]

Thus the link with Spinoza is rather tenuous. Indeed in 1998 Cupitt dismisses a comparison of solar ethics with Spinoza. Cupitt's "energetic Spinozism" is very different from what Spinoza envisaged in that when motion, contingency and temporality are brought to the fore there can be no "theological" totalization of everything. Spinoza is dismissed because of his totalizing tendency towards rationalization and completeness. Cupitt will allow no summing up of everything, for naturalism of whatever form (Spinoza's included) can never claim to be more than a transient literary creation, dependent upon metaphor and always capable of a variety of readings. Solar ethics (like Cupitt) is too elusive to be tied down to any thoughts of unity or totality. Solar ethics surpasses all distinctions and is beyond any totalizing theory. It is neither a form of law-ethics nor is it grounded in a vision of a cosmic moral order, but is purely expressive and theatrical.

Cupitt's concern *after* God is to rid ethics of any metaphysical grounding or undergirding. In particular, he is critical of theologians like Martin Buber and Emmanuel Levinas. It is significant that solar ethics will not endorse Levinas whose emphasis on the "Other" has been appropriated by many postmodernists including, as I have already discussed, Bataille. For Cupitt this is to fall into the trap of setting up yet another dualism — something he wishes to avoid by bringing to an end all distinctions. There can be no hint of anything beyond what we are. There is no Kantian noumenal self, Buberian *I and Thou* or Levinasian infinite "Obligation." There is no "Other," either within or outside the self, which calls one to act. That would be a return to some sort of metaphysical thinking. It is only by bringing to an end *all* of these distinctions that people can be truly happy. In the tradition of religious naturalists Cupitt proposes the way to happiness not by giving the human self a unique metaphysical status and then delivering it from the world, but rather by melting it down into the flux of the world. The self does *not* transcend the flux of phenomena. We are *all* part of a struggling cosmos.

Cupitt is obviously commending an unconstructed self, and people who are pure communication. Solar people are those who put on a "good show" and who communicate expressively a life-affirming presence. One can read these people as signs. Hart correctly identifies Cupitt's inter-weaving of his language-communication thesis with the expressive-ethical. This occurs in an almost revelatory way when Cupitt's "reading" of someone at a party (as one would read a sign) introduces another metaphor for solarity — the fountain. He relates how he saw a woman who in his eyes was totally solar. "Every bit of her was broadcasting information, radiating messages. Dress, body-language, facial expression, gesticulation, high-speed talk — she was all communication (and was) emitting light, sparkling, shining, radiant, dazzling. The phrase came to me: 'A human being, a fountain of signs.'"[58]

Cupitt uses the metaphor of the fountain to describe the expressivist way of living. Perhaps surprisingly, he chooses the Irish philosopher and Bishop George Berkeley (1685–1753) who is famous (or infamous) for his argument that idealism can generate a proof of God's existence. Cupitt is, of course, not interested in debating "immaterialism" or whether trees exist independently of one's perceiving them, but simply "borrows" the image of the fountain from the end of *Three Dialogues between Hylas and Philonous*:

> the water of yonder fountain, how it is forced upwards, in a round column, to a certain height, at which it breaks and falls back into the basin from whence it rose, its ascent as well as descent proceeding from the same uniform law or principle of gravitation. Just so, the same principles which, at first view, lead to skepticism, pursued to a certain point, bring men back to common sense.[59]

The "common sense" for Cupitt is his anti-realist stance, and the image of a fountain that renews itself is his expressivist doctrine that everyone and everything is a flux of language-formed events. Later, this "common sense" will be promoted as meaning that *everything* is embedded in ordinary language. But for now the fountain is a useful metaphor for the world as "a constantly-maintained uprush of energies that arch upwards, spread, scatter and are borne away and lost," and *this* fountain is never switched off.[60] Recently, Cupitt has updated the metaphor of the fountain with reference to an installation "sculpture" by the artist Damien Hirst, in which a ping-pong ball is supported on a rising column of air from a tilted-back hairdryer.[61] Still, the same point is being made: existence has no foundation, and everything is to be merged into a continual pouring out and passing away.

The images of the fountain and the sun thus reinforce Cupitt's concern that just as the world is "a continuously outpouring, self-renewing stream of dancing energies-read-as-signs" so are human beings. Indeed, in Cupitt's naturalistic vision of the world, human beings are commensurate with the world. Everything (which includes everyone) is literally caught up in being "energies-read-as-signs." This is a religious ethic because it gets rid of the dualisms that (false) religion (especially the type of Christianity that he labels "cosmic terrorism") has always sought to impose. Solar ethics allows freedom where once there were chains of bondage, symbolized by those men wearing "big hats."[62] Domination, whether by a Divine Being or ecclesiastical structures, is anathema to the solar ethics that allows one, as John Shelby Spong incisively puts it: "to do what you were created to do without regard for recognition, permanence or reward."[63]

Cupitt's metaphor of the sun rests upon six "pointers" that allow one to escape the traditional binary contrasts in terms of which our culture and our world view have heretofore been constructed. These pointers are both ethical and religious, since they enable one to cope with the contingencies of temporality. Thus solar ethics has a therapeutic effect, enabling one, as Bataille insisted, to say "yes to life." Here are the six pointers:

1. **Living beyond the distinction of living and dying** (in Christian language, "dying, we live"). This means giving up notions of life after death and instead affirming the life we have now. Having accepted one's own transience, one can put away selfish concerns about the future of one's existence, and thus expend oneself in the direction of others.

2. **Living beyond the distinction between noun and verb, substance and activity, being and doing.** The implication here is that "what you see is what you get." We are the performance that we put on. We are our lives.

3. **Living beyond the distinction between the ideal and the actual.** Once again Cupitt insists on avoiding the Platonic distinctions of a "morality out there." Self-expressive outpouring is all there is: there is no-one, no thing, no ideal to which one should be compared.

4. **Living beyond the distinction between inner and outer.** This re-echoes Cupitt's postmodernist idea of a decentred self: there is no "inner" self that is more real than the "outer" or apparent self.

5. **Living beyond good and bad; the saved and the lost.** Here Cupitt quotes Matthew 5:45: "for he makes the sun rise on the evil and the good." Demythologizing this verse, Cupitt argues that to be solar, one

must not discriminate in these black and white terms. People are a complex mixture of creative and destructive forces. Like that of the sun, the energy they produce can burn either for good or ill.

6. **Living beyond the distinction between the Way and the End, the journey and the destination.** Cupitt's ethics is very close at this point to Rudolph Bultmann's theological position of "realized eschatology," where eternal life received in faith is a present, existential reality and not a future anticipation.[64] Indeed, Cupitt exclaims: "We should see ourselves as living *already at* the End. . . . We should live expressively, outing ourselves, shining, burning, and going down with all guns blazing."[65] However, one should remember that even though theological statements must also be anthropological statements, Bultmann would part company with Cupitt when the latter dispenses with *any* transcendent Other. Significantly, Cupitt further remarks that solar living replaces traditional ideas of Transcendence and self-transcendence. Again, he reminds his readers that there is only one level of reality; nothing exists beyond *this* world.

Solar ethics is made prominent in *After God* (1997), which contains restatements of Cupitt's position that "we ourselves are the only makers of meaning and value," and that we should live by dying all the time, heedless like the sun, and in the spirit of the Sermon on the Mount (Matthew 5–7). Solar ethics is a radically emotivist and expressionist reading of the ethics of Jesus. Cupitt here refers to Jesus' images of people as shining lights or hilltop towns. It is interesting that he later finds an "inconsistency" in the Sermon on the Mount, claiming that within it co-exist two different religions: one recommends "cautious, secret, inward church-spirituality" (for instance, Matthew 6: 1–6), while the other advocates "all-out, expressive, solar spirituality" (Matthew 5: 13–16). Cupitt naturally comes down on the side of solar religion, but wonders why there has been no discussion of this glaring inconsistency.[67]

Once one has discarded all supernatural props and frames, ethical living and "postsainthood" are achieved by self-exteriorization, self-outing, and self-shedding; it is thus we make meaning and value. Life can't be possessed or clutched at, and we can get ourselves together only by leaving ourselves behind. Cupitt makes a verbal play on "leaving ourselves" — i.e. the self is decentered; and his references to "self-outing" are obviously an allusion to "gay" motifs. These allusions are not lost on David Hart, who re-echoes them in his appropriation of solar ethics. It is to this consideration that I now turn; specifically to the question of how solar ethics can be put into practice.

The practice

Only one attempt has been made to give practical application to Cupitt's solar ethics. In light of the dedication of *Solar Ethics*: "For the members of Sea of Faith," it is particularly fitting that one of its founding members should have taken up the challenge of using the "visual ethics" in the notoriously complex area of sexuality and sexual ethics. Seizing upon the language of "self-outing" and "self-exteriorization," David Hart's *Linking Up: Christianity and Sexuality* applies solar ethics to the issues that deeply affect his own gay and radical Christian identity. It is noteworthy that Hart's book was originally entitled **Radical** *Christianity and Sexuality*, but on publication "Radical" was omitted from the title, though "Radical Christianity" is retained *within* the text. The book also extends far beyond specifically gay issues, with sexuality including many sexual sub-cultures (bi-sexuality, transvestism, androgyny, etc). He attempts to "link up" what have historically become disparate worlds — sexual theory and ethics with the theology and practice of Christianity.

Hart's thesis is that the traditional binary opposition of male and female must be superseded. Sexuality has more to do with a series of temporary situations than a fixed or final condition. He endorses the postmodern understanding that there is no fixed position — just movement — and "truth" is only as we know it today (and may change tomorrow). Thus he wants to by-pass the current debate as to whether sexuality is an inherited characteristic (from chromosomes) or the product of socialization. Hence we must go beyond all distinctions of sexuality, especially categorizing people as either homosexual *or* heterosexual. Since the situation is far more fluid than such an either/or categorization admits, we have to transcend these distinctions. It is a radical approach that calls into question the binary distinctions that both Western philosophy and Western societies have regarded as defining the only way that one should live. In particular, this has been reinforced by the doctrines of the churches. Hart affirms Michel Foucault's thesis in *The History of Sexuality* that power is something exercised "from innumerable points, in the interplay of non-egalitarian and mobile relations," and by producing multiple sexualities, society can then classify, distribute and assign moral ratings. "And thereby the individual who practices certain forms of sexuality can either be approved or marginalised, disciplined or normalised by a classification which society itself has produced and polices."[68]

Using Cupitt's solar image, radical Christianity can now break the mold and go beyond the distinctions that society and the churches have given us to define our sexuality — and by implication how moral we are.

Following Foucault, Hart wants to avoid being restricted to only socially constructed and approved forms of sexual expression. These categories should be resisted from *within* the structures of power. Likewise, radical Christians must work from within Christianity to change power structures. They must deconstruct the sexual categories that are paraded before people by ecclesiastical authorities, and supplant the categories that both society and religion use to classify and morally appraise people. Thus we witness the realizing of one of Cupitt's hidden agendas in writing *Solar Ethics*: aware of sexual liberation movements such as feminism and gay pride, he wrote *Solar Ethics* in the hope of giving them some ammunition with which to be *transgressive* and propose new Christian sexual ethics.

Radical Christian sexual ethics accepts the instability of postmodernism, and wants people to be free to move backwards and forwards along an endless Foucauldian spectrum of sexual options throughout their lifetime. People are not determined to be either homosexual or heterosexual for their whole lifetimes, but may have different preferences at different stages in their lives. Someone who has been in a heterosexual partnership that comes to an end may subsequently have a homosexual relationship or vice-versa. During one's lifetime one may have many different sexual preferences. For Hart this is already happening within Western societies, and Christianity must incorporate this shift in morality both liturgically and doctrinally.

Hart's Christian sexual ethics thus goes beyond the traditional Christian ideas of marriage "till death do us part," "nuclear" families, and all attempts by religion to impose final standards or totalizing ideas. Hart's agenda adopts the postmodern concept of "creating" and "choosing" values. We face rapid developments in our world, but we also have a choice: do we continue to maintain the language of nature and law, or do we propose a new model of ethics reflecting the postmodern ethical situation? The discussion of sexual ethics leads Hart to reassess Christian ethics.

Hart uses five of Cupitt's six features of solar ethics to help illustrate a new way of ethical living beyond the traditional distinctions. First, living beyond the distinction between living and dying helps people in a practical way to approach their own death in a more integrated way. In acknowledging that "to live is to die and to die is to live" we recognise the necessity to make best use of the time available for ourselves and for each other. To accept that this is our one and only life means that we have to act in an ethically responsible way. Second, living beyond the distinction of noun and verb means that we "neither label ourselves by a particular type of sexuality (absolutely) nor . . . deny that our sexual activities help to constitute the person that we are." The inference, as shown above, is that we are sexual beings, yet that our sexual preferences can change depending on circumstance and lifestyle. Third, living beyond the distinction between the ideal and the actual avoids Roman Catholic casuistry and the legalistic pretence of Protestantism. This is especially relevant in many ethical problems that the churches face in attempting to endorse highly problematic "ideal" commands for Christian couples, such as "no sex before marriage" or "do not use contraceptives." Since many couples do not accept such teachings, the Church becomes compromised, and its role reduced to that of play-acting ceremonial. Radical Christianity can go beyond this, and by negotiation the actual and ideal are discussed and explored. Fourth (and closely related) is living beyond the distinction between "good" and "bad" people. Division and exclusion — the "insiders" and the "outsiders" — seem to be part of the agendas of most churches and societies. Hart cites Cupitt's reflections on the teachings of Jesus, which provides an example of how *not* "to divide humanity into us and them, the sound and the unsound." Fifth, living beyond the distinctions between the way and the end, the journey and the destination, reflects Hart's affirmation of Leonard Woolf's dictum that "It is the journey not the arrival that matters." Again Hart, like Cupitt, is not expecting life after death — we have only this existence to cope with, life in the here-and-now. No final destination awaits us. Hart finds echoes of this in the Judaeo-Christian tradition ("Dust thou art and to dust thou shalt return") and, like Cupitt, in Saint John's insistence on eternal life *now*. Moreover, he argues that both Christian and modern ethical thinking, including Kant's autonomous moral person, is content with ethical living and requires no recourse to the rewards of a future life.

Does all this result in totally libertarian ethics? Hart is not so persuaded, for he acknowledges that moral codes are still required, especially in places of education and work. He avoids the either/or of short-term heedlessness or long-term planning by a typically Anglican ploy of embracing a fluid Tradition that includes many different viewpoints. This Tradition has no one unchanging essence, but rather many and varied ways of appropriating and interpreting it. This puts him at odds with feminists like Daphne Hampson, for whom Christianity is irredeemably locked into a sexist Tradition that cannot be reformed. Its system is so all-inclusive and its way of thinking is so masculine that it cannot adapt to changed circumstances. Following Nietzsche's observation that Christianity is not an ethic but a system, Hampson concludes that the overthrow of patriarchy would shatter the whole Tradition.

For Hart this is not the case. He argues that Christianity is not a fixed Tradition, but is adaptable; and unlike Hampson, who is prepared to let the Christian Church go, he urges radical Christians to remain and defend their corner. If the Christian faith has always been only a human invention, then it is no less valid for feminists to seize the wheel of the vehicle now from the patriarchs who considered themselves entitled to steer it in the past. This is a better course to follow than trying to re-invent the wheel. However, he argues, we must go one step further than the gender distinction. It is not simply a matter of replacing the former patriarchal system with a matriarchal one as proposed by some feminists. Rather, *both* systems are ultimately flawed because they each adopt a fixed position and set the other in binary opposition. Such a situation is obsolete in a postmodern world. We must end these binary oppositions, he urges, and solar ethics will provide a good way of transcending all distinctions. This theme will be discussed in more detail later in this book.

The important point here is that for Hart, solar ethics is commensurate with the Christian ideal of living-and-dying for others; it functions as "a guide to our engagement with an equally fractured world," for it provides a vision of living beyond any distinctions. Hart endorses the Sea of Faith Networks' catchphrase that "religion is a human creation," and thus concludes that Christianity, including its sexual theory and ethics, *can* be remodelled effectively.

However, for some evangelical Christians, Hart's book has proved to be too subversive. After its publication in 1997 a well known conservative Christian bookstore purchased and pulped all copies of *Linking Up*. It is therefore difficult to find in print — such is the perceived threat of putting solar ethics into practice!

****

Cupitt confidently asserts that *Solar Ethics* is a "supposed final position." One may ask how the postmodern Cupitt can enunciate a "final position" in a world of difference and flux. Is he sawing off the very branch on which he is sitting? Perhaps he is nearer the mark with his declaration in *After All* that he is not writing the Truth, but what he says is true for *now*. Indeed, in a characteristic move he concedes that *Solar Ethics* leaves unresolved the problem of how short-termist one can be. In an Endnote to the book — which was discussed by his Cambridge students as it was being written — a student, Rachel Muers, declares that for the workaday-world solar ethics is too bohemian and short-termist. Long-term planning, disciplines, and codes of practice are needed in the workplace to avoid total anarchy. Cupitt admits that perhaps he has dismissed moral codes philosophically, and has forgotten that they are needed in social and economic life. Even solar people have to conform to some rules. Yet, how in practice does one combine solar heedlessness and short-termism with the need for at least some long-term planning of *one's own* life?[69] Hart solves the problem by stating that encoded ethics are transitory, applicable only to certain groups and "few can be for all times and all places." As I have shown, he uses the (Christian) Tradition as that which can be fought against and reformed because it is not fixed forever. Cupitt adopts another approach, although it takes him five years to resolve the problem. He does so by combining solar "personal" ethics with humanitarian "social" ethics in his figures of the solar performer and the selfless professional.

Phase 5: Humanitarian "social" ethics (2000 onwards)

To his parting plea in *The New Christian Ethics* that "we *have* to do better" and "invent a new world" Cupitt responds twelve years later in his assertion that secular postmodernity has begun to show how to live *after* God. More than simply "adding to the world," postmodernity has "realized" the religious humanism espoused by Jesus in his Kingdom theology. "God" has become disseminated into *this* world in postmodern, humanitarian "social" ethics. It is a bold statement, yet one that an acute observer of Cupitt's movements could have anticipated. As early as 1994, in a paper presented at the Sea of Faith Conference in the United Kingdom, Cupitt prepares his readers for the tack that he is going to take. He argues for the distinction between Kingdom theology and Church theology, and then suggests that we are now ready to embrace a Kingdom that has *already* come. This does not preclude the conflict and suffering that, as he argued in *After All*, are built into our world. However, we have now come to the realization that ordinariness is outsideless and is of value. Kingdom theology does not look to a future kingdom either here or elsewhere, but returns us to ourselves, overcoming metaphysical evil and making us content with trying to renew the world here-and-now.[70]

In *Kingdom Come in Everyday Speech*, "returning to everyday life" is revealed in the way human beings now express themselves in humanitarian acts, coming to the aid of others without any thought about their race, colour, creed, or personal merit. Today people show little or no hesitation in acknowledging a moral call to help their fellow human beings in distress anywhere in the world. Cupitt points to the general acceptance of the idea that "for postmodern humanitarianism, thoroughgoing anti-discrimination is axiomatic."[71] People reject the idea that someone of a

different race, creed, or gender doesn't deserve our attention. This has
been shown most convincingly in the global response to the tsunami(s)
that caused so much loss of life in South East Asia and Africa on
December 26, 2004. Whilst there might be pockets of resistance to this
stance from religious fundamentalists, racists and nationalists the march
of globalization is gradually eradicating such tribal conceits. This can be
seen in the figure of the selfless professional — the *unperson* — symbolized by the "United Nations peace-keeper," the "aid-worker," or the
"client-centred professional" who keeps his/her own personal beliefs in
check in the course of serving other human beings of whatever ethnic or
religious background. In such acts of compassion, people acknowledge the
nihil (they simply *do not ask* whether the needy person objectively *merits*
assistance). In humanitarianism, secular postmodernity has combined
humanism with nihilism. Just as in traditional realist theology God gives
value to worthless sinners simply by loving them, so in the kingdom world
everyone has a similar power to create and assign value simply by caring
about others. Thus "God" is the original non-realist. Cupitt has no need
of ethical codes and systems from such usual sources as Plato, Aristotle,
Utilitarianism, Situation Ethics, and Canon Law etc. In and through the
language of everyday speech, humanitarianism has emerged from within
Western culture, and he is most happy to endorse it. It is radical theology;
and it is *good news* waiting to be read.

Both styles of what may be labelled "postmodern saints" — the "selfless, dedicated professional" and the solar artist/performer of *Solar Ethics*
— may be conjoined in one person, as in the case of someone like Nelson
Mandela. In such a fusion Cupitt finds the answer to the above noted
query from Rachel Muers concerning the applicability of solar ethics in
the workaday world. Indeed, the merger of the solar performer and the
selfless professional might also be seen in the postmodern person typified
by some Californians whom Cupitt himself had laughed at twenty years
previously. Rational and disciplined physicists during the work-week, on
the weekend they might become expressionists, perhaps cruise the gay
scene, chant in ashrams, or head off into the desert for earth-festivals.
Cupitt admits that it took him years to recognize that it was acceptable to
"learn the habit of moving back and forth between the worlds of work
and leisure, negation and affirmation, the active and contemplative
lives."[72] Why *shouldn't* there be an element of plurality in the moral life?
The solar performer and the selfless professional may each be the "necessary other," and by mixing the two styles one may achieve a synthesis of
short-term heedlessness with long-term planning. Why not? Expressivism

and Humanitarianism co-exist — the joy of burning up in the present moment is fused to self-effacing public action.

Cupitt's radical agenda has led him to look for a synthesis of personal and social ethics, enabling us to live *after* God. The former Kierkegaardian, autonomous individualist has become both an expressivist solar artist/performer accepting transience and creating new "lifestyles" in *this* world, and the selfless professional committing him/herself to a professional ethical code of selfless dedication in the service of others. It is an adroit and satisfying resolution to a long search for a way to live by a prophet of *this* world. It is also to be noted that both solar "personal" ethics and "social" disciplined humanitarian ethics are rooted in the ethical teaching of Jesus. The expressivist solar performer echoes the words of Matthew 5:16: "let your light shine before others," while the quiet selfless professional reminds one of the injunction to do good deeds in secret (Matthew 6:2–3). However, it is important to note that these two styles may exist separately. One doesn't have to fuse the solar performer and the selfless, dedicated professional. In practice many artistic people are solar performers, and many quiet professional types are happy to be quite unshowy. Cupitt's point is that both types typify postmodern people who simply affirm their values without needing to be propped up by any supposedly objective ground of value. But there remains the question of whether this synthesis is credible. In the next section, I will assess two crucial issues. First, how does Cupitt's ethical analysis compare with current realist/non-realist ethical approaches? Second, we must evaluate the success of Cupitt's ethical position in addressing what has been dubbed the "ethical paradox of postmodernity," or the "moral maze," the fact that living *after* God sometimes leads to a situation in which "functionally, we are not morally disengaged, adrift, and alienated; we are morally obliterated. We are, in practice, not only moral *illiterati*; we have become morally vacant."[73]

Chapter 2

Cupitt's ethics and his critics

Two competing "armies" have drawn their lines in the battle of post-modern ethics — the realists and the anti-realists. Realists believe that some things and situations have inherent moral properties whether or not human beings at a given time or in a particular society recognize this to be the case. Such moral absolutes as Truth and Goodness are independent of our own cultural interpretations, and stand waiting to be discovered. Anti-realists, on the other hand, hold that values are invented or projected by people. The distinction between "inventing" and "discovering" is at the heart of the conflict.

For the ethical realist, choosing the anti-realist option means accepting that "we are traveling blind, stripped of our moral compass . . . not only in society, but increasingly in the Church as well."[1] For the ethical anti-realist, the realist option means adopting the "herd-morality" of people who slavishly follow the prescriptions of those in authority, and laying oneself open to Nietzsche's ridicule. Cupitt, as I have shown in chapter 1, affirms inventing/creating as the source of ethics, yet with the important caveat that ethical valuations are always an intrinsic part of culture and encoded in language. Unlike some anti-realists, Cupitt does not think that we ever have to begin from nowhere. Rather, the task is to evaluate and revise the ethics that our culture has already produced. In arriving at this position, Cupitt for all intents and purposes discards three current models of ethics that might have been viable alternatives to his personal solar ethics and social humanitarianism. These are to be found in the writings of Iris Murdoch, Alasdair MacIntyre and Richard Holloway. I will analyse these ethical models, showing why Cupitt has insisted that they are flawed. It is fruitless to critique ethical systems based on Biblical fundamentalism, because nothing their proponents argue would resonate with Cupitt's agenda.

Realist ethics, but a non-realist theology (Iris Murdoch)

David Edwards in *Tradition and Truth* suggests that Cupitt's stance on ethics is akin to that of the novelist and philosopher Iris Murdoch. Edwards' comparison is, however, wide of the mark. To be sure, Cupitt and Murdoch are theological non-realists in holding that human life has no external vantage point and share a commitment to being religious without believing in God; nevertheless, they differ considerably in their approach to ethics. Indeed, Cupitt has told me that Iris Murdoch used to say; 'I don't believe in God, but I do believe in religion'— by 'religion' meaning attention to the Good.

Iris Murdoch describes Cupitt as "a very brave and valuable pioneer and a learned and accessible thinker, who stirs up thought where it is most needed."[2] Like Cupitt, she endorses contingency and actively seeks to engage with it. However, to overcome this state of being she turns back to Plato and his idea of the Forms, especially the Form of the Good. Instead of a plurality of voices competing in the ethical market-place, contemplation of the Good is the best replacement for the now defunct notion of an objective personal God. Underlying this approach are two suppositions: first, the already stated idea that "God is dead," and second, the validity of the traditional Christian concept of "sin" (that Murdoch wants to retain but that she asserts society has lost). This she equates with the Freudian concept of *ego*. She sees Freud as having given a modern interpretation of the doctrine of original sin, with "the psyche as an egocentric system of quasi-mechanical energy, largely determined by its own individual history, whose natural attachments are sexual, ambiguous, and hard for the subject to understand or control." So, "in the moral life the enemy is the fat relentless ego."[3] For Murdoch, human selfishness is the chief sin that must be overcome.

Like Cupitt, Murdoch rejects the idea that humanism will save humankind from selfish living. Rather, by contemplation of the Forms there will be "patiently and continuously a change of one's whole being in all its contingent detail, through a world of appearance toward a world of reality."[4] Change of being provides support for both moral contemplation and moral action. According to Murdoch, if one tries to act well, one receives help from the unconscious mind. Following Plato, she considers that the supreme Form is that of the Good which is defined as "an active principle of truthful cognition and moral understanding in the soul." It is a "reality principle" by which we can guide our lives in the assurance that there *are* absolute standards that take the form of general moral rules: "do not lie," "do not steal," "be helpful," "be kind." The reality principle also assists us in choosing the most appropriate course of action in specific situations. It enables the "true and just seeing of people and human institutions, which is also a seeing of the invisible through the visible, the real through the apparent, the spiritual beyond the material."[5]

Murdoch, like Cupitt, sees life as an engagement with the world as it is, but relies on Plato's myth of the cave in *The Republic*, to consider that it is a progressive spiritual journey from appearance to reality. She views the ultimate Good as "somewhere beyond" and asserts that "it is an empirical fact about human nature that this attempt [to attain ultimate goodness] cannot be entirely successful."[6] To be consistent with Plato, Murdoch "employs the language of the ontological argument to argue that God (the Good) cannot simply be one thing among others, but exists of necessity."[7] Just as in traditional theology aseity (self-generated existence) was ascribed to God, so it now ascribed to the Good. There must always be a sense of ultimate mystery (something Cupitt rejects); indeed, the theologian Stanley Hauerwas labels her "mystical" and criticizes her mystical interpretation, arguing that Christianity is much more historical than Murdoch will allow. Moreover, he considers that the world as portrayed in her novels is too lonely and individualistic, pointing out that Christians constitute a community of people who believe in a God who forgives sin, and who meet together to acknowledge that fact.

Though Murdoch departs from Plato by not relating the hierarchy of the Forms to the various categories and classes of citizens, for her the Good will always be imperfectly instantiated in the world. Indeed, in a move resembling Cupitt's turn from the academic to the everyday world, Murdoch elevates the wisdom of the "ordinary person" over that of the professional philosopher. Ordinary people recognize without much hesitation that some ways of behaving are better than others, and there is not usually much discussion about which direction leads to the Good. Conversely the ordinary person can recognize that which contravenes the Good — evil, cruelty and indifference to suffering. (It is interesting to note that she thereby counters one of Alasdair MacIntyre's objections to Plato: that knowledge of the Forms is accessible only to the elite).

The nub of the disagreement between Murdoch and Cupitt is that for Murdoch, values are not created by one's choices, and people's intuition of the reality principle suggests to them what is good and what is not good. To free ourselves of our natural egoism, contemplation of the

Forms (with transcendence understood *only* in a moral sense) makes available to us "standards, which are not dependent upon our individual, self-centred perception of the world."[8] This is where Cupitt rejects Murdoch's idea of the Good: in *Odyssey on the Sea of Faith*, as I have shown, his whole flowing project is a denial of transcendent values, Platonic or otherwise. As Elizabeth Burns observes, Cupitt discards "Platonic views such as those of Murdoch on the grounds that transcendent values can have no relevance for us."[9]

Indeed, the disagreement between Cupitt and Murdoch must be yet more emphatically expressed; for the ethical anti-realist Cupitt, it is not simply that transcendent values have no relevance, but that *transcendent values do not exist*. The only values that exist are those that are embedded, and continually renegotiated, in language by human beings. There is no moral order, except that which arises in different cultures and societies as a result of their own inventions. There is no one true morality but rather many ethical systems that we have fabricated ourselves. No outside "measuring-stick" exists against which to regulate human behavior, nor (as Cupitt argues against Murdoch as early as 1986) can anything external to us "cure us of egoism."[10] Cupitt's catchphrase has consistently been that "we have to do that for ourselves." We have to create our own ideas of goodness and salvation. They are not to be found outside us. Indeed, Cupitt criticises Murdoch for making goodness, like the God portrayed by Anselm, something whose "face is blank, its nature mysterious" so that, for human beings, "goodness is impossible, non-existent, not on the map at all and wholly beyond our reach."[11] To be sure, the early Cupitt in a book like *Christ and the Hiddenness of God* (1971) might have been more than willing to find a space for mystery and transcendence but he has now moved on. In 2000, referring to Iris Murdoch he states explicitly: "I love the end of mystery. . . . I love being precipitated wholly into Now. . . . A Platonist, (Iris) Murdoch hated the thought of a world in which 'nothing is deep'. . . . But I say this state of total exposure is the *telos*."[12] For Cupitt, there is nothing either "out there" or "hidden" within human beings that it is "Good" to contemplate. Moral realism and metaphysics are dead. Nihilism is our permanent human condition: the world is one in which everything changes, peters out and has no fixed value beyond what we ascribe to it at the moment.

Christian realism in ethics (Alasdair MacIntyre)

Alasdair MacIntyre's *After Virtue* has now become a classic in the study of ethics, but people commonly forget that it was originally part of "a work still in progress."[13] MacIntyre's primary aim is to challenge emotivism in its many forms. He thus lays down a challenge to Cupitt's solar ethics, which Cupitt freely admits is "a form of emotivism."[14] Like Iris Murdoch, MacIntyre takes as his starting point one of the founding figures of the Western philosophical tradition, but this time it is Aristotle rather than Plato who inspires the attempt to revive a forgotten morality of the past. He develops a form of Virtue ethic that describes what sort of persons we should become — that is, he explains the move from "untutored-human-nature" to "human-nature-if-it-achieved-its-*telos*." Unlike Cupitt, MacIntyre envisions a specific *telos* or goal to human life: one linked to people's membership in the local (religious) communities that stamp them with their identities, and furnishes them with a purpose for living. In a move interestingly reminiscent of Cupitt, MacIntyre sets up a Kierkegaardian *either/or*, insisting that there is *only one* choice. It is *either* to follow emotivism with Nietzsche as the prototype *or*, as he prefers, to show that the Enlightenment project should never have begun and the answer has been there all the time with Aristotle.[15]

The key to MacIntyre's trilogy is to be found in capsule form at the beginning of *After Virtue*, where he resumes the search begun in *A Short History of Ethics* for a criterion by which to judge what is ethically acceptable. Without some such standard we are left with emotivism: this is an unacceptable situation in which "the invocation of one premise against another becomes a matter of pure assertion and counter-assertion."[16]. This is a dire situation for MacIntyre, because for him emotivism opens the door to someone whose rhetoric might sway the minds and hearts of the populace to evil rather than good — the archetypal case being the Nazi appropriation of Nietszche's *Übermensch*.

MacIntyre lays much of the blame for the rise of emotivism on the failure of the "Enlightenment Project." In the Enlightenment, as reality was fragmented into distinctive and competing spheres, the individual replaced the social as morality was moved from God's hands to the human sphere. People could now behave as they chose. According to MacIntyre, "the interrelatedness of all aspects of reality, and of all people within an objective moral system, was destroyed as morality was uprooted from its traditional and divinely sanctioned context."[17] We must return, he urges, to a more originary Virtue-tradition that does not repudiate all things social (virtues and practices) and things historical (narrative and tradition), for we need a *telos* by which to live and criteria for making moral judgments. Without virtues, practices, narrative, and tradition — with no way to discover the purpose of human life — one is the captain of a rudderless ship. Aristotle's theory provides the way of living from within a tradition or community that is the necessary framework for making sound ethical judgments. The Virtue ethic builds upon a shared heritage nurtured in "heroic narrative." Heroic societies offer two lessons. First, morality is always to some degree tied to the socially local and particular (thus the aspiration of modernity to a moral universality freed from all particularity is an illusion); and second, virtue can exist only in the context of a tradition.

MacIntyre argues that everyone is part of some tradition and that whether Aristotelian, Augustinian, Thomist, Humean, post-Enlightenment liberal, or something else, one can speak *only* from within that tradition. Further, he says, traditions are vindicated or impeached by how they cope with "the epistemological crisis" that results from an encounter with another tradition.[18] Very simply, if a tradition can provide a more reasonable or rational answer than other traditions to the question of what constitutes the good life, then it will survive. MacIntyre claims that since by definition emotivism does *not* stand within a tradition, it cannot provide a more adequate answer. In the end, then, it must be "a doctrine only possible for those who regard themselves as outsiders, as uncommitted or rather as committed only to acting a succession of temporary parts. Hence theirs is not so much a conclusion about truth as an exclusion from it and thereby from rational debate."[19]

MacIntyre is, of course, emphasizing both a realist and a narrative approach to ethics. The realism is reflected in the assumption — in contrast to the Nietzschean "perspectivist" approach — that the heroic stories informing one's tradition have objective value. MacIntyre would understand heroic stories not in a postmodern way as a "fiction" to be dismissed as one person or group's (incomplete) interpretation, but as part of a narrative tradition that has sustained people. Aristotle's advance over Plato is that "the moral structure is intimately linked with social relationships."[20] The self becomes what it is in heroic societies only through its role as a social creation, not an individual one.

In the course of his writings MacIntyre looks specifically to the Roman Catholic community and tradition to provide an adequate narrative to find answers about how to live the good life. In *Whose Justice? Which Rationality?* he promotes the writings of St. Thomas Aquinas above those of Aristotle, and he himself becomes a convert to the Roman Catholic Church, which he views as a community that embodies the Virtues. This answers Stanley Grenz's specific criticism that MacIntyre advocates an "open-ended" search for the good life.[21] In his third book,

MacIntyre defends tradition against the genealogist's suspicion (especially Nietzsche's) of the community as encouraging "slave morality." Following the Thomist tradition, he stresses that the self exists in relation to a community to whom it is accountable for "actions, attitudes, and beliefs" and which provides the self with "the unity of a story with a beginning, a middle, and an end."[22] Thus, according to MacIntyre, being within a Roman Catholic community has distinct advantages over the anomie of the Nietzschean individualist.

Cupitt's first response to MacIntyre was aimed at *After Virtue*. It is no surprise that in 1982 he defended Nietzsche against MacIntyre's Aristotle. For the early Cupitt, the autonomy of the individual is paramount. The Nietzschean individualist is concerned solely with the will-to-truth, and unmasks all social fictions of "human life as potentially a meaningful story, of a stable human character, of the good for man, and of the moral precedence of society over the individual."[23] However, as I have shown in chapter 1, this emphasis on autonomy is replaced in the mid-1980s by the acceptance of a more de-centered person, one who is a product of his/her culture/society. Indeed, Cupitt would now agree with MacIntyre that society takes precedence over the individual and would be extremely wary of equating the will-to-power with the will-to-truth. As I will argue in chapter 4, Cupitt is *still* a member of the Christian community and tradition, but he would not endorse the Thomist cardinal virtues of justice (rectitude), wisdom, courage (fortitude) and moderation (self-control). While acknowledging MacIntyre's success in creating public interest in ethics, Cupitt dismisses his thesis as an effort to achieve what the Monastic orders did from the sixth to tenth centuries. MacIntyre is a countermodern and nostalgic neo-conservative enamored of a past that cannot be recreated. It is a return that is doomed to failure.[24]

Essentially, the contention between MacIntyre and Cupitt is the realist versus anti-realist debate. For Cupitt, MacIntyre is guilty of the Realist assumption that *only* realism is rational. Cupitt asserts that anti-realism is *also* rational. The anti-realist endorses Nietzsche's project of the critique of all values, asking people to begin by studying the overall valuation of life — i.e. of *everything* — that is already built into their language. As he states in *The New Christian Ethics*, "life is valuation." By this he means that as an inherent element of culture, value is omnipresent. Indeed, "the will-to-live just *is* a will-to-value."[25] The role of the Christian in this is to attempt an almost Nietzschean revaluation of values. The main difference between MacIntyre and Cupitt is that for Cupitt there can be no return to a better age or moral philosophy, for one has to deal with the situation *now*. Like Edith Wyschogrod he would view MacIntyre's thesis of a return to a monastic ethics or the Aristotelian good life as "the myth of the tabula rasa (that) leads to impossible dreams."[26] Moreover, it is not a matter of trying somehow to smuggle ethical or moral codes into what is wrongly assumed to be a valueless world. What Cupitt proposes is the opposite. He follows Nietzsche's saying in *The Will to Power* that "all sense perceptions are permeated with value judgments." Valuation comes first, is omnipresent, and creates everything. Everything that we say, do and think involves valuations and is therefore creative. Morality must give up the task of attempting to restore values to a world supposedly bereft of them. Instead, we should see our task as one of understanding, sorting out, and criticizing the creative valuations that we are always and every-where making.

Furthermore, Cupitt would not be in the least worried about the claim that emotivism is "the doctrine that all evaluative judgments and more specifically all moral judgments are *nothing but* expressions of prefer-ence, expressions of attitude or feeling, insofar as they are moral or evalu-ative in character."[27] He would retort that all valuations are expressions of feeling and there is nothing wrong with that, for people use differential feeling responses to structure the world. We are creatures of feeling; and our values are not absolute or objective values, but, as the modern idiom has it, simply *human* values. So Cupitt locates all value in our emotive response to life here and now.

Other commentators have made specific criticisms of MacIntyre's thesis. In particular, it is noted that Aristotle's "ethics is just a detailed elaboration of a very orthodox Greek view of aristocratic living." It rein-forces undesirable attitudes of racism (friendship with non-Greeks was only a matter of utility); sexism (man rules by merit but hands over to his wife such duties as are best "suited" to her); speciesism (animals cannot be happy for they have no reason); and ageism (nobody would want to befriend the old). Likewise, it is argued that Aristotle's moral theory is elitist in that *only* "magnanimous men," "honourable politicians" and "philosophers" can appreciate the Good Life.[28] Thus, Aristotle's teachings are sufficiently culture-bound that, as Bertrand Russell observed, "the suf-ferings of mankind, in so far as he is aware of them, do not move him emotionally."[29]

Cupitt would agree, then, with D. Z. Phillips that MacIntyre's project is a flight into "romanticism" in its attempt to give a unified account of an historical excursion from "moral coherence" (Aristotle) to "moral incoherence" (post-Nietzsche).[30] This latter thesis is rejected on the his-torical grounds that ancient cultures were far from being as morally homogenous as MacIntyre would want us to suppose. Likewise, if present-day culture is rendered morally incoherent by incommensurable competing moral traditions, how can one arbitrarily announce (as MacIntyre does) that his thesis is the best way of "settling the issue and . . . generating a moral tradition in a vacuum?"[31] Does this not show the present-day culture eminently capable of providing the necessary resources for moral coherence — a capacity he has denied in declaring it morally incoherent — and thus render his thesis inconsistent? Phillips concludes with the observation that in the area of morality "we actually proceed, individually and collectively, in ways far more ragged than MacIntyre would have us believe."[32] No criterion that can be plucked from "outside," "beyond," or from a previous age can provide immediate answers to the ethical problems of today.

This "ragged" nature of ethics is what Cupitt, following postmodernism, would call the "death of God" or the "death of Tradition." Once we have dismissed the appeal to an ancient and unified inheritance (whether Aristotle, Aquinas, or God), then a form of emotivism or expressivism must replace it. This is what it means to live *after* God. Surprisingly, perhaps, it is a former Scottish Episcopalian Bishop, the Right Reverend Richard Holloway, who comes closest to Cupitt's position in *Godless Morality*. Here he acknowledges that even in the case of Christians, "God" must be kept out of morality. Phillips' "ragged" morality is similar to what Holloway terms "ethical jazz."

Godless morality (Richard Holloway)

Richard Holloway, the former Anglican Bishop of Edinburgh, wrote *Godless Morality* as a response to the raving homophobia of bishops at the Lambeth Conference in 1998. He was dismayed that this Conference, which meets only once in ten years to decide on the future direction of the Anglican Communion, should condemn homosexuality as a sin. Although a few dissenters spoke out, the majority of bishops simply quoted the Bible and invoked moral absolutism to justify hatred of a sexual minority.[33] Holloway's considerable experience of medical ethics committees, where moral issues were debated strictly on the basis of scientific facts and human welfare, made him wonder to himself, "Which world do I belong in?" He had to choose the medical world, and in *Godless Morality* he argues for a human approach to morality on the grounds that an ethical system driven by religious zeal is almost always demonic.

The tabloid press in the United Kingdom was predictably outraged that a Bishop had spoken out on such issues as sexuality and drug-taking. David Boulton makes the apposite point that they were aggrieved that

Holloway should have discussed topics that now "belong" to the media — sex and drugs — and even used such an earthy word as "shagging" for casual sex. A corollary implication is that such newspapers view themselves as the kind of morality arbiters and commentators on the Zeitgeist that the churches once were. Only the "more serious papers" tackled the pertinent issue of how a representative of a metaphysical tradition could reach conclusions identical to those of someone without the benefit of such a tradition.[34] This is the crux of the issue for Holloway, and his reason for writing the book was to show "that we must disconnect religion and God from the struggle to recover some elements of a common ethic."[35]

Holloway makes a distinction between moral pluralism and moral relativism, affirming the former while denying the latter. He insists that common ethical principles can emerge from differing moral systems. Whereas God has in the past been posited as the final arbiter ("micromanager") in all ethical matters, Holloway prefers to leave God out of the picture and rely on human reason. Thus his book "is an attempt to offer a human-centred justification for a particular moral approach. It is a morality without God."[36] Morality becomes like a jazz session, constantly being re-invented, with lots of improvisation in response to differing situations and new developments in science, medicine and technology. Affirming Nietzsche, he deplores (as does Cupitt) a slave morality that renders humans unable to choose and reliant on Divine fiat or the power of the State. Adopting a stance like that of the Sea of Faith Networks, he views morality as a human creation. An emerging morality will incorporate a principle of consent so that "justifications have to be offered for moral restraints upon individuals," while at the same time recognising that such restraints are necessary for the well being of others and for harmonious co-existence.[37] He then attempts to create human ethics that incorporate this *principle of consent* in the areas of Sexuality (chapter 2), Gay and Lesbian issues (chapter 3), Drugs (chapter 4), Abortion and Euthanasia (chapter 5) and Reproductive Technology (chapter 6).

Holloway's ethical stance is essentially a restatement of an Anglican *via media* position — steering a course between extremes — and though not grounded in postmodernist thought, is very reminiscent of Cupitt's standpoint in *The Long-Legged Fly*. Holloway does this by affirming (without clearly elucidating the point) a "general application of Aristotle's doctrine of virtue as a mean between two extremes."[38] This idea of virtue seems to reflect a cursory reading of Alasdair MacIntyre, and to portray Aristotle as an Anglican apologist for a middle course from which a new morality of consent emerges. To this he contrasts the conceit of official religious systems that lack the capacity to embrace the huge diversity of humanity, all the while insisting on their way as *the* only way. For Holloway, Aristotle's ethics can be summed up as the middle way between "absolute prohibition and absolute license" so that the "virtuous person lives a balanced life."[39]

As the previous section surely indicates, I doubt whether MacIntyre would accept such an interpretation. According to his analysis, Aristotle's ethics involve much more than simply adopting virtues that help a person to live a more balanced life. Holloway lamentably mentions nothing of *telos*, practice, narrative, and tradition, which are the central core of MacIntyre's thesis. Moreover, Holloway is insistent that religion must be kept separate from ethics. This would be anathema to MacIntyre, and as a Christian interpretation of MacIntyre states: "If virtues are cultivated by striving for excellence in the practice of practices, then we are unable to grow in Christlikeness unless we participate in Christianity's practices."[40]

Holloway's thesis becomes even more inconsistent in that, while calling for the adoption of a religionless and godless morality, he still affirms an objective God who is *more* than the projection of our best values. Without stating his position very clearly, he places himself somewhere between Process theology and panentheism. He argues that the idea of God as a micromanager of humanity must be replaced by a more dynamic understanding of a deity who accompanies creation in its evolving story after the manner of a pianist in a silent movie.[41]

Holloway's book is thus the direct antithesis of Iris Murdoch in that he wants to retain an objective (almost Deist) realist God, yet promote anti-realist ethics. It flies in the face of the indubitable fact that religion has always had ethical implications, and ends up with religion that has no room for ethics, and ethics that has no room for a religious tradition's perspective (whether that religion is either realist or non-realist). It falls between two stools and satisfies no one. On one side, the realist Christian traditionalist who affirms belief in God is mystified, because without an ethical content what kind of religion is left? On the other side, while endorsing much of Holloway's transactional, democratic and consensus-evolving ethics, Cupitt recognises that his argument is "unstable," and suggests that Holloway hasn't pursued the implications of anti-realist ethics to their necessary conclusion of dispensing with belief in a realist God. Cupitt has consistently warned that ethics will bring the downfall of belief in a supernatural God. Although Cupitt endorses Holloway's book as "brave and necessary" he thinks that in refusing to acknowledge that religion, too, is a human creation, and thus abandoning belief in God, Holloway has not gone far enough. Holloway's position comes closest to that of Cupitt in his next book, *Doubts and Loves*, especially in his insistence on the theology of life, Kingdom values, and the moral value of following the way of Jesus as opposed to believing traditional Christian claims as to who he might have been. Indeed, he seems to espouse a position a bit to the left even of Cupitt, for he begins to purge himself of all residual Christian language and thinking. However, he falls short of rejecting belief in a Supreme Being.

Ethics has obviously dented the confidence of the ex-Primus of Scotland, and Cupitt can now recommend that there are *only* two consistent theological standpoints: *either* fundamentalism, in which the unchanging dictates of God (including his ethical injunctions) must be obeyed, *or* a thoroughgoing non-realist theology and anti-realist ethics that are continually being re-negotiated.

Theological non-realism and anti-realist ethics under fire (Joseph Runzo)

The major critique of the inconsistency of holding on to both theological non-realism and anti-realist ethics has come from Joseph Runzo. He identifies that there are two major protagonists who support non-realism in theology and anti-realism in ethics. First he highlights the work of Gordon Kaufman, whom he thinks is Kantian when he says that that "God in Godself (is) noumenal and transcendently unknowable."[42] Hence, rather than deliberate on epistemology or metaphysics (because God is ultimately the mystery that surrounds us) the concern of any God-talk is how to understand the ethical concerns of human beings. Accordingly, God is better defined in a non-realist way "as the unifying symbol of those powers and dimensions of the ecological and historical feedback network which create and sustain and work to further enhance all life."[43]

According to Runzo, Kaufman's emphasis on theological non-realism aims to divert the theist from idle speculation about God to concentrating on the pressing ethical concerns of a world facing ecological and nuclear disaster. However, it seems highly problematic to label Kaufman a thoroughgoing theological non-realist in Cupitt's sense of the term. Admittedly Kaufman is hesitant to use the symbol God as a literal reference to an existent being, yet he wants the concept God somehow to exceed the sum of the current values — i.e. for him there is an ultimate referent. For Kaufman, then, God (understood symbolically) holds in tension a connectedness with people's struggle to be human *and* that which transcends humanity. In fact, Kaufman himself in his later writings, remarks that "when the symbol 'God' is interpreted as identifying and holding together in one the ultimate mystery of things and the serendipitous creativity at work in the ecological order of which we are part, it can provide a valuable focus for human devotion, meditation, work in today's pluralized world."[44] Lloyd Geering points out in *Tomorrow's God* that this is "third-order theology" which admits that religious language is a human creation and that people must consciously reconstruct those human symbols to personify their supreme values and ideals. However, this "third-order theology" does not preclude the possibility that there might be some reality beyond the symbol. This symbol might not convince orthodox Christians, but Kaufman's aim, like that of John Hick, is to engage with other faith traditions. Therefore, his God is not strictly non-realist, for there is still *something/someone* beyond the limits of our intellectual (not experiential) powers — ultimate mystery. What Runzo fails to mention is that Kaufman recalls Wittgenstein in positing mystery as that which draws the limits to human imaginative constructions. For, "in reminding ourselves that God is mystery to us, we allow God in God's concrete actuality to be whatever God is, quite apart from our conceptualizations."[45]

Runzo's choice of Kaufman as an advocate of non-realism is thus less than appropriate, for Kaufman keeps open the possibility of an ultimate reality, recognising that this ultimate mystery remains unknowable. Cupitt leaves no such door ajar.

The object of Runzo's second attack is Cupitt. Written in 1992, it relies on an engagement with Cupitt's *The New Christian Ethics*, and is admittedly outdated. I refer to it here because many of Runzo's arguments reflect the same hostility that is *still* engendered by Cupitt's ethics. Runzo outlines five "internal deficiencies" in Cupitt's non-realist Christian humanism. I shall summarize his argument and offer rebuttals taken from Cupitt himself.

First, he argues that if Cupitt's ethics are non-cognitivist, then a "purely secular non-cognitivist meta-ethics" is consistent, but a "religious ethical non-cognitivism" is "self defeating." He likens this to self-deception, maintaining that in most religions God has an objective referent, and the sacred scriptures are realist in intent, with ethical injunctions derived from a transcendent deity.[46]

Cupitt would counter that non-realism about God is not self-deception, but an up-to-date use of the symbol. The mere fact that we no longer posit an objective referent does not obviate the *use* of the symbol, especially if that use still has value. Indeed, Cupitt puts his case more strongly, arguing that *only* the non-realist can truly say "My God" because, "only the person who thinks that God does not exist can really know how to praise God, worship God, love God, and thank God aright. Provided that we put metaphysical nontheism first, the religion of Being may permit a certain reinstatement of language about God."[47] Following Mark C. Taylor's thesis in *About Religion*, Cupitt compares "God" to the way that gold functions in economic systems "to safeguard the meaning and value of signs by providing a secure referent." When this objective referent is discarded then "meaning and value no longer are determined by reference to a transcendental signified but now emerge through the diacritical interplay of freely floating signifiers."[48] Cupitt differs from Taylor in arguing that worship can still go on even when people admit that "God" is only a sign, just as economic exchange happens without the protection of a "real" gold standard. Thus he can respond to Runzo that "God is simply a sign, just as money is simply a sign or a flow of signs. And religion is surprisingly little affected. Worship goes on without a realist God just as easily as economic exchange goes on without the backing of gold. What's the problem?"[49]

Second, Runzo argues that anti-realist ethics provides "little check against moral anarchy" in that Cupitt's historicist and relativist perspective lacks the "criterion" test. Lacking an external measuring-stick, one has to rely on "parochial homocentrism" with ideas of truth and value seen as socio-historically conditioned and relevant only to our *present* needs and purposes. Runzo asks: "How could we *know* that there is nothing beyond *our* possible knowledge?"[50] He also is skeptical of Cupitt's alleged denial of shared, cross-schema moral standards, adducing the existence of generally accepted trans-world moral standards — for example, that cruelty is wrong.

Here Runzo has misunderstood Cupitt, who is arguing that society/culture draws the lines or the boundaries that characterize what the values are to be, but once drawn they ought not to be regarded as being "unbudgeably fixed." Cupitt is not advocating moral anarchy, but an ethic of living-and-dying for others. The charge that there "appear to be general moral standards" is countered by Cupitt's insistence that by practicing solar ethics (immersing oneself in the flux and outpouring of life and forgetting ourselves) we put others before ourselves. His *Christian* humanism still affirms *Christian* values about being part of one body, the human race. He would also add that the scope of future moral and epistemological change is limited by the fact that we cannot imagine ourselves ever being able altogether to transcend ordinary language, temporality and society. Ordinary language already commits us to a basic picture of the human situation, within which we must work. We have some leeway for modifying and reinterpreting this basic world-view, but we cannot expect ever to escape it completely. It is also worth noting that Runzo's idea of "trans-world moral standards" must be tempered with the recognition that moral standards, however they might be conceived (and they are not always conceived in the same way), exist *only* where they are both claimed and acknowledged![51]

Third, Runzo is correct when he notes that Cupitt's ethical agenda is not to overcome sin, but nihilism. But he does not expand upon what this means for Cupitt and the implications for his ethics. As I have argued above, Cupitt's relation to nihilism has passed through many phases, and his ethics are focused on helping people live in an era for which there is no vertical axis, but only the horizontal. Cupitt affirms that we should *embrace* nihilism (if that term is still to be used); and by accepting it we will overcome what the term is pointing to — the "death of God," the arbitrariness of life, contingency and temporality. Runzo argues that Cupitt's Christian humanism could be as adequately served by reference to scientific or secular humanism and wonders why Cupitt could not be a secular humanist rather than a Christian humanist. We have met this criticism before; it betrays a total misunderstanding and perversion of Cupitt's position. As I will show in the next chapter, he considers the "religious" dimension to be of crucial importance. Runzo accuses him of self-deception in appealing to a system of belief that he has clearly castigated as destructive and oppressive. Runzo's argument seems to suggest that it is impossible to affirm the "affective" aspects of Christian ethics without reference to the alleged "destructive cognitive" aspects. At the time when Runzo was writing, the thrust of Cupitt's radical agenda was to *reform* Christianity and to assert those aspects of it that are life-affirming, while rejecting those that are life-denying. Runzo simply presupposes that this task is impossible. It is also bizarre that as a critical realist, Runzo would not similarly pick and choose which aspects of the Christian system he would want to affirm and which to reject. It is unlikely that he would be advocating Christianity *in toto*. The sticking-point for Runzo is that like other critical realists, he considers Cupitt to have overstepped the mark by dispensing with God, and thereby rejected any moral standards.

Fourth, Runzo claims that Cupitt considers belief in an objective God "inimical to the essential autonomy of ethical action." Arguing that this is a misinterpretation of Christian teaching, he concludes rather weakly, that "non-realism, then, is internally defective insofar as it is based on the erroneous assumption that obedience to God necessarily *entails* loss of autonomy."[52]

As I have shown before, this argument might be directed at the early Cupitt; but he has moved on, and for the postmodern Cupitt we are not wholly autonomous, self-made monarchs of all we survey. For the recent Cupitt, human living is highly *situated*. Precisely because humans are social beings, non-realism and autonomy are not synonymous — in fact the opposite is the case.

Runzo's fifth and final criticism is another version of the criterion argument: it asks what standard or criterion anti-realists can use to decide upon the correct way to behave towards others. According to Runzo, one can appeal only to a "matter of luck" or "natural inclination." Likewise, he argues that to add "Christian" to what are in effect humanitarian values is inconsistent, since in his estimation Cupitt has dealt the death blow to Christianity (see argument 4).

This, of course, is to misunderstand Cupitt. He reiterates that values are implicit in everything one does and is. Values are there already, needing to be assessed by people to see if they are still applicable. Moreover, Cupitt considers Christianity profoundly humanitarian! At the heart of Jesus' message was the call to create a more just and humane world and to advance Kingdom values that accept the worth of each human being.

Underpinning these five arguments is Runzo's major theme that only theological realism can change world-views; for him it is superior to (secular) humanism and non-realism because it adds "another" dimension. He approvingly cites Sallie McFague, who in *Models of God* says that "to have faith in God is to believe that the universe is neither benevolent nor indifferent but is on the side of life and its fulfillment."[53] He argues that with realism there are *objective* standards (apart from what humans happen to think) which determine what is moral — i.e. ultimate morality is grounded in an ultimate God. He claims that this makes it easier for realists to oppose evils such as sexism and avoid the necessity of war. This is an extraordinary assertion, for even a cursory historical survey reveals Christian realists whose understanding of God has been blatantly sexist and others who have invoked a warlike deity. Indeed, a document such as the "Papal New Millennium Apology" produced by the Roman Catholic Church admits that theological realism has countenanced slavery, the oppression of minorities, killing fields in countless countries, the oppression of women, and the persecution of those who choose to worship a different Divinity (or not to worship at all).

For Runzo, being a theological realist also assures one of adopting the moral point of view, whereas a non-realist's choice of the correct moral point of view is a matter of "happenstantial good fortune." The Christian realist takes the moral point of view because he/she is "both autonomously committed to this stance towards others *and because* [he/she] loves the things that God loves."[54] Runzo seems to be using the first part of the celebrated Euthyphro Dilemma derived from Plato: something is good/moral only because God commands it to be good/moral. For non-realists, the counter-argument within the Euthyphro dilemma is that standards of goodness/morality can exist independent of any belief in God; they require no realist God to support morality.

Even more extraordinary is Runzo's already mentioned distinguishing of different ethical stances *within theological realism* and equating ethical pluralism with a God who "creates and sustains . . . a staggering diversity of laudable human moral convictions."[55] An obvious rejoinder would be to ask, "How does one decide which of these moral convictions are *really* God-given? Is it all, some, or none?" Ironically, one is led back to subjectivity and into the arms of Cupitt! To use Runzo's own example, how many Christian realists would endorse McFague's new models of God? How many of them would be comfortable with a "more female model of responsibility and care" or God as "mother," "lover," "body" etc? How would they choose which ones are acceptable? Runzo's argument collapses because he now needs a criterion when he has already insisted that his realism has a criterion!

Another equally valid argument is that emotivism/non-realism generally respects the ethical point of view of others better than those theological realists who proclaim that theirs is *the only* correct way to behave. In short, realism (whether critical or otherwise) is no guarantee of non-authoritarianism in ethics. To Runzo, Cupitt would reply, "What *difference* does the supposed backing of an objective God 'on the side of life and its fulfilment' *really* make?"

Runzo's criticisms of Cupitt again fail because he is not pitting sword against sword, but sword against pitchfork. His critical realist position is another way of promoting a more compassionate understanding of an objective God. Unfortunately, it will fall on deaf ears. In fact, his contentions are very similar to those of Brian Hebblethwaite, who holds that Cupitt's ethics is "implausibly Promethean in treating humanity as the inventor of right and wrong, and at the same time it is wilfully blind to men and women's needs for resources of transformation and sanctification from beyond. It is also in danger of total collapse, if ethical distinctions themselves are part only of the surface of things, to be dissolved in the flux of experience."[56]

Hebblethwaite and Runzo are mistaken in requiring Cupitt to endorse transformation "from beyond." For Cupitt, ethics are indeed "Promethean," and the questions that this chapter has been working towards must now be addressed: "How adequate are Cupitt's ethics for those who reject any external arbiter and are content with the 'outside-lessness' of existence?" "Do Cupitt's ethics collapse in the face of the post-modern 'flux of experience?'" "Are Cupitt's ethics a viable postmodern approach to living in postmodernity?"

Cupitt's criticism of Cupitt!

Theologians seldom (if at all) take the trouble to critique their own writings. Cupitt is an exception, freely admitting that all his books have been much corrected first drafts and that he starts each new book from a perceived fault in the previous one. He also recognizes that his study of ethics has sustained two major criticisms. First, it is alleged that his solar ethics can work only in a Western, liberal, capitalist society. Second, it is stated that his formulations disintegrate in the face of the world's mani-fold evils and injustices. Are these criticisms justified? And how has Cupitt responded?

(a) A naïve "western capitalist?"

...I know what will be said. I'm being naively utopian about the excesses of our late-capitalism and our consumerism. I'm denying (or at least playing down) the manifest evils and injus-tices that are everywhere as rampant as ever. My postmodern solar ethic of free self-expression runs into acute difficulties when different cultural groups, each seeking to affirm itself and its val-ues, clash head-on. Markets, whether in ideas or values or signs or goods, never get to be so "free" as to solve by themselves all problems of *power*. On the contrary, markets will be manipulated by various power-interests unless they are carefully regulated; and the regulators need moral principles to guide them – which surely shows that thoroughgoing market relativism can never by itself be the basis for a social theory. And so on. I do believe that these objections will be made, and that either they rest upon a misun-derstanding, or I have already replied to them.[57]

True to his own inimitable style, Cupitt thus sets out the objections that will be presented by others against his combination of solar ethics and humanitarianism. Clearly, he is confident that his ethics offer a credible way of living *after* God. Indeed, he asserts that he has already countered the usual objections.

Cupitt points his reader to a specific section, "The regime of the sign," in *The Time Being* (pages 72–82). Here, he up-dates the argument in *The Long-Legged Fly* that finds a path between the extremes of legalism and lawlessness, and sees "culture (as) the single most important constraint upon freedom."[58] Unlike some of his postmodern commentators Cupitt is optimistic about Western culture (late capitalism or postmodernity), stating that it is a system that "manifests a most extraordinarily potent synthesis of the principles of order and freedom, self-indulgence and social control."[59] He rejects the pessimism of Jean Baudrillard and others, outlining four reasons why one should not be too fearful of Western culture:

- People have shaken off realism with the realization that absolutes no longer exist, and thus they can change moral values.

- As social controls have been loosened, individuals have more freedom than previously. The super-abundance of employment opportunities, consumer goods, etc. is an indication of this freedom.

- The rate of social change as people continually redescribe their world also shows the increase in freedom.

- Moreover, today people who re-invent themselves after a major setback (e.g. loss of employment, divorce, mental breakdown etc.) are accepted and even admired, whereas in previous generations they would never have been given a second chance.

The gist of this is that, because it is so plural and democratic, modern Western society has great internal resources for criticizing and correcting itself. However, before we fall into the trap of using labels such as "naïve utopian" (which Cupitt himself thinks will be used against him) we must adopt the approach that Michael Tanner advises for evaluating Nietzsche, namely that "one needs to read the whole book to see what it means and then to read [his] other books to see what it *really* means."[60] We must remember that Cupitt will always want to criticize any unifying system, including Western culture. It is in this context that one can underst and Cupitt's claim that postmodernity is "Enlightenment-squared, hyperbolic Enlightenment."[61] By this he means that postmodernity is an Enlightenment critique of the Enlightenment project — with the resultant awareness that it is a mistake to portray postmodernity as narcissistic and indolent. "On the contrary, *la lutte continue*, but now we battle not against supernatural foes but against what our own past has made of ourselves and of our world."[62]

Thus, the prevailing moral codes must be subjected to continual criticism; its work never ends. Similarly, one can understand that Cupitt is politically a "radical democrat" urging "continual renegotiation" of the way that people live.[63]

Even some from within the United Kingdom Sea of Faith Network have censured Cupitt's optimism about Western culture.[64] What his present-day detractors fail to note, however, is that this debate concerning Cupitt's alleged blindness to the suffering of oppressed minorities has been raging for the last decade or so. The complaint is connected to a very early reproach, noted by Cowdell (following Kosuke Koyama), that there was a difference between "theology done at 70 degrees and theology done at 120 degrees,"[65] and a later admonishment by Hart that "it's all rather provincial."[66] In short, it is alleged that Cupitt's project needs to be informed by those contexts/religions that stand outside Western culture, and especially by those movements (like Liberation theology) that engender hope for oppressed people in the Third World.[67]

A spirited defence of the non-realism implicit in much liberation theology from South Africa, including that of Steve Biko (the founder of black consciousness) and the theologian Albert Nolan, is given by Ronald Nicolson in a paper presented at a Sea of Faith Conference in the United Kingdom as early as 1992. Nicolson argues that far from hindering a sense of liberation, non-realism can be a corrective for any would-be liberationists. It can prevent them from believing that their own "human construct or interpretation [is] divinely revealed and therefore beyond questioning."[68] Interestingly, he points out that the Afrikaaner founding fathers themselves adopted a liberation theology that fused the teaching of John Calvin (1509–1564) with the socialist theology of Abraham Kuyper (1837–1920), and was based on a realist conviction that "God was on their side in the struggle against international colonialism and capitalism."[69] Thus the white liberationists' belief in an objective Being itself led to the establishment of apartheid. How ironic that a realist-type liberation theology should result in a people's suppression! Nicolson infers that liberationists (of many political persuasions) need to learn from non-realism that "their language about what God has done [is] really language about what they themselves [have] accomplished."[70] Non-realism inhibits the use of religion to buttress oppressive regimes. If non-realism allows people to realize that " they are on their own in this struggle and must for their own sake retain hope and faith in their ultimate power to become subjects and not objects, [then] false hopes will not be raised and despair may defiantly be kept at bay."[71] This can be seen especially today in South Africa, where many of the promised hopes of the new government have not been achieved. The ending of "White-Only" rule has not meant an instant end to oppression and injustice, particularly for those of mixed-race descent. Realist dreams (whether Marxist *or* Christian) have not materialized as quickly as expected. For many African Christians the question still remains: "Where now is God?" Perhaps non-realism is more *realistic* in acknowledging that political outcomes are created by human beings!

Nicolson has correctly pointed to Cupitt's insistence on non-realism as a philosophical/theological methodology that avoids "the problem of arrogance" (that I will liberate you in *my way*, because I am God's agent for *your* redemption), and sees that "liberation" is a continuous human work of creating and re-creating a more just and human(e) world.

Cupitt would also acknowledge his own Western cultural bias, but would respond that, as he indicated in *After God*, the key features of the emerging global culture (for good or ill) are shaped by what is happening in Western culture.[72] These need to be scrutinized and challenged from where they began. As Philip Knight notes, although "it contains much to criticise, and is need of continual reform, it is the only effective system of social and economic polity by which any of us have any hope of realising the justice which Jesus suggested we seek."[73]

For Cupitt, then, willingness to help the world's oppressed is by and large Western and capitalist, but it is also liberal and humanitarian. While he perhaps needs to point out some specifics of the downside of the global march of "liberal Western democracy" (e.g. the lack of accountability of some multinational companies and the eradication of certain indigenous cultures), it is unfair to categorise Cupitt as detached from the daily suffering of oppressed peoples. His theology is still *done* at 120 degrees, and the confines of a Cambridge College are no guard against spiritual discomfort. Dinah Livingstone's description of Cupitt as "a retired English don, with many unmistakeable characteristics of a retired Cambridge don, rooted in English philosophy and that pleasant way of life" is ill-judged. As I have shown in *Odyssey on the Sea of Faith* Cupitt has not opted for "the pleasant way of life" and his radical humanitarianism is very much concerned with creating a more harmonious and equitable planet for all its creatures.

But what about evil; can his ethics respond to it?

What about evil?

Perhaps the most strident criticism of Cupitt's ethics emanates from those who raise the problem of evil against him, claiming that he has ignored or glossed over moral and physical evil. But Cupitt is keen to assuage such doubts. First, he links the death of God with the modern-day problem of a Heideggerian fear of contingent, temporal be-ing. Instead of a divine omnipotent God, people now fear the deep insecurities of mortality and transience, and accordingly clutch all the more obstinately at certainties, authorities and absolutes — often reverting to religious fundamentalism and belief in eternal bliss after death. For Cupitt, solar living is the only way to conquer the fear of death. This world is the last world, this life is our last life; therefore, we must commit ourselves to it completely. There is nothing ahead to save up for.

Getting people to shake off these false securities and embrace insecurity will lead to Cupitt's second and salient line of attack — "metaphysical evil." Taking his cue from the philosopher Leibniz he understands metaphysical evil as "the very idea that there is something unsatisfactory, wrong, and beyond our power to rectify, in the human condition as such."[74] Although fully aware that Christianity has rejected Manicheanism and now asserts that finitude in itself is not evil, he nevertheless argues that Christianity retains a residual belief that true disciples are really citizens of another and unchanging world. If only we could get rid of the fear of life's insecurities *and* the fear of metaphysical evil, that would really change how we relate to this world and our fellow human beings. His brand of religious humanism is not self-centered. Indeed, "we will not make a good world by asserting ourselves and throwing our weight about. On the contrary, we should relate ourselves to Being, to Language and to our world as amenable partners. Let it be."[75] His secular Trinity is a metaphor for a communitarian ethic.

In a paper presented at the Sea of Faith U.K. Conference in 1999 Cupitt reiterates that he cannot accept "the problem of evil" as people normally suggest it to him. Especially at times of local or national disaster, others expect God to intervene and save the innocent. They imagine the world to be a well-run school or patriarchal household with a stern but fair Father-figure watching over and keeping them safe. When this doesn't happen, they are shocked and distressed. In language reminiscent of biologist Richard Dawkins' observations that "DNA neither cares nor knows" and that the universe is "neither evil nor good in intention,"

Cupitt affirms the purposelessness of the world at the "micro level." No one knows which atom will decay next or which person will be struck down with a deadly disease. It is random and unpredictable.[76]

He solves "the problem of evil" by once again returning to his non-realist theology and anti-realist ethics. He insists on solar "personal" ethics that emphasises the acceptance of our own mortality, and humanitarian "social" ethics that ends the binary opposition of "us" and "them"; these give us enough to live by *after* God, which is the same as *after* realism. Cupitt thus endorses a non-realist understanding of evil, accepting life as a package deal of good and evil, and the recognition that evil is something that people have created themselves without any outside or external help — for example racism, nationalism, and oppressive moralism.[77]

Cupitt's self-criticism leads to his self-description as an "ethical non-realist." The only way to live *after* God is to struggle against the evil that people have created themselves. The important point is that we need to give up the idea that finitude, contingency, and temporality are somehow deeply *wrong* and unsatisfactory. When we have learnt a solar acceptance and affirmation of our own transience, then we will be free to deal with the moral evil that has been humanly created; and by so doing we can reinvent and re-create *this* world.

Conclusion

Edith Wyschogrod identifies a "fault line" in postmodernism dividing philosophers of "difference" (Levinas and Derrida) from philosophers of "ecstasy" (Deleuze, Guattari, Genet), arguing that only philosophers of difference "can provide a language and interpretive context for saintly existence."[78] Following Derrida, she wants to promote the "primacy of the other," though not in terms of a transcendent "Other," but "the primacy of the other person and the dissolution of self-interest."[79] It amounts to bringing down to earth Levinas' "Other," and postmodern saints are those who show altruism in an age that has grown cynical and indifferent to the sufferings of others. It is a familiar plea made even more strident by a philosopher like John Caputo, who equates "other" with a sense of "Obligation" that "comes over me and binds me."[80] Answering the appeal of obligation to the other, (for example, a child is who is suffering needlessly), is not a response to something/someone infinite, but to something/someone finite. Obligation is itself a *hermeneia*, an interpretation that this is how one should respond and a "factical fact" that "has made its mind up to have a heart."[81]

True to his project, Cupitt stands astride this alleged "fault line," encompassing both "ecstasy" and "difference." He would endorse the ecstatic saint — symbolised by Bataille in *Blue of Noon* — who expresses him/herself in solar living.[82] *Blue of Noon* was written at the time of the rise of fascism in Europe and after the breakdown of the author's own marriage. A violent, disturbing tale, the novel explores the ambiguity of sex as a force of subversion, and is a journey of excess identifying with both victims of oppression and the seductiveness of its victors. The excessive expenditure (symbolized by sex, vomiting, drunkenness etc.) is intended to highlight that one must not devalue any part of *this* world, even those bits which one might not find immediately agreeable. As I have shown above, this expenditure is for Bataille "the sacred" which can generate concern for alterity. Moreover, as Cupitt remarks, if we devalue anything "we thereby also devalue a bit of ourselves."[83] For Cupitt, the best way forward is to avoid negative and moralistic attitudes and try to be as generous as we can. Some people seem to require excess or waste that others may despise, but the answer is not to go to the other extreme and mean-spiritedly praise prudence or restraint. And yet, as Wyschogrod points out, there remains Bataille's question about how "altruism is generated"; and one needs to "'fill' in what remains unthought in Bataille."[84] For Bataille, and indeed for Cupitt, two questions need to be addressed: "To what or to whom is the subject of expenditure indebted?" "How does this indebtedness come about?"[85]

As I have reiterated in this chapter, Cupitt fills out the "unthought" by appealing to the postmodern situation that "radical humanism is becoming an obvious fact of life, and it has brought ethical humanitarianism in its train."[86] This is an ethics of difference where people perform selfless deeds, in and for the service of others, irrespective of racial or credal affiliation. One has no recourse to Caputo's sense of "Obligation" because it an unsatisfactory concept. The patriotic American soldier in Vietnam doubtless felt "obliged" to commit atrocities: he was defending freedom and fighting communism. That belongs to the "old" moral vocabulary that has now been replaced by a new morality of human rights. Wyschogrod's "fault line" becomes filled in, and her own search for a postmodern saint is realized in Cupitt's selfless professional and solar performer. Cupitt has thus provided his readers with a viable postmodern strategy for living in *this* world *after* God. What more could religion (and especially organized religion) have to offer? Isn't it now time to live not only *after* God, but also *after* the Church? It is to these questions that my next section is addressed.

Chapter 3

Four ideas of the meaning of religion

Cupitt still attends the Eucharist at Emmanuel College Chapel every Sunday. He enjoys the Eucharist as a sort of Kingdom meal; matins and evensong, however, he regards as monastic services, and he doesn't approve of monasticism. Although he has relinquished his licence to officiate because of the Anglican Church's ruthless treatment of Anthony Freeman (see chapter 5), and often been called upon by opponents to withdraw from clerical status, he has never resigned his priestly orders. He remains within the embrace of the Anglican Church and both retains and accepts the title "the Reverend." The loss of belief in an objective God does not entail abandonment of ecclesiastical belonging. His most recent writings have moved in the direction of the Kingdom, but his hope is still to reconstitute the church, though he is alarmed by its increasing theological fundamentalism. He is concerned for the role of fellow radicals in reforming the Church when a priest can be thrown out of his job and his house with no proper trial or appeal or recompense. Indeed, can radicals with views similar to his find an acceptable place within what seem to be the increasingly narrower confines of the churches? Is his agenda too subversive for the churches? Have his philosophical and theological writings taken leave of the Church? Is his post-Christianity a reworking of the Christian Gospel or a total departure from it?

In the next two chapters I will explore these questions and argue that his reformist agenda can still find a place within the Church. It is my contention that to repudiate this unsettling but challenging radicalism would be to miss an opportunity for dialogue with a postmodernity that views with increasing scepticism *any* religious understanding of life and which is epitomized in the quip, "If Jesus is the answer, what is the question?" Few other theologians try to engage the postmodern condition with Cupitt's religious zeal and fervor. As I argued in chapter 2, his embrace of postmodern nihilism is intended to find forms of religious expression that will endure or overcome that situation. Moreover, he insists that today's secular postmodernity does not understand its own religious roots. Cupitt is one of that rare breed of philosophers whose writings have tackled head-on what others have ignored. Graham Ward may allege that "it no longer seems necessary to argue for postmodernism's fascination with things religious,"[1] but John Caputo is nearer to understanding the Zeitgeist. He reminds us that many postmodern philosophers talk about 'the other,' but have side-stepped religion, since the subject is seemingly "just too, too other for them, too 'tout autre.'"[2]

The central question posed is whether Cupitt's idea of religion is, to adopt Caputo's words, "too 'tout autre'" for mainstream Christianity, and even for the allegedly broad spectrum of beliefs permissible within Anglicanism — a breadth of view immortalized by the 19th Century English author Thomas Hardy in *Far From the Madding Crowd* when he has Jan Coggan say, "There's this to be said for the Church (of England), a man can belong to the church and bide in his cheerful old inn, and never trouble or worry his mind about doctrines at all."

As I have shown in the previous volume, Cupitt's odyssey has taken many twists and turns. David Hart correctly notes, with specific reference to Cupitt, that "the biography of a radical thinker is of necessity discontinuous."[3] Just as Cupitt's ethics have passed through various phases, so Cupitt's ideas about religion have changed. In the space of twenty years, he has gone from radical Anglican apologist to post-Christian. And this fascinating journey is not yet over. In this chapter I will outline how Cupitt's four ideas of the meaning of religion have taken shape. In the next I will discuss his advice for beginning, even at this late hour, the task of reforming Christianity. In particular, I will seek to determine whether it is to be undertaken with *or* without the churches.

Idea 1: The religious requirement (1980s)

Cupitt's purpose throughout his writings has been to hang on to religion, but to divest it of supernaturalism. In the 1980s he advocated belief in what he labels: "the religious requirement." This position even found its way into a popular English novel, *Paradise News*, by David Lodge. Lodge's hero, Bernard Walsh, is described as an agnostic theologian or unbeliever. He is a former Roman Catholic priest who turns to teaching theology in a non-denominational college after a crisis concerning lack of belief in supernatural doctrines. Walsh admits a fascination for Cupitt because "in a series of books, he grimly sawed away at the branch he was sitting on, until there was nothing left between him and thin air except a Kierkegaardian 'religious requirement.' There is as far as we are concerned no God but the religious requirement, the choice of it, the acceptance of its demands, and the liberating self-transcendence it brings about in us."[4]

One may ask: "Why the need for a religious requirement?" A fellow radical theologian, John Hick, departs from Cupitt when the latter wants "religion to 'become autonomous,'" and that "the religious requirement does not depend upon any external power or authority."[5] Once Cupitt has gone beyond a way of living advocated by Dietrich Bonhoeffer — *etsi deus non daretur* (even if God is not there) — to a demythologization of God into spirituality, then, for Hick, a religious loss necessarily ensues. Language with an (objective) theistic referent is quantifiably different from that employing a (subjective) human self-referent. It is the difference between seeing hope only for a spiritual elite and extending it to the whole human race. Very few are able to pursue the ideal of selfless love if no transcendent divine Reality exists and if this present earthly life constitutes the entirety of human experience. For the majority of humankind life has been and remains a harsh struggle for survival. Only belief in God and eternal life can provide the necessary basis for hope. Without the Divine referent humanity is ultimately reliant upon itself and that is not sufficient to overcome the vicissitudes of life.[6] Conversely, it is Cupitt's claim that once people are freed of the need for metaphysics, religious humanism can help them accept and cope with whatever *life* serves up.

Peter Mullen takes up Cupitt's cause by arguing that just as in the works of a composer such as Schoenberg music can become atonal, random, and apparently liberated from its technical foundations, so Cupitt has been "redrawing the categorical boundaries."[7] Religion does not have be about supernaturalism, any more than music must have the solid base of a key signature to be called music. He points to three reasons why people might have a religious experience, yet not wish to ascribe any supernatural origin to it:

- Scientific "discoveries" are revelatory; yet require no "God-hypothesis."

- Psychologically it may be objectionable to posit the supernatural causation of a human experience, since that renders the experience impersonal or absurd.

- The "insistence of contemporaneity" is undeniable. God is no longer considered an appropriate explanation for such events as the arrival of rain or the achievement of peace between warring factions; and prayers in favor of such causes are now interpreted as assents to "solidarity and goodwill."

Mullen endorses Cupitt's de-supernaturalization of Christianity, advising that "we have nothing to fear from a thoroughgoing psychological description of religious contents of the kind which Cupitt recommends." Following Wittgenstein, he permits theistic language for those who still find it an appropriate "language-game." However, he thinks that in the future fewer and fewer people will be able to assent to the metaphysical propositions that Christianity presently requires.[8]

This is the crux of "the religious requirement" debate instigated by Cupitt with the original title of *Taking Leave of God* — **The Autonomy of Religion**. The battle-lines are drawn between those who affirm the value of what will be dubbed "godless religion" and those who cannot comprehend such a move. Cowdell is skeptical whether this religious requirement without God can be substantiated. He muses that if, following Cupitt (and Sartre), people are now confident to dispense with God, why should they not move beyond religious affiliation of any kind? It is a significant query that anticipates much of what will preoccupy Cupitt up to the present-day. Indeed, Cowdell's ruminations may be coming to pass in some Western countries. According to the latest census figures in the United Kingdom, Australia and New Zealand, fifteen to twenty per cent of their populations now describe themselves as having "No Religion." Today many declare that they *are* "tough enough" to go it alone, having dispensed with *both* a Divine Being *and* mainstream religious affiliation.

Probably due to his reading of Foucault, Cupitt is wary of any forms of control or power politics, and so he advocates religion that is anthropocentric and voluntarist. This appears in *The Sea of Faith* (1984) and *Life Lines* (1986), in which he argues that religion, like art, must be followed "for its own sake." He is also faced with another problem: how does one communicate a sense of meaning to those who, as he notes in a scene from his *Sea of Faith* television program, must confront the transitory nature of life? Recalling his experiences as an Anglican Curate visiting patients in the wards of the local hospital, he ponders anew the significance of "non-realist" religion in such situations. Presented with the undeniable facts of sickness, death, and the void, he closes one of the episodes with a definition of his religious requirement: "religion (is) a way of affirming the value of human life from the first breath to the very last.

It is up to us to give it that value and to affirm human dignity in the face of an indifferent universe."[9] Significantly, Cowdell mentions this incident as the defining moment when Cupitt came to the realization that religious actions were to be done for their own sakes, disinterestedly. The religious act itself was intrinsically good, regardless of any subsequent payoff.

Confronted by the nihilistic void, transience, and the fact of death, Cupitt's "religious requirement" develops into a "discipline of the void." This is both a way of coping with, and a celebratory acceptance of, one's life without any metaphysical underpinning. He boldly claims that "religious activity has now to be undertaken just for its own sake, as an autonomous and practical response to the coolly-perceived truth of the human condition. This is true religion: all else is superstition."[10] Cupitt's religion is not for the faint-hearted and remains firmly rooted in the Christian faith. It is a serious undertaking. Perhaps he would now admit that it is a little too serious for someone who in the next decade is promoting "ultralight" religion. It is anything but a religion for the comfortable, and the aim of its stories and liturgy (interpreted in a non-realist way) is to affirm human values in a seemingly hostile and inhumane world. By this Cupitt means that we must confront the nihil or the void, and he begins to outline the necessary religious discipline to cope with this dire situation.

Idea 2: The discipline of the void (1989–1992)

In *Taking Leave of God* Cupitt announces that his new religion will take the form of Buddhism combined with the spirituality and values of Christianity. This means that we must do without the answers to metaphysical questions, and instead put the practice of religion first. This concept comes to fruition in the period from 1989 to 1992 when he argues that for postmodern Christians it is the godless abyss or void that must be confronted. Indeed, "the message of both Christianity and Buddhism (*Die to the self!* and *There is no self!*) is that to gaze steadfastly into the Void purges us of anxious egoism, and liberates us for love and creativity. There are plenty of hints of this in the religious tradition: the Wholly Other, the Absurd, the Sea without a shore, the Divine Darkness, the Dark Night of the Soul. You must collide with something Unthinkable that unselfs you, and it is the Nihil. Poetically speaking, the Abyss is merciful and gracious. It puts us to death and raises us to life again."[11] Traditionally religions have attempted, through their myths and rituals, to defer or deny the void, but this is a form of escapism that no longer works for postmodern people. Instead we must welcome the void in the manner of Jesus who stared into nothingness on the cross. By embracing the void we overcome our fear of metaphysical evil. Thus a "discipline of the void" is needed to train people to welcome the void.

This discipline has two main ingredients. First, it is specifically aimed at those who wish to depart from the traditional Christian emphasis on escaping from the world into inwardness (for example the practice of going on retreats). It is designed to help those who are looking for "worth without worship, mysticism without the Mystery and the Word, (and) nihilism while remaining utterly nihilistic."[12] Although his opponents have dismissed this stance as untenable, it resonates with many who still attend Church and can find meaning in a desupernaturalized and socially-relevant Christian tradition. Through its liturgy, stories and sacraments they are attracted to a human life that calls for "a sacrifice costing not less than everything" rather "than attempt to survive unaided the bruising of human dignity and compassion of which their world largely consists."[13] But this is not Bishop John Robinson's idea of "ecstatic anthropolatry," not a conflating of the religious realm with the domain of interpersonal relationships to arrive at *disponsibilité* — being for others. Cupitt doesn't want religion to worship the human absolutely, for the cosmos embraces more than humanity! The distinction between humanism *per se* and religious humanism is an extremely important one, and as will become apparent in the next section, it underlies much of his emerging post-Christianity.

Second, the "death of God" is more than the death of outmoded ideas or models of God. There is no supplementary "God of the gap" left over. There is no Tillichian "God above God." No "additional blank" or mystery surrounds life, and religion is not about trying to find God (or anything else) beyond the human realm. The world is outsideless: there never was a metaphysical world — it was just a nostalgic feeling Cupitt now derides as an illusion. The void is what the Buddhist means by emptiness, nothingness, or Sunyata; it is the experienced character of life itself. Hence, he advocates "a religion of life in the sense of a spiritual discipline that enables us to accept and to say yes to our life as it is, baseless, brief, pointless and utterly contingent, and yet in its very nihility beautiful, ethically-demanding, solemn and final."[14]

To counter those critics who say that he has now departed from Christianity, Cupitt points to Kierkegaard's "astounding idea that God has become just a historical contingency, something as accidental and gratuitous as me" and that his "extreme incarnationalism brings him unexpectedly close to a kind of world-affirming Buddhism."[15] However, he goes even further than Kierkegaard because he is combating a different enemy. Whereas Kierkegaard was fighting against the philosophical rationalism of Hegel, Cupitt is confronting the very nihilism we must worship!

In 1992/93 the "discipline of the void" becomes subsumed under the general banner of religious humanism as he attempts to avoid being identified as simply a humanist. Indeed, he subsequently admits in *The Religion of Being* that in the decade leading to the new millennium, his struggle was to convince others to find in expressionism a new account of the *religious* life. He has often been dismissed as merely a humanist in disguise, but this is again to misread him. Humanism is too individualistic a notion for Cupitt, and he does not find anything in the prevailing humanism that meets with his approval. As early as 1987 he warned that "we must be wary of 'humanism,' because it is easily misunderstood as a proposal to put "Man" (whoever *he* is) in the centre as the supreme and only arbiter."[16] This caveat is linked to his non-endorsement of the Western Enlightenment project. He proposes a *religious* response to secularism, one that distinguishes between Western secularism and religious faith. The latter has an "irreplaceable something" (usually defined as "spiritual values") with which to overcome nihilism. Religion has the task of giving to modern culture the spiritual substance that it so evidently lacks. The turn to postmodernism includes a turn to religion that challenges the Enlightenment project's assumption of the demise of religion. Indeed, John Caputo notes that two recent books — *The Postmodern God* and *The Post-Secular Philosophy* — have "pressed the claim that 'postmodern' must be understood to mean or at least to include 'postsecular;' that the delimitation of the claims of Enlightenment rationalism must also involve the delimitation of Enlightenment secularism."[17] Religion is still needed, and postmodern writers have pointed towards new forms of religion: one thinks, for example, of Jacques Derrida's *Religion without Religion*, and Lloyd Geering's *Christianity without God*. But, again, that is to anticipate Cupitt.

It is perhaps more appropriate to say that in the early 1990s he chooses to go in the direction of humanizing Christianity (i.e. to define a Christian/religious humanism). The "death of God" leads not to despair, but to an emphasis on *this* world and coping with the pain of others, with a special focus on the Passion of Jesus — which becomes a central motif for helping suffering humanity. This is Christian humanism as opposed to humanism. That is the distinction that his opponents have failed to understand; as he remarks, the "religious conservatives . . . use boo-words like 'Western individualism,' 'relativism' and 'humanism.'"[18] Cupitt's use of the idea of "the discipline of the void" lasts only a few years. Perhaps the word "discipline" has too many associations with the authoritarianism that he denounces within traditional Christianity. It certainly sits uneasily in his postmodern insistence of an "ultralight" religion. Accordingly, he rarely if ever uses the phrase again, and for much of the 1990s prefers to be known as a *religious* humanist.

Idea 3: Religious Humanism (1992 onwards)

In a significant paper presented at the Sea of Faith U.K. Conference in 1991, Cupitt highlights the distinction that has historically been made between humanism and religion: the former is identified with this worldly materialism, and the latter with spiritual other-worldliness. He nevertheless refuses to acknowledge such "conventional binary oppositions," and argues that Christianity itself can be understood "in a humanistic, materialistic and this-worldly direction." First, he identifies within the Hebrew Biblical tradition an intrinsic Jewish humanism found in the Patriarchal narratives and the Court History of David (Genesis 1 and 2 Samuel) where God retreats into the background and "in the foreground there is a drama of human relationships." From both this and a tendency to conflate ethics with religion there emerges a pragmatic vision of life that is this-worldly and dramatic. Second, he argues that the New Testament expands these themes and introduces three other humanistic ones:

1. **The Incarnation and Pentecost, with Christ becoming a human person**. The symbol of the Trinity becomes "a symbol of the death of God, that is, of God's self-giving and his disappearance into the human realm."
2. **The internalization of Christ's suffering and death within the believer.** "The Christian's psychological conflict and stress become the labor-pains of a new humanity in a new world."
3. **The End of Religion.** Since Jesus promised the Kingdom, not religion, "the institutions of religion are only tools, and have only an interim function."[19]

Cupitt thus contends that the old transcendent sacred is now dispersed into humanity. The divine comes down into the human world. Theology is translated into anthropology, and the doctrine of Christ is the doctrine of us. All that which was originally said of God becomes a sort of template for the construction of modern selfhood. We become ourselves by living our lives, going out into expression, and passing away. Cupitt wants to keep many of the old categories, but give them new humanistic interpretations and thereby generate a human-centered religion.

Having humanized Christianity, Cupitt tackles the obvious objection: "Why should one still *bother* with religion?" His answer is that the ancient religious myths and stories are even now needed to help people survive in the nihilistic age where all "ideas go into the melting pot." In responding to Richard Rorty's neo-pragmatic liberal ironism, religion provides the "more resources" that Cupitt needs "to maintain the right to . . . private self-creation alongside a social concern 'to make our institutions and practices more just and less cruel.'"[20] It will be religion that acknowledges its human origins, just as we recognize the myths and stories that humans have lived by throughout the centuries as human creations whose main purpose was to urge people not to be afraid of the nihil. Religion is a human language by means of which we try to give symbolic meaning to life.

Cupitt's "religion is a human creation" thesis was appropriated by the emerging Sea of Faith Network in the United Kingdom with its 1989 "Statement of Intent" — that of "exploring and promoting religious faith as a human creation." His New Zealand sojourn in late 1991 provided him with an opportunity to work through the implications of what he put succinctly into question form: "The question I am raising is this: modern society is very highly reflective, very highly conscious. It is a pluralist society, a society which is a marketplace of ideas and a society in which we are highly conscious of the beliefs and the factors which influence our own thinking. In such a society can religion still exist, in the consciousness that it is only human?"[21]

Cupitt's naturalistic view of religion constitutes his affirmative answer. Repeating the rejection of a transcendent God and insisting upon the "outsidelessness" of existence, he points to the social implications of religions. In most societies, to use Lloyd Geering's phrase, religion acts like superglue. It provides the myths, the symbols, and the practices that shape peoples' vision of the world and enable them to construct their own lives. Yet by admitting that these myths are human creations and have a human history, we avoid the debilitating idea that these beliefs are "*idées fixes*." Following Wittgenstein, Cupitt declares that beliefs are "tools" which can be changed, discarded, and rethought in order to foster "human emancipation." Anticipating *The Religion of Being* he singles out the Society of Friends as a forerunner of "a beliefless but creative Spirit-Christianity," with "God" becoming disseminated in the lives of human beings and "distribut(ing) himself as Spirit in human relationships."[22]

Here is a postmodern spirituality with the "death of God" becoming not an unnerving loss, but a liberating experience. Religion is a dream of a fully humanistic world that we hope is now coming into being. Linked to this — indeed a vital expression of this new religion — is the creation of new values in social life and the public world. This was discussed in chapter 2, but it should be noted again here that Cupitt's religion works in the same way as his transactional ethics, by trial and error as you go along.

It was mentioned at the beginning of this chapter that Cupitt dislikes monasticism; and this comes to the fore when he argues that the new religion must restore the body. By this he means discarding all hidden Platonic soul language, and replacing it with his idea that the self is the totality of the signs one displays. The self is not located "within," but is culturally inscribed and read from the actions of the body when we express ourselves. Monasticism, which emphasised rejection of the worldly passions and a discipline aimed at mastering the body, is replaced by a religion of expression. That does not mean self-expression must be self-serving, but as Cupitt has often made clear, it is a new understanding of the self as "the public expressive self." His radical religious humanism thus again steers a course between humanism's excessive emphasis on the self and monastic Christianity's constrictive world-denial. The self is essentially social, inter-relational, exterior, and on show. We have to put on a good show by following the example of Jesus: living by dying and becoming ourselves only by losing ourselves in acts of compassion for others. Indeed, Cupitt claims that the new religion will be "saying yes" to what historic Christianity denied. He contends that his religious humanism is consistent with the teachings of Jesus in the Sermon on the Mount, a program that he deems to be short-termist, and conducive of both the internalization of spiritual truths and a religion that reconciles us to life in *this* world. These are the "key" elements for the launching of post-Christianity.

Idea 4: Post-Christianity — a new world religion? (1994 onwards)

Cupitt's first sustained use of the terms "post-Christian" and "post-Christianity" comes in 1994 with the publication of *After All*. Daphne Hampson takes issue with his terminology, claiming that he has confused people by characterizing a secular position as post-Christian, "since this term has now come to be widely used by those, such as myself, who hold a spiritual position in continuity with the Western tradition which has however discarded the myth of Christianity."[23] Aside from the obvious retort that Cupitt would deny the immutability of any terminology, Hampson has misunderstood his special use of the phrase. To be sure, he sometimes uses the phrase "post-Christian" to refer to Christianity's loss of influence on the consciousness of the Western world, and to acknowledge the rapid decay of its authority and legitimating narrative.[24] However, he also uses the term to indicate what a self-reformed Christianity might be. Here he is not proposing "secular" as opposed to Christianity, but rather Christianity that has re-invented itself from within, just as postmodernism has invented itself out of the self-criticism of modernism. Not only is his post-Christianity still religious rather than secular, but it is continuous with Christianity. The emerging global society that promotes the values of the kingdom — humanitarianism and ethical concern for others — is Christianity's self-realisation.

The importance of this point cannot be underestimated, for it now forms the keystone of Cupitt's relationship both to his own Christian faith and to the emerging new religion. It adds the necessary spur for Cupitt to remain *inside* the Christian tradition, confident that Christianity has within itself the capacity for self-transcendence. His post-Christianity, then, is not a radical break from the past, but a natural development of the tradition. Cupitt is not so much a destroyer of the tradition as one who calls the Church back to the origins of its faith and its founder. The Church has distorted the message of Jesus and made him into someone he never claimed to be — the divine pre-existent Logos. It has emphasised another heavenly world and a life of discipline under authority instead of the Kingdom of love and justice to be established here and now on earth. Indeed "Jesus was not a Christian, but a post-Christian. Post-Christianity, the Kingdom, preceded the church and will also succeed it."[25]

Cupitt is confident enough to claim that Christianity is the *only* religion that looks to its own demise and replacement by something greater (the Kingdom). Christianity is the sole major world religion with a strong radical tradition of self-transcendence: it hopes one day to become something more than itself. The Hindu, Muslim, and Jew take it for granted that their religions are unalterable entities. The believer may have various relations to it, but in itself the religion can't change. He/She wouldn't think of proposing to reform or radically modify it. Yet Christianity displays an innate propensity to point beyond itself: the church must eventually give way to the Kingdom.[26] What Cupitt is proposing is not new. These ideas were foreshadowed long ago by theologians like Adolf von

Harnack in *The Essence of Christianity* (1900); and the progressive Unitarian educationalist Charles Eliot (1834–1926) in his emphasis upon what became known as "the social Gospel."[27]

Cupitt's post-Christianity, then, contains the following essential ingredients:

- Christianity's capacity for self-transcendence
- The Kingdom as the expression of this "greater reality," with its themes of "immediacy, non-hierarchy and democracy"
- Jesus as the one who proclaimed a spirituality and a revaluing of values in the here-and-now, a teaching that is succinctly expressed in the Sermon on the Mount

Allied to this, as he outlined in *After All*, are the twin paths of "active" and "contemplative" religion by which one becomes so immersed in this world and its problems that religion is redescribed as a way of world- and life-affirmation. He is concerned to ensure that this new religion can confront all the pain and distress that he encountered in the late-evening visits to the wards of the hospital in Salford, and that he has personally experienced in Addenbrooke's Hospital, Cambridge. Like Jesus in the Sermon on the Mount, he affirms "joy in affliction" and is convinced that his religion can face the ultimate challenge of "preparing for death and overcoming the fear of death . . . by making the world so beautiful that one could die content."[28] This religion can pass through the fires of suffering because it has carried Cupitt there too, and has proved sufficient to the task. The question to be posed in the next chapter is whether it will do the same for others.

Contrary to the approaches of conservative theologians like Stanley Grenz (*A Primer on Postmodernism*) who have defended the Christian metanarrative against the iconoclasm introduced by Jean-Francois Lyotard, and post-liberals like George Lindbeck (*The Nature of Doctrine*) who have withdrawn into the cultural-linguistic narratives of particular communities, Cupitt proposes religion that embraces postmodernism. With postmodern irony he quips: "a seriously postmodern definition of true religion: religion that makes you smarter than your god."[29] In *After God* (1997) Cupitt catapults religion into the postmodern minefield, opposing the prevailing postmodern assumption (described above by Caputo) that with the "death of God" religion too must become extinct.

Ultimately, he says, the salvation of religion will be "a new world religion as a new way of feeling and living our own relationship to the world of our common experience."[30] Cupitt asserts that he has been presenting this new religion since 1994 and that it has a "philosophical core" which can be labelled: "solar living." This was defined and examined earlier in this book, but here it should be noted that in Cupitt's view religion, like ethics, has more to do with "a way of living" than with organization and hierarchy. It is at this point that a serious tension appears within Cupitt's idea of the future religion — a disjuncture that takes him well beyond Cowdell's portrait of an apologist for radical Anglicanism. Put very simply, it is whether Cupitt's post-Christian religion is a revision of Church Christianity or a new religion altogether?" From 1997 onwards his writings seem to present three different positions, which can be broadly categorized thus:

1. "Yes" to new world religion and "Yes" to revising local (church) religion
2. "Yes" to new world religion, but "No" to any hope of revising local (church) religion
3. The emerging new postmodern world religion as post-Christianity

The first position is advocated in *After God* where Cupitt seems hesitant to commit himself (and others) to the emerging expressive religion that unifies and builds up a common world. He prefers to hedge his bets. On the one hand, he promotes "a solar process pouring itself out into symbolic expression in its world, (so that) astoundingly, environmental ethics and postmodern spirituality turn out in the end to coincide. Our spiritual life, our quest for redemption, and our world-building activity all turn out to be the same thing."[31] Yet on the other, he advises people to follow their own local (church) religion, especially a minimalist non-realist version of Christianity. This seemingly ambiguous position must come as no great surprise to anyone for Cupitt has always been wary of "one-man religion" and feared for many years that he might be proclaimed the founder of a new religion.

Then in 1998 the vision of a new world religion begins to take shape, and the second position emerges with a swing away from the revisionary stance of *Radicals and the Future of the Church*. He announces that "until very recently it was a matter of great grief to me that the Church seemed unwilling and even unable to reform itself: but now it seems that people in general have decided that there is not enough left to salvage. Reform isn't worth trying for: let the dead bury their dead. It wasn't I who decided that it is now too late, but the general public."[32] Cupitt's assessment of the demise of the Church is based on the prevailing cultural abandonment of Christian beliefs, and is endorsed by statistics from Western nations on the decline of belief in God and the practice of mainstream Christianity. He is sufficiently persuaded to state that a "fresh start" is needed. His sketch of post-Christianity is a reiteration of that philosophical core which he has variously described as "energetic Spinozism" (*The Last Philosophy*), "Poetical Theology" (*After All*) and "Solar Ethics" (*Solar Ethics*). It entails a naturalistic way of living that is accepting of the here-and-now, and calls for a switch from dogmatic to poetical theology that "ennobles" people's existence. In a foretaste of his third religious position, Cupitt wonders whether "the modern secular world, increasingly emancipated from the constraints of religious law, represents not an abandonment but a fulfilment of religious faith?"[33]

In a move towards some sort of synthesis, Cupitt weds postmodern spirituality to post-Christianity, seemingly ambivalent and unconcerned about whether what emerges is an offshoot of Church Christianity or something else. That consideration is secondary to the importance of religion being a vehicle to help in the formation of responsible human beings and communities. He has always maintained that his non-realist religious agenda is to direct us in symbolic language to try to create a particular kind of world. In a paper presented at the Sea of Faith U.K. Conference in 1998 he contrasts the "old" and "new" spiritualities. He argues that "classical" spiritualities were world-denying, while postmodern ones are focused exclusively on this world and are a "movement into it." Again, Cupitt reiterates that his "expressivist" religion is consonant with postmodern spirituality in that it can put an end to all dualisms and allow one to embrace the flux of language-formed events. And yet he is insistent that religion is therapeutic and "is halfway between ethics and art; indeed, it is a sort of performance art in which we act out a representation of what our life might be like."[34]

The reference to "performance art" harks back to *Creation out of Nothing* (1989) where, as I outlined in *Odyssey on the Sea of Faith*, Cupitt draws inspiration from the work of the artist Richard Long, whose landscapes become living liturgies. Postmodernist spirituality and post-Christianity thus coincide, as they both become "the creator(s) of a new sacrality that is strictly 'on the level.'"[35] Post-Christianity becomes democratic. Cupitt's *bête noire* — the hierarchy, cosmic terrorism, and authoritarianism of traditional Christianity — can be replaced by a religion that is judged pragmatically. Religious teachings and practices should be evaluated in terms of the kind of person and kind of world they tend in practice to produce.

Central to Cupitt's new religion is his insistence that it must be free of greed for power. In *The Religion of Being* he links both political and religious democracy to the postmodern outlook. It is a familiar plea, and highly consistent with his evaluation of traditional ecclesiastical organizations as being oppressive, tyrannous, and deniers of freedom. Moreover, the main functionary of such organizations — the priest (and this with Cupitt himself still an office-holder) — is characterized as "an institutionally-accredited person . . . (who) is simply not expected to think, or to change anything."[36] In a paper presented at the Sea of Faith U.K. Conference in 1999 he draws a distinction between this situation and his own role as a priest communicating *with*, but no longer officiating *in* the church. He says that from the Church's point of view, he is only a marginal Christian. He has moved on from where Cowdell found him in 1996 as a priest still presiding at the Eucharist and he stands on the organization's periphery, prophetically calling others to a new religious liberation, teaching that religious truth cannot be canonized in fixed doctrines or forms of words, but needs to be continually reminted by the invention of new metaphors.[37]

Cupitt's new post-Christianity, then, while it is a radical departure from the old tyrannical religion that has emerged from the historical mission of the Church, is still Christian, because Jesus' message was aimed at establishing Kingdom Christianity. Cupitt insists on the crucial distinction between Church Christianity and Kingdom Christianity. He intimates in 1998 that the former Congregational Union and the present Society of Friends are examples of the democratic, creedless churches that he would favor.[38] In particular he endorses the Quakers for having shifted from "the Church" to the Kingdom almost three centuries ago. This may be reflected in the significant number of Quakers who are members of the Sea of Faith Networks. He reports that one fifth of those attending a Quaker Conference were also members of the Sea of Faith (U.K) Network. It is also worth pointing out that many Sea of Faith members are Unitarians who consider that their organization comports with Cupitt's advocacy of a creedless and democratic church.

As I shall further discuss in the next section, it may questioned whether this distinction between Kingdom and Church Christianity should be so rigidly maintained or whether some Church Christianity has *already* become Kingdom Christianity. Cupitt polarizes the two positions by quoting the well known saying of Albert Loisy who was excommunicated from the Roman Catholic Church in 1908 for his "modernist" views

that: "Jesus preached the Kingdom — but it was the Church that came."
For Cupitt, Church Christianity is coming to a slow and painful but
inevitable end; and it is the Kingdom that must become the focus as it
was in the days of Jesus. Again, he describes postmodernity as
"Christianity's final expression, now coming into being," and insists that
"we should be looking out for the signs of the long-awaited post-ecclesiastical age."[39] He is not too worried about what the new post-Christianity is
to be called or what "brand label" is ascribed to it, but he is keen to avoid
religious versions of nationalisms or tribalisms; and is content to wait and
see what emerges. Postmodernity, the Kingdom, and post-Christianity
become intertwined in a vision of "the world" (i.e., the human social
world) as a place where

- Everything is transient, everything is contingent, everything just
  pours out and passes away.

- Reality is a ceaseless flux of communication.

- On its inner surface the flux resolves itself into a network of persons,
  who include you and me: on its outer surface the flux is "screened" as
  the objective world, the life-world, the world of experience.

- The divine is the light that irradiates everything; it is everything's being, intelligibility, and bliss.[40]

This is what Cupitt's new religion will have to contend with and par-
adoxically will become — a religion of communication creating new and
more wonderful ways of both individual and corporate living and be-ing.
This is the new religious world-picture, and it is up to everyone to make
that world-picture as attractive as possible.

Conclusion

It can be seen that the "religious requirement" has today become the
development of a "new communally-evolved system" that will be continually open to re-negotiation, but will hold out something of value for people to live by. Cupitt's post-Christianity (Kingdom) is, to borrow a Biblical
phrase, both a threat and a promise. It is a threat to those neo-conservative theologians like John Milbank who remain within ecclesiastical
Christianity trying to "open up a space" in postmodernity to restore the
primacy of the traditions of the Church. It is a promise to those who like
Lloyd Geering accept that a new global religion has already begun to rise
out of the ashes of Christianity. If Christianity has the capacity to super-

sede itself and become the Kingdom then, according to Geering, "the humanistic and secular world is to be seen as the legitimate product of the ever-evolving Christian culture of the West."[41] Church Christianity was always meant to be *only* temporary and with the advent of secular humanism it can secede to the Kingdom and Christianity can fulfil its original promise. Indeed "out of the chrysalis of Christendom there is currently emerging a new kind of society — a global, humanistic and secular society." This secular global world is a 'sign' of "what Jesus once talked about in terms of the Kingdom of God." The Church is becoming increasingly redundant as global, humanistic and tolerant secularism, under the influence of the Christian message, takes over its role and establishes a Kingdom of peace and justice, irrespective of creed, ethnicity and sexuality.[42]

Cupitt too spells this out in *Reforming Christianity*. He berates the Church for being "stuck up its cul-de-sac" unable and unlikely to reform itself; and considers that it is consigning itself to the heritage industry. He sees the immense progress that has been achieved by those who are outside the Church yet who have been influenced by Christianity — "human emancipation, human rights, humanitarian ethics."[43] This is the reformation of Christianity — a desupernaturalized, secular, Kingdom religion. The crucial point to note is not that humanism has developed by itself out of a reaction to Christianity, but that secular humanism is "Christianity's own struggle to advance from its relatively warped ecclesiastical to its final, 'kingdom,' stage of development."[44] The demise of the Church is not the end of Christianity, for Christianity is still unfolding in secular humanism. What we are now witnessing is a change of dispensation, as the Church's own inner logic brings it to an end and Christianity becomes its long-awaited, post-ecclesiastical, Kingdom form. Cupitt can even see small signs that the Church itself is changing, in the way that it has altered the emphasis in its rites of passage (baptism, confirmation, marriage and death) from another world to affirming *this life*. But the thrust of his argument is that the Church's downfall will be gradual and he is not too distressed at its passing because Kingdom Christianity is replacing it.

He would, however, be perturbed if the consciousness of the West were to suffer the loss of Jesus as an ethical teacher.[45] He still has an intense devotion to Jesus and his original message which emphasised the founding of the Kingdom. It in this context that one must understand Cupitt's renewed interest in searching out the historical Jesus and his increasing attraction to the work of the Jesus Seminar of the Westar Institute. For Cupitt, Jesus dies as a god and returns as a human teacher with a revolutionary Kingdom message: "[T]here is no common and compulsory doctrine or moral code at all, except a general love of life and commitment to world-affirmation." This is the new religion.[46]

In the following chapters I shall explore whether this in fact does amount to a parting of the ways, and whether it leads to taking leave of the Church. These topics have been discussed not only by Cupitt, but also within the Sea of Faith Networks. I will include insights from this latter group to show the dramatic effect of Cupitt's ideas both on those who wish to remain within the churches and on those who have left the churches, having found them beyond redemption.

Chapter 4

Taking leave of the Church?

The setting

In *The Sea of Faith* (1984) Cupitt exposes the tension experienced by Christians who belong to the Church and yet live in a highly secular, scientific and global world. It is an all too familiar situation as churchfolk try to reconcile the traditional religious language celebrating a defunct medieval world-view with an emerging postmodern consciousness that dissolves everything into the flux of the here-and-now. The language of religion begins to lose its descriptive force and social authority. To relieve this tension people seem to have followed three paths.

First, this dissonance leads some to an extreme reaction against the scientific and secular culture, a response that manifests itself in various forms of religious fundamentalism and has been well documented by Karen Armstrong in *The Battle for God*. Second, those like Michael Goulder have concluded that organized religion must be abandoned, since the churches are "locked for ever in the ice-floes of theological contradiction" and the only honest course of action is to leave.[1] As I have shown in this book, Cupitt provides a third option. It is to recognize that religion everywhere is by its very nature a human creation, and as such remains very important to us — even though philosophical and historical criticism have demolished all our received religious beliefs, including God. We can still use to good advantage the myths, doctrines, and rituals of religion, but in a non-realist way.

This third path is perhaps the most difficult position of all, and Goulder has been a vociferous opponent. He has raised the popular cry that non-realism is atheism in disguise and that no amount of academic

91

double-talk can make it otherwise. Similarly, but on the other side of the theological divide, Daphne Hampson represents those who are mystified why anyone would want to affirm both the continuity of Christianity and the discontinuity of its essential underpinning — a realist understanding of God. Hampson, labelling herself a "non-Christian realist," is convinced of the continuing validity of the term "God" in referring to an objective reality and "not an idealized notion of human beings." Yet, because of her feminist critique of Christianity, she must separate herself from the Christian tradition. Finding it irredeemably sexist, she leaves the Church, having found other strategies for survival.[2] As in the case of Mary Daly's dramatic announcement to the congregation at The Harvard Memorial Chapel in 1971, the only possible route is "to affirm our faith in ourselves and our will to transcendence by rising and walking out together."[3] Daly's argument is that the women's movement is an "exodus" community in which people can express their ideas of transcendence without being constrained by the irredeemably patriarchal Christian tradition.

This "feminist, non-Christian realist" view has itself been questioned by Christian non-realist feminists. Beverley Clack takes a page out of Cupitt arguing that the feminist emphasis on *thea*logy (the Goddess) "need not involve accepting a referential account of the way in which religious language operates."[4] She highlights the work of feminist writers such as Carol Christ, Jane Caputi and Starhawk, who interpret the Goddess not as a divine female being, but as a symbol of human values and the significance of that understanding for women. Carol Christ, for instance, sees the Goddess as "a symbol [which] aids the process of naming and reclaiming the female body and its cycles and processes."[5] For Clack, the implication is that a non-realist feminist *thea*logy avoids the simplistic replacing of a male divine being with a female, and allows the Goddess symbol to be flexibly interpreted and thus appropriated into the life of the individual. And because it refers to human ideals and values, feminist non-realist religious language takes us beyond the point of men having to worship a male God and women needing a Goddess; it prompts *both* men and women to explore what it means to be human. Understood non-realistically, *all* concepts of "God" or "the Goddess" are human expressions of human values, and in exploring these human values both genders can search for meaning and integration, eschewing the separation experienced when God and Goddess are understood in a realist way. Daly's and Hampson's assertion that Christianity and the Church are irredeemably sexist evaporates when we adopt non-realism. We recognize that these symbols of power and patriarchy are *only* human symbols,

devoid of divine authority and capable of being revised. Equally important, women can use their symbol of the Goddess to challenge inappropriate human ways of being that currently cause people discomfort.

The debate about whether lack of faith in an objective God should
preclude Church membership also surfaced at the 1999 Methodist
Conference in the United Kingdom. Delegates discussed a proposal by
the Reverend Dr. Stephen Mosedale that those who did not *yet* believe in
an objective God might still join the Church. Mosedale's argument was
based on outreach and evangelism. He wanted to admit to membership
those who might be affiliated with the Church by using its facilities
(youth group, mothers and toddlers meeting etc.) but who were unable *at
that time* to assent to certain propositions of belief. Although the motion
was defeated, it brought into focus the parameters of belief: either "one
could see this as the measure of a church quite desperate about its declining membership or as a sensible sign of realising that religious commitment is not just about assenting to a proposition."[6]

So what are the pertinent objections to remaining within the
embrace of a traditional church while yet espousing non-realism? I will
identify four such objections.

Reasons for taking leave of the Church

Doctrinal integrity

Perhaps the most frequent criticism levelled at those who wish to be
both non-realists and church members is that doctrinal integrity and
church membership are inseparable. This has been elucidated in various
ways by Cupitt's main critics — Michael Goulder, Brian Hebblethwaite,
Stephen White and Rowan Williams.

For Goulder, such a position is "paradoxical, and such paradoxes are
only for the very clever." Academics might be able to perform the necessary mental gymnastics, but ordinary people would feel that there is something counterfeit about offering prayers and participating in a liturgy to a
non-existent God. Without an objective God Christianity becomes a
sham. If belief in God is not a defensible position, then Christianity is
not a "valid option."[7] For Hebblethwaite there are two distinct differences
between metaphysical (realist) and expressivist (non-realist) views of
Christian religion. First, the values and ways of life are not the same. He
argues that the love of Mother Teresa of Calcutta for the poor and desti-
tute is demonstrably different from that of the secular relief worker.
Second, there is a difference between those who have the resources of a

higher Being to support them and those who hold that one must realize these values oneself.[8] For White the practice of religion (worship, prayer, ethics) and spirituality must have a referent; otherwise, it becomes "the egocentrism which Cupitt so much detests."[9] He endorses Williams' argument that Cupitt's religion becomes solipsistic in that "religious language collapses in upon itself when it tries to make spirituality a religious goal."[10] Williams himself sums up the seemingly contradictory position asking: "Can the functions of classical theological language actually survive the denial of ontological reference beyond the speaker?"[11]

A club with rules

Closely allied to the defence of the doctrinal integrity of Christianity is the argument that being a member of a church is like belonging to a club with rules. There is a limit to how innovative or religiously experimental we may become. To use the Biblical analogy, one cannot step over the "line drawn in the sand." There "*is* an orthodoxy in force in the church and individuals' religious viewpoints are judged against it. The authority of the church and its hierarchy is credal and defines and limits acceptable behaviour and forms of expression [and] *members and officials of the club are bound by the rules.*"[12]

An obvious example of this stand is the dismissal of the Reverend Anthony Freeman from his parochial position by the Right Reverend Eric Kemp (the Anglican Bishop of Chichester) after the publication of *God in Us*. Moreover, in the "traditionalist" reply enunciated by the Right Reverend Richard Harries (the Anglican Bishop of Oxford) in *The Real God*, Freeman's Christian humanism is alleged to be not only incompatible with Christianity but also a perversion of the Truth. As Harries states, "the arguments put forward by Anthony Freeman do not stand up to examination. God is real and it is possible to know this. The assumptions of post-modernist deconstructionism are fallacious. Questions of meaning and truth remain on the agenda."[13] The clear implication of this is that non-realists are not only erasing the line in the sand, but also peddling heresies!

This is made even more explicit by Andrew Moore in an article in which, after a sympathetic examination of those who might wish to be both members of a church and the Sea of Faith Networks, he shows his Barthian colours. He cites Karl Barth's (in)famous double-edged definition of heresy: "By heresy we understand a form of Christian faith which we cannot deny to be a form of the Christian faith from the formal standpoint, i.e., in so far as it, too, relates to Jesus Christ, to his Church, to baptism, Holy Scripture and the common Christian creeds, but in respect of which we cannot really understand what we are about when we recognize it as such, since we can understand its content, its interpretation of these common presuppositions only as a contradiction of faith."[14] While granting that non-realists ought to be welcome to attend church, he refuses to allow them to hold official or teaching positions. He argues that permitting Christians to accept non-realism would mark the end of the churches. Implicit in the outward welcome to participate in the worship service of a particular church is the intrinsic and irreducible commitment to affirming the objectivity of God and the historic faith in God's Trinity.

Moore's argument is also used against liberal theologians who are permitted to discuss theological controversies within the confines of a University Faculty of Theology, but not "outside" — and certainly not amongst "the faithful." This is similar to the furore over David Jenkins who, after his consecration in 1984 as the Anglican Bishop of Durham, made public theological controversies that he had discussed openly as a Professor of Theology at the Universities of Oxford and Leeds. Once he became a bishop it was decreed that personal discipleship should be wholly subordinated to the demands of the representative nature of the new role. These are rules of the church that no one can overstep without being identified as a heretic. In effect, the essence of religious orthodoxy has become, not a theological, but a philosophical doctrine — metaphysical realism — against which Cupitt has been battling for twenty or more years!

Feminist challenge — create a church elsewhere

As indicated above, some radical feminists have asked why anyone would wish to stay in the Church at all. Hampson argues that she and "a whole circle of friends" could not belong to a male-dominated patriarchal club and remain in an organisation that "has been the undoing of woman in Western culture." The Church, simply put, is there to legitimize patriarchy and Hampson (unlike David Hart) does not want "to stay and fight our corner," but urges men to join with women in fashioning a new Christianity and a new Church outside the ecclesiastical boundaries.[15]

This stance of "creating a church elsewhere" has been expressed very cogently by two members of the Sea of Faith Networks. Teresa Wallace argues that churches need to be "reborn" as places of "natural refreshment," so she recreates "church" in situations as disparate or even incongruous as the cancer ward, the bathroom and listening to Brahms. For Wallace, the real meaning of "church" is found wherever "real live flesh-and-blood people" and their concerns are explored and made mean-ingful. It is serving one's neighbor just as effectively without the frame of the churches.[16]

Anne Padley puts forward the argument that if asked, "Is God real?" most church members would answer "Yes," and very few would reply, "Don't care." The churches and church members don't really want non-realists in the pews. Padley declares that "the feeling is mutual," stating bluntly that she "could no more sit among a congregation of realists than (she) could sit in an ant-heap." She objects to the values of realists who believe that they have the Divine power on their side. This is offensive and drives a wedge between her and them. While admitting that her ideal church will never exist, she suggests that a church composed only of non-realists might be the answer.[17]

Churches are intellect-free zones

The proposition that churches are "intellect-free zones" is put for-ward by Alison Webster. The cut and thrust of theological debate seems anathema to the churches, most of which have "disowned theology in a fit of anti-intellectual pique." Webster asserts that contemporary creative religious thinking is being practiced only at the margins of the Academy and within radical networks. We should not look to the churches for engagement in the difficult questions of faith, but rather to "those per-spectives which have been marginalized — the lay, feminist, gay, people of colour, interfaith."[18] Indeed, the Anglican Church's distancing or sidelining of Cupitt is indicative of how it has closed ranks when con-fronted by revisionist writing. As Cupitt himself noted in a foreword to *Odyssey on the Sea of Faith*, many in the upper ranks of the Church who were once his friends now avoid him, because associating with him might jeopardize their careers.

****

These four cogent arguments suggest that those convinced by Cupitt's radicalism should steer clear of any church organization. The reasons range from intellectual and doctrinal integrity to simply not being wanted, but the message seems to be that the churches do not need non-realists and vice-versa. Only those afflicted with some sort of martyr-complex, extremely thick-skinned, or illogical would want to remain. Non-realists who contemplate remaining in the churches would do well to listen to one feminist's observation that women who stay in the Church give the same reasons for doing so that battered women give for staying in an abu-sive relationship — "they don't mean it; they said they were sorry and would be better; they need me/us, we can fix it if we just try harder and are better; I'd leave but how can I survive outside; we have nowhere else to go."[19] Perhaps the words of the poet Philip Larkin sum up the "stay out of the church" position:

> we cannot revive old factions
> we cannot restore old policies
> Or follow an antique drum.[20]

So why might one stay? Rather than comment on each of the four reasons individually I will put forward reasons why a non-realist might choose to remain a member of a church. In the course of this exposition, I hope in large part to counter the above objections.

Reasons against leaving the Church

The original vision

In 1989 David Edwards describes Cupitt as having undergone something similar to a "Victorian clergyman's 'loss of faith'" and calls for his resignation from the Anglican Church.[21] Cupitt replies that Edwards has missed the point of his writings, which is not to eradicate the Church but to reform it. The best place for reforming that institution is from inside. Moreover he is able to stay within the Church as a non-realist because "Anglican formularies nowhere say either that the Church is infallible or irreformable, or that priests have got to be metaphysical realists."[22] It is a bold and telling statement, and one that the Church authorities have never challenged. It also shows that revision of the Church is a major component of his original vision. Indeed, even in 2001 he is still prepared to endorse what he had written in *Radicals and the Future of the Church* about reforming the Church.[23]

From the outset Cupitt's aim is to answer the question of how in postmodernity a church is still possible. He identifies the conflict between individual and group belief. He asks whether the individual who knows that the group will eventually become an enemy of "truth and freedom" should wander the countryside, or just keep silently doing one's own thing, or go public?[24] At one moment he is pessimistic, noting that all one can do is stay and attempt to update the tradition without very much expectation of success. Then he becomes up-beat, latching on to the notion Mark C. Taylor espouses in *Altarity* of a religious thought that exults in *différance*. There emerges a vision of "a church that will rejoice in being highly pluralistic, a tapestry of diverse Christianities all adding up to an aesthetically beautiful, morally-variegated and ever-changing whole. Why *shouldn't* the faith mean something different to each Christian?"[25]

In 1989 Cupitt's proposal for remaining in the Church and revision-ing it from within has two main components — ethics and human rela-tionships. Ethically speaking, the Church is needed because "it is a theatre in which we solemnly enact our deepest feelings about the human condi-tion."[26] Furthermore, the churches have in the past served as a useful cor-rective to the power of the State, which down through history has often been a cruel and oppressive institution. They have exercised their prophetic role in defending humanitarian priorities and individual human rights; their agapeistic values can counterbalance the selfish utilitarianism of the state. Thus, lacking a powerful objective God, Cupitt resorts to an argument from antiquity: the churches are ancient organisations that have stood the test of time as fraternities embodying communitarian values that can challenge oppressive State legislation. The obvious retort to this is that the churches have exhibited just as much authoritarianism as the State, and have themselves often embodied the very power that one criti-cizes the state for employing.

Through his second concern, human relationships, Cupitt seeks to address this issue. He argues that a new order of personal relationships is needed, and he looks to Romantics and anarchists to supply inspiration. We fight not for a new creed but to discover a new basis for human rela-tionships. So far, religion may have been disciplinary and repressive; but now there *must* be another form of religion. Citing feminism as one of many forces leading a revolt against patriarchal rationality, its structures of authority, and its pyramidal rank orders, he envisages the new churches being the same as the postmodern world: "a living horizontal network, a multicellular ferment of communication."[27] The religion of the future is "dispersing God into people, people into their own communicative activ-ities, and the cosmos into an unceasing, endlessly self-renewing process of communal artistic production. *Our* work of art."[28]

Cupitt reiterates that no advantage is to be gained by breaking away from ecclesiastical structures. One should try to reinterpret one's own inherited vocabulary in mainstream Christianity rather than in the "thin-ner and artificial language of some new and smaller group."[29] People might dream of solving the problems of the universe in some group with the sup-posedly correct creed, but Cupitt doubts that there is such a group — or such a creed. And such a dream likely leads to idolatry of the group.

Rather, he advocates that we should remain in the Church, but keep our eyes wide open!

Although he has now shifted slightly from this position, he remains generally hopeful (when not somewhat despairing) that the churches might be revised and reformed from within. His original vision of *Radicals and the Future of the Church* is still with him, even if in a diminished form.

Retaining the bathwater, not the baby

It is often protested that non-realists are "throwing the baby out with the bathwater." Non-realists would reply that they simply wish to splash in the bathwater without the baby! The bathwater of religion (ethics, spirituality, worship and prayer) does not require an external deity in order to "affirm the value of human life from its first breath to its very last." If all religions are human constructs, then one can demythologize the supernatural and still offer a powerful program for faith. Christianity isn't about saving one's soul, but about losing oneself in the work of love. It is a creative and redemptive work by which value is bestowed upon people who would otherwise lack it. Love saves the world and justifies the poor, the wicked, and the ungodly. We now have to do the work of God.[30]

It is self-evident that Christian ethics do not need a referent to be meaningful or effective. Hebblethwaite's argument that Mother Teresa's love is greater than that of the secular humanist (see above) comes to grief on the fact that love is still love whether its source is Mother Teresa, or a non-realist, or a secular humanist. If God is the "religious ideal" which equates to the Christian understanding of God as love, then "the Christian specification of the religious ideal makes agapeic (disinterested, or 'solar') love the highest value."[31] The doctrinal and ethical objections can be countered when humanism is combined with a religious under-standing of the human condition. Religious humanism allows one to enter the nihil of one's own and other people's lives and embrace "it" and them; indeed, by so doing, one effectively transforms that situation. Retaining the bathwater can be the key to Christian living.

Non-realism and worship

One of the bathwater ingredients that non-realists often find incon-gruous or paradoxical is worship. Why belong to a church and join in wor-ship? If there is no objective God, are non-realists not worshipping themselves — their own egos? Can one avoid the seemingly inherent "cosmic egotism"? Robin Gill is most adamant that the chief aim of

Christian communities is to gather for worship, and that this is much more than assembling for Cupitt's "bleak dictum of we make truth and we make values." He attacks Cupitt for "mak(ing) little sense of Christian communities as worshipping communities."[32] David Hart offers an incisive riposte:

> If we accept the central thrust of the non-realist argument — that God should be conceived as nothing more or less than the human creation and articulation of the area of our deepest concern, the religious requirement — then we have to understand that the words of our liturgies and the practice of our rituals is our attempt to gather together with our chosen community of spiritual "soul-friends" and give expression together in symbolic form to our deepest spiritual yearnings and our human longing for some understanding of the "vast expanse of interstellar space, galaxies, suns, the planets in their courses, and this fragile earth, our island home."[33]

The implications of this credo have been fleshed out by Cupitt and others within the Sea of Faith Networks.[34] Cupitt points to the fact that over the centuries Love has replaced God as the object of worship in many Christian traditions. This is nowhere better reflected than in some of their hymns. Non-realist worship is *already* evident in hymns that personify Love as God and begin with "Love," "O Love," "O perfect love," "Come down, O Love divine," "Immortal Love," etc. Many such hymns clearly express non-realist theology: Love is God, Love takes human form in Christ, Love conquers and redeems all things. There is no God but Love, and to believe in God is to believe in the divinity of Love. Non-realism has long been part of the Christian tradition.[35]

Anne Ashworth reinterprets for non-realists the traditional Christian "ingredients of prayer and worship" — Adoration, Confession, Thanksgiving, Intercession, Petition, Meditation, Dedication and Benediction. Apart from Meditation, all these liturgical elements were originally forms of worship addressing a transcendent deity. However, the loss of a supernatural God does not make these forms of worship obsolete. So, for example, Adoration (which is normally interpreted as adoring that which is greater than ourselves) is not the celebrating of an objective God, or reducing God to oneself as is the case with humanism; we can still adore something greater than ourselves. Ashworth enjoins that "we celebrate . . . the oneness of the cosmos and the beauty of the earth. . . . Our capacity for awe and wonder has been stretched to fresh horizons."[36]

Likewise, instead of seeing Confession as a mode of inducing guilt that can cause psychological harm, Ashworth turns to Cupitt's *After God* to appropriate his "Eye of God," whereby one checks out one's life from the point of view of an ideal observer. We don't need a religious professional such as a priest to pronounce forgiveness. We can evaluate how we are performing in life by imaginatively looking at ourselves from a distance. We do it everyday in other areas of our lives — our employment, marriage etc. — and so why not in religion? And the one who is serious about self-evaluation will become a better person.

Other Sea of Faith people have produced non-realist material to help non-realists in worship. A parish church in New Zealand has its own hymn-book of non-realist hymns. A "funerals pack" including an anthology of readings and a booklist, along with various thoughts on planning funerals, was issued by Sea of Faith (UK) in 1998, and proved so successful that it was updated and re-issued in 2002. Likewise, Ronald Pearse wrote the following introductions for use in Anglican Eucharistic services to re-interpret its central act of worship in a non-realist way:

At the welcome:

A responsible spirituality is important for our health
and for well-being of the world.
It can be supported by following
a way of life within a fellowship
The Christian church is a fellowship
and maintains and renews itself in a fellowship meal – the
eucharist – the service for which we are now gathered.
In it we honour our historic myths and practice
discerning and using with integrity
our traditional themes of incarnation and of death-and-res
urrection,
and taking the opportunity of new insight
to orient ourselves afresh in honesty, love and creativity.

Before the creed:

We value and honour our heritage
and we are also mindful of the call*
to proclaim the faith afresh in each generation.*
We recite the Nicene Creed,
A fourth century response to that call

Which interpreted incarnation in the terms of the world-
view of those days.

Let us commit ourselves to an on-going interpretation of
our faith.

Before the eucharistic prayer:

For the healing of the nations,
for our wholeness and health
and by ancient words and actions
we bring the symbol of the Christ, the symbol of death-and-
resurrection,
into the present
into ourselves
and into the world of our concern.
(*The Canons of the Church of England, C15)37

Here then are some practical uses of Cupitt's radical religion, applied
within an ecclesiastical setting, with the liturgical practices of the
churches reenvisioned and reinterpreted in a way that he would approve.

It has been my aim in this chapter to provide reasons for affirming
Cupitt's radical religion and his apologia for church membership. The
arguments of those refuters who urge non-realists to leave the Church are
well-intentioned and not without cogency. To remain within the Church
after embracing non-realism is no easy undertaking; this option can appeal
only to those who are willing to contend vigorously against an increasingly hostile audience. Moreover, several unresolved tensions need to be
carefully investigated by those who would look to Cupitt's writings as a
source of inspiration about the religion of the future.

Chapter 5

Unresolved tensions

In this chapter I will identify and discuss four unresolved tensions that confront a non-realist who is attracted by Cupitt's ideas about religion. Suppose the aim is to translate theology into anthropology and the old Christian doctrines of Christ into doctrines about ourselves and our religious task: Will the tradition admit of such flexibility? Have Western people any need of religion at all? Do people want religion that is exclusively centred on this world? Can we really take up the role of religious artists and recreate our faith tradition?

Inheritors of the tradition?

Ronald Pearse understands the predicament of a non-realist within the Anglican Church. As a retired priest he now sits in the pews of his church, squirming at its failure to meet the needs of vast numbers of people who have no meaningful philosophy of life or any significant community in which to live and express a faith. He feels that the Church has let them down badly. In particular he is scathing in his reproof of the Church's silence about the impact of scholarly Biblical research over the last two hundred years, a dereliction that has kept people in the dark and offered only an infantile presentation of the great Biblical themes. Pearse advocates going to church wearing a sprig of rosemary (a symbol of remembrance) to remind oneself to be honest about what one really does and does not believe.[1]

Pearse wants to be allowed to reinterpret the Christian tradition in two important ways. First, he explicates the doctrine of death-and-resurrection not in terms of survival after death, but of how one's present life may be a victory over the all-encompassing despair that many experience.

Second, he recovers the theme of incarnation by understanding it as the "projection of our values and ideals . . . as God-in-us." Here is a non-realist reading of the tradition that is *still* evangelistic in that it purports to have identified within that tradition a non-realist message that is sufficiently meaningful and intellectually honest for people to live by.

Anthony Freeman and Stephen Mitchell take this a step further in two ways. They both provide pastoral reasons for affirming non-realism and church membership. Mitchell presents religious stories and rituals in a non-realist way. For him, the traditions of the Church are relevant to the problems faced by most people in their everyday life (illness, unemployment, bereavement etc.). For both, re-enacting the rituals of faith helps to "fire our imaginations and empower us to work through these very human issues." Christianity provides feelings of solidarity in an otherwise hostile world.[2] Freeman sees other pastoral implications as well. His plea (made more poignant as a result of his own eviction by the Anglican Church) is for "the Church to be open to non-realism as a permitted starting point — not something to be imposed, but something to be allowed for those who find themselves at that position."[3]

Adrian Moore (see chap. 4) makes a distinction between ordinary church members and church officials (including clergy), arguing that the latter should not be permitted to be card-carrying non-realists. Freeman counters this stance by pointing out the potential advantages of a non-realist priest officiating at the eucharist and at funerals. Far from desecrating these rites, he argues, a non-realist priest may be pastorally more effective in healing the theological rifts concerning the interpretation of both the central ritual of Christianity and the final rite of passage. In the former case, the plethora of interpretations prevents any consensus as to what exactly happens in the eucharist, and yet it remains the principal celebration of many Christian churches. The eucharist has spiritual value all of its own, independent of any theory of what it *might* mean, and thus the non-realist priest is in a better position to be pastorally sensitive to the many varied beliefs of his parishioners. It is also to be noted that in the matter of the presence of Christ in the Eucharistic elements (bread and wine) realists and non-realists have long coexisted in the Church. Indeed, throughout Church history eucharistic theology has been a battlefield. The Roman Catholic Church has taught the "*real* presence" of Christ in the Mass (the doctrine of Transubstantiation), whereas the Protestant churches have generally leaned toward a non-realist, symbolic, and non-supernatural understanding of the consecrated elements as *signs* of Christ's body and blood.

This capacity for heightened sensitivity to people's doubts or outright skepticism is perhaps even more evident in funeral arrangements. Citing actual bereavement situations, Freeman argues that the openness and sensibility of non-realism allows a non-realist priest to be more effective in the Anglican Church, which the vast majority of British people still view as "their church," even though they may attend only the traditional rites of passage. Confronted with the agnosticism and atheism of a populace who nevertheless turn to the Anglican Church for an appropriate funeral ceremony, the non-realist priest might be more competent in meeting their needs than one with a more "orthodox" belief system. Indeed Freeman wonders how theologically conservative ministers are able to minister to those people who call upon the Church at times of bereavement and yet who have no wish to adopt a realist faith.[4] It is significant that Moore, who is more interested in conversion than the lack of "orthodox" beliefs of many people in the United Kingdom, never mentions this pastoral advantage of the non-realist priest.

Even more contentiously, perhaps, both Freeman and Mitchell believe that they are in the vanguard of a Christian faith that is *a legitimate expression of the Christian tradition*. This is nowhere better expressed than in Freeman's controversial *God in Us*. Here his intent is to argue for ecclesiastical non-realism, provocatively (like Pearse above), upholding the Preface of the Declaration of Assent (made by every priest of the Church of England at their Ordination) to "*proclaim afresh*" the faith "*in each generation*."[5] This is necessary, he proposes, because our way of life is significantly different from that when the faith and its liturgies were originally composed. There must be a new expression of faith; otherwise the "fictional faith" will be perpetuated much after the manner of those who are members of English historical societies. Adopting postmodern literary views on interpretation, Freeman explains that "in presenting the faith to this generation I am bound to be presenting a *different* faith from that which my forefathers presented. Not just a different *interpretation* of the same essential core, but a *different faith*. This is because there is no essence or inner core. Re-interpretation is not like taking the shell off a nut. It is like peeling the layers off an onion: the interpretation goes all the way down. All is interpretation. That *is* the essence."[6]

Moore notes that Freeman's understanding of interpretation is the key to his belief that he and other non-realists are the inheritors of a tradition that can be continually created and re-created. Thus, the texts of the Church have to be interpreted "afresh by each generation" and he interestingly (at first) agrees that it is "obscurantist nonsense to allege that people like Freeman are betraying the faith of the church by continuing in orders."[7] Though he later amends this stance by rebutting Freeman's claim that Christianity lacks an indispensable core or inner essence, he has correctly identified the non-realists' claim that they *too* are legitimate heirs of the tradition. They believe that they have every right to continue within the tradition and should not be forced outside it by the conservatives. If religion is a human construction, if God is created rather than discovered, and if language interprets reality, then they can reinterpret Christianity. Indeed, from the perspective of Freeman and Mitchell "they are the true torch-bearers for the gospel."[8] Here is the crux of the argument: "Is non-realism a legitimate or illegitimate position to hold within the churches?" "Are non-realists practitioners of Christianity, or do they preach a radically different Gospel?" "Will/Can the churches ever admit such a position?"

In many ways the non-realists seem to be fighting a battle in which everything is against them. Cupitt, himself, as I mentioned earlier, is ambivalent about whether non-realists can find an appropriate and cordial role within the churches. The way he has been shunned by both the Church hierarchy and the Academy should be sufficient warning to anyone who contemplates following a similar path. Furthermore, an increasingly conservative Anglicanism in retreat from its former "breadth" of belief reflects its declining influence and its decreasing number of adherents. Ironically, its demise and that of the other mainstream churches may be viewed as a significant result of the ebbing of radicalism within those organizations. As the churches turn inward upon themselves in an attempt at self-preservation, the search for self-definition leads to stricter doctrinal orthodoxy. As the churches contract, they increasingly resemble sailors patching a leaky ship; any admission of weakness or uncertainty will be letting the side down. In a few cases, to be sure, dwindling attendance leads to a lessening of doctrinal orthodoxy as churches emphasize "fellowship" and "journeying" in an effort to accommodate new members; but it is fair to say that the majority of churches have become more stringent in upholding "orthodox" teaching.

I suggest that if it is to be tolerated, radicalism like Cupitt's generally needs a numerically strong Church, one in which it is not perceived to be threatening or subversive. A struggling Church is no lover of radicalism and is ill-prepared to entertain untested doctrines within its walls. On the other hand it might be proposed that no more than a few thousand radicals could conceivably provide an urgently needed stimulus to the many churches around the world that find themselves in retreat. What is certain, as I will argue in chapter 6, is that the churches would have more to gain than lose by including these radical searchers. Any church that excludes or ignores its radicals (those Wilhelm Dilthey called the 'disquieting voices') will be the poorer. Even Moore recognises this, and sees it a mistake to reject their views outright. Moreover, their ideas deserve a hearing "because we should never complacently assume that the church's expression of its faith is perfectly in order as it stands."[9] Here, then, is both a motive and a protocol for "orthodoxy" and radicalism to enter into a mutually beneficial dialogue.

However, perhaps there is a greater threat to both orthodox and radical expressions of faith: that people have no need of mainstream Christian religion and will abandon it altogether.

Is religion needed?[10]

This is exactly the question that Cupitt poses in a paper presented at the Sea of Faith U.K. Conference in 1999. Confronted by evidence from Europe, Australia, and New Zealand that "[Christian] religion plays no visible part at all in the lives of the majority of the population," and that the traditional statistics of observance such as baptisms, confirmations and Easter Communions are currently declining at a rate of almost twenty-five per cent every decade, Cupitt asks: "What is religion for — and is it still worth bothering with?"[11]

Clearly the question is not whether religion has given up on people, but whether people have given up on religion. If religious language (whether as doctrinal creeds *or* as that which generates our world) is perceived by an increasing percentage of the population as meaningless, that is of vital concern to organized religion, and especially the churches. When an estimated 76 million people in the U.S.A tuned in to the last episode of *Seinfeld* that was, in the words of its producers, a "show about nothing," one cannot help wondering whether television has replaced religion in the Western world. Are people today so quiescent that they no longer even ask "What is the world?" "What are we: how is it with us?" "How should we live?" The absence of such basic responses to our situation is the nihilism that Cupitt foresees, and perhaps in the Western world is very close — if it is not already here.

Cupitt's religious task, I have maintained, is the same as that of the churches, and of theology: to persuade people to endorse a religious outlook. Is it creative faith that will save people, or do they need above all belief in an omnipotent God? This is the "mission-field" that theologians and institutional churches must now recognise *after* Cupitt. More significantly, perhaps (and may I suggest that this is the real Nietzschean terror), the answer that Cupitt *and* the churches fear most is that the general populace is perfectly happy to be caught up in the whirl of a "non-religious" society and so senses no need for recourse to any mainstream religion. Here is reality for the majority of people, especially in the Western world. Cupitt's religious endeavours are a timely wake-up call to theologians that the "non-religious" option is now very deeply embedded in Western societies, and as Heidegger would say, it may already be "too late." The secularist hegemony is established; can there be any turning back?

Moore correctly describes Cupitt as an "evangelist for religious values in a technocratic, postmodern, and nihilistic society."[12] The implication is that a society with a religion freed from metaphysics is healthier than one with a religious metaphysics or one without any religion. At present it seems that the former (fundamentalism) and the latter (nihilism) are the preferred options of most people. Nihilism has devoured Europe and the Antipodes. Fundamentalism, especially of an Islamic variety is attempting to establish total hegemony in Asia and the Middle East, and has challenged the power of "the Infidel" America with chilling consequences. Cupitt voices the concern that another option is sorely needed — religious humanism.

Death and the new religion of life

Hans-Georg Gadamer notes that the central problem that all religions address is the need of people to face up to their own mortality. Human beings are the only creatures that *know* that one day they will die.[13] How to deal with the facticity of death has been a major preoccupation for Cupitt from *Taking Leave of God* onwards. Significantly, he connects this knowledge of one's own death to the question of *how* one is going to live — having accepted that "all this is all there is." Cupitt finds an answer in Heidegger: temporality and "religious calling" are linked. The sense of our own mortality "acts like a religious vocation: it galvanizes us into realizing that we must make something of our lives while we have time."[14] It is, of course, a scandal that despite this realization Heidegger not only embraced National Socialism but also failed subsequently to admit his own disastrous error.

Cupitt thus emphasises that people must create religions that find blessedness and acceptance of life in the here-and-now. Any new religion must abandon all pretensions of belief in an afterlife and immortal souls, and affirm that there is only *this* world.[15] One crucial piece of evidence which shows how people in the Western world have begun to embrace this new thinking is the way that "ordinary language" has changed as we have moved from a God-centred to a life-centred outlook.

In *The New Religion of Life in Everyday Speech* Cupitt argues that the arrival in language of a flood of new idioms about life shows the extent to which people have made "life" the new religious object. As was shown in *Odyssey on the Sea of Faith*, Gregory Spearritt identifies a tension within the book, for Cupitt acknowledges that pessimism about life is also a significant belief. The 2002 figures from the Australian National Bureau of Statistics, for example, reveal the suicide rate for males aged 15–24 years rose from 27.9 per 100,000 in 1988 to 30.6 per 100,000 in 1997. The high rate of youth suicide within a country like Australia inclines Spearritt to prefer the pessimistic analysis.[16]

Not only must we face this unresolved tension about whether people are optimistic or pessimistic about "life," but one must ask whether people are ready to adopt a religion that entirely excludes any notion of a future life. Indeed, one must ask what kind of religion ordinary people need to help them in their lives. Cupitt, as will have become apparent, does not give any specifics as to *exactly* what the "religion of the future" might be, but makes the general claim that religion overcomes nihilism, and gives value to life. In religion we develop shared meanings, purposes, and narratives. Religion's least concern is with offering eternal happiness in the face of our own death.[17] It is left to people themselves, adopting the role of the religious artist, to work out what this means. For some that is an opportunity that they are willing to embrace with open arms; others need more of a conceptual framework within which to work.

Disposable and undogmatic religion — the artist?

In *The Revelation of Being* Cupitt claims that he wants to invent a universal-human kind of religion, and then give it away![18] Only by taking it in the postmodern sense of having no fixed position can one begin to understand this paradoxical claim. Once one has a religion with a fixed position, it becomes authoritarian and undemocratic — the very antithesis of his lifetime's work. However, this involves the corresponding difficulty of trying to work out what *is* the "truth for the moment" and the religion of "the time being?" This problem arises from his insistence that religion must fulfill the following criteria: "religion should make our life seem to us to be intelligible and valuable. In religion we seek a picture of the world and of ourselves with which we can be content. We want to know what we are, how we fit into the overall scheme of things, how we should live and how we can be happy. Religion should give us a world-picture and a way of life that are attractive, and that make sense."[19]

The latest move to post-Christianity is not a New Reformation like the battle cry of theologians in the 1960s, but a demand for *new religious thought*. It is here that he tries to solve his problem of how to create what I would call a "disposable religion" by reigniting a theme that has preoccupied him since *Taking Leave of God*, namely that religion must become like art.[20] I agree with George Pattison when he says that art "is not merely an occasional source of illustration but integral to the shape of his theological project. This is because, for Cupitt, the world of art does not just provide a useful analogy to what is going on in religion: it actually shows the kind of religion — and, indeed, the only kind of religion — that a postmodern world can get along with."[21]

Cupitt's early ideas of the creative "religious" artist develop into the concept of the artist who "is not at all aggrieved by the news that reality has become all fictional, and that difference, the sign, and secondariness come first."[22] Using Derrida's concept of *différance*, Cupitt argues that the artist becomes the role model for the renewal of religion because "the vacancy at the Centre of all things and the vacancy at the centre of the self coincide. The artist journeys into that darkness and nothingness. . . . Yet art is an affirmation of life precisely in its acceptance of death and secondariness."[23] In other words, by relinquishing realism and admitting that there is nothing except contingency and immanence, one enables creativity to begin. This may seem perplexing, and yet there is virtue in it in that religion is coping with outsidelessness, transience, and death — nihilism, the Cross!

There are, of course, many styles of artists, and Cupitt first seizes on the work of Paul Cézanne because he would not be troubled by the thought that a supernatural God was dead. Indeed, Cézanne "understood that the object with which painting is concerned is not anything external to painting, but just *la peinture*."[24] So too, religion must be undertaken for its own sake, disinterestedly. Moreover, Cupitt warms to those artists who can brighten the world for people (as in the Paris School of painters from Monet to Matisse who invested everyday scenes with the radiance of Paradise) as well as those who can point out the poignant elements of life (as in tragic art).

This artistic celebration of *both* joy and tragedy is a theme often overlooked by Cupitt's detractors. Some have objected that he seems to be attracted only to tragic artists, especially in view of his claim that Mark Rothko "just invented works of art that are great religion."[25] Yet Rothko committed suicide, seemingly unable to accept what Cupitt views in his art as affirming — the contingency and utter horizontality of life. Surely it is significant that after his move from "the discipline of the void" to a lighter, solar religion in *After God* (1997), Cupitt seems to abandon Rothko. This answers George Pattison's criticism that Cupitt's reliance on Rothko's paintings makes his religion too "tragic" and that "art which would be religiously significant [is] summonsed to such tragic serious-ness."[26] Cupitt would now insist that his ultralight religious humanism points beyond the Void.

In an interesting comparison between himself and a fellow postmod-ern theoretician, Cupitt explains his discomfort with the "negativity" of the American (a)theologian Mark C. Taylor by pointing out their diverse artistic preferences. Cupitt laments Taylor's choice of American abstract Expressionism (Pollock, Rothko and Newman) concluding "very pes-simistically with Anselm Kiefer."[27] Ironically, this is the very argument with which Charles Pickstone attempts to refute Cupitt, contending that his "horizontal" religion is so indebted to American Abstract Expressionism that he has forgotten "other schools of art," which might point towards a different understanding of religion.[28] Since Pickstone's article dates from 1994, it fails to appreciate Cupitt's shift away from the harsh American abstract expressionists to the more joyful French post-impressionists and German expressionists that now fit more easily into his "solar" religion.

Cupitt's list of artists in *After God* begins with Vincent van Gogh, turns to the post-impressionists through the symbolists and German expressionism, arriving not at pessimism but "the world as outpouring energetic process" — solar.[29] Indeed, Cupitt further praises van Gogh's works because "towards the end, he was painting the Revelation of Being and solar living every day."[30] By this he means that the secularization of society — or the humanization of the Christian vision — is not an irreli-gious but a religious movement. What has happened in art is a good indi-cation of the dissemination and scattering of once specifically religious ideas into the secular sphere. A deconstructed religiosity is widespread, and has much influenced modern art ever since the Impressionists. Cupitt was led in this direction in the mid-1980s when he first saw many of Monet's late paintings in France and visited the famous lily ponds at Giverny. He thought how joyfully 'Empty' was that late-impressionist vision of the world, and how like that of Buddhism in its suggestion that Europe was even then going over to what he calls "the mysticism of sec-ondariness" — a mystical love for everything transient and fleeting.

Monet painted his water lilies at Giverny to express visual delight in immediate experience; and that is what religion should do: go light, delight in life, delight in experience, delight in the way the world continually pours out and passes away. This emphasis on "visual delight" also silences Pickstone's second "problem" that Cupitt's writing about art is "curiously disincarnate, languagey." For Cupitt, visual experience and language are interlinked. Seeing is from the first interwoven with language and interpretations: it comes to us pure, contingent, and chaotic, but is formed into a world by human interpretation.

It would seem that the following equation expresses Cupitt's understanding of religion:

SECULARIZATION OF SOCIETY ≠
SACRALIZATION OF LIFE ≠
POSTMODERN CONDITION ≠
KINGDOM OF GOD ≠
POST-CHRISTIANITY

Post-Christians are like artists continuing the temporalization and religious humanism of what was once a strictly Christian vision. The post-Christian artists are those who try to find religious meaning in the process of democratization, laicization and secularization; they advance "polydoxies" which are continually discarded lest they gain the status of "orthodoxy." Post-Christianity thus becomes "protean," "mobile" and "errant"; it resists any final definition or totalization, a quality that Cupitt recognizes as annoying to his critics.[31] This is the revelation of being as be(com)ing — the combination of non-realism and radical humanism. It can be seen, then, that "art provides the saving analogy which leads Cupitt out of the impasse of despair."[32] This begs the questions posed earlier: "Will this satisfy people's religious needs?" "Is this enough by which to live?" "Is constant re-invention and re-creation of a universal humanism the religious task?" "Are religious people artists?"

The major critique of Cupitt's understanding of art has come from George Pattison. He elicits four "themes" from Cupitt's writings that seem to epitomize the questions raised above. The first he entitles "Art as religion," and contrary to Cupitt he contends that art has neither replaced nor filled a void left by the demise of religion. He is not persuaded by Cupitt's endorsement of Nietzsche's paean to "Art, nothing but art! It is the great means of making life possible . . . the great stimulant of life."[33] He questions whether "art needs religion more than religion needs art" and whether art can by itself replace religion as a guide to living.[34] The second theme "Surface and depth," is important for Cupitt in that all is "horizontality." Following Bataille, he sees Manet as making the transition to "art on the level." Pattison questions this interpretation of Manet, contending that far from being one-dimensional, he creates a "metaphysical shock" that encourages one to look deeper. Although Pattison concedes Manet's painting "Dead Christ with Angels" might be interpreted "horizontally" as the humanization of Christ, he views it as a painting of "the deepest pathos."[35] Third, Pattison questions whether the artist is truly a creator: Is it not rather that "art (is) essentially a responsiveness to the givenness of colour and form?"[36] Pattison's calls his fourth theme "The end of tradition." Here it may well be questioned whether Pattison has fully understood Cupitt for as I have argued above, Cupitt does not so much abandon tradition as attempt to reform it.

Pattison argues that art is dependent upon religion (religious/spiritual ideas) for its powers of creation and for its epiphanies of the sacred attending "to the God who is yet to come."[37] He thus identifies himself as a critical realist, one for whom art points towards the Ineffable, which is God. For Cupitt those epiphanies are not of God, but of humanity. Art shows how truly human people can become. Pattison's positing of a "God of beyond" in horizontal art is another version of the attack that has failed, the attempt by those who try to represent realism as being more benign — in short, the "critical realist" position of White and others (see *Odyssey on the Sea of Faith*). The resulting conversation operates on different levels and the parties to the dialogue pass each other by.

So, where is the greatest tension for Cupitt? I propose that it is to be found in asking whether he can avoid his own image of the proliferation of religions in the same way that "widely different works of modern art coexist in the art gallery."[38] Is Cupitt's "expressionism" so all-embracing? His writings exhibit two conflicting ideas. Though he asserts that "meaning is always somewhat ambivalent, plural or indeterminate," he also acknowledges that: "we are trying to synthesize conflicting forces."[39] He seems to want to accommodate his late-1980s "let a hundred flowers bloom" scenario to a more radically democratic position in which the "final vocabulary" is open to constant re-negotiation. He is unsure about the vast array of New Age cults and spiritualities that have entered the religious supermarket, for they have created formless anarchy and often commit the same error as traditional religions by producing dogmatic teachings dispensed by gurus and shamans.[40]

To this problem Cupitt offers a fivefold response: (1) still using the traditional religious practices in the short-term, (2) practicing meditation, (3) active solar living, (4) poetical theology — i.e. retelling old myths in new ways, and (5) attempting to create a universal human religion. But this is rather like having a bet each way.[41] If notions of the gods have become disseminated by language across and within cultures, then why limit oneself to a universal humanism? Simply put, the secularization of religion has not reduced the number of religious options, but rather has resulted in their proliferation. Indeed, according to the Australian writer David Tacey a "spirituality revolution" is taking place. It seems that people are *already* creative religious artists with a corresponding array of "artistic" religions helping to guide them through life. It could be argued that while many of the "newer" religious practices fulfill Cupitt's undogmatic criteria rather better than the "historic religions," Cupitt *still* looks chiefly to Buddhism and Christianity for his inspiration.

Conclusion

In conclusion, Cupitt seems to be caught in a dilemma from which he finds it difficult to extricate himself. Should he abandon completely his Christian past and surge forward into a new religious humanism that could go anywhere, or should he still try to reform the Christian tradition that he obviously holds dear? The former move will take him into the unknown territory of competing or co-existing with many spiritualities for which he has little time or inclination, fearing them to be an intellectual mess and which reinforce the platonic distinction between this world and something better elsewhere. The latter way is made equally unpalatable by the strident evangelicals at the helm of the churches and unwilling to proclaim a Gospel that allows any room for his particular form of radicalism. This oscillation between optimism and pessimism concerning the Christian tradition is one that leaves Cupitt's religion somewhere between a rock and a hard place. Cupitt himself tries to write off the tension as simply a symptom of living in postmodernity that artists continually point to:

> The lesson to be learned from artists . . . is that in postmodernity we are all of us . . . in an ironized, both-believing-and-unbelieving relation to our own religious tradition. Artists explore and play with the many different nuances of irony now found amongst us, and the fact that they find a public — often, a very large public — shows that we are all of us in varying ways ironized non-realists nowadays. We at-least-half know it's only myth, but many of us remain very attached to it all nonetheless.[42]

Recently, he has advocated "informal religious associations" for people needing a community where they can share stories that explain their "present religious situation."[43] One might conjecture that some churches have already begun to function that way. Although I have argued in this chapter that the churches have become more doctrinally orthodox as their membership has dwindled, some churches have gone against this trend. In Australia, for example, a few Uniting and Anglican churches are beginning to emphasize "fellowship," "community," "sharing your story," and "kingdom values" rather than an orthodox understanding of "God." It may well be significant that these churches are quite close to what Cupitt has envisaged as the religion of the future. Likewise, Cupitt has admitted that the Quakers have been the "only serious Christians" because "they abolished the whole religious sphere of life (the church, the clergy and the sacraments); they affirmed the value of life, to the point of being strict practitioners of non-violence; they were the chief pioneers of our modern humanitarian ethics; and they sought to be politically supranational."[44] I wonder if this may convince Cupitt that it is now time to follow his fellow Anglican priest and radical writer Graham Shaw out of the Church and into the Society of Friends? Or, will his love for the eucharist as a kingdom-meal prevent such a move? Perhaps, as he freely admits in *The Long Legged Fly*, he is fated to be "one of the last ecclesiastical theologians."

If Cupitt finds the churches oppressive, then to whom can he turn to find the necessary companionship, freedom of opinion and intellectual stimulus in which to debate this tension? For the last decade or so, he has been affiliated with three groups of loosely associated individuals in his own country and in the Antipodes — the Sea of Faith Networks. Cupitt's dilemma over taking leave of the Church is echoed by that of the Networks: Are they the churches of the future, or are they merely irritants to the mainstream religious traditions?

It is to those Networks that I now turn.

Chapter 6

Cupitt, the origins and development of the Networks

Introduction

> ...I for one am indebted to Don [Cupitt] for creating a *milieu* in which religious ideas can be considered with openness and without fear of reproach. Here there is no dogmatism, no seeking for easy answers, but a place where it is possible to discuss with people of imagination and tolerance that which can be taboo within a traditional church setting.[1]

This sentiment expressed by many members of Sea of Faith indicates that the Networks provide a much less intimidating forum for the discussion of difficult religious questions than does organized religion, for they afford a context where no heretical statement is too shocking and no contemporary idea too disturbing. For some like Teresa Wallace (quoted above), the new religious freedom is linked to the pioneering work of Cupitt, whereas others in Sea of Faith think it is time to take leave even of Cupitt and push the boat out into deeper and rougher seas. Moreover, the expansion of the Sea of Faith Networks to three countries has unleashed the creative talents of a number of new religious writers. That its collection of literature is both increasing and relatively diverse is evidenced by the books, articles and conference papers listed on its three websites. Cupitt is no longer the lone prophet battling single-handedly to gain a hearing for non-realism or for a non-supernatural interpretation of Christianity.

It is often erroneously thought *either* that the United Kingdom Network is the only Network *or* that it is the major Network and the others are branches of it. Writing in 1995, Anthony Thiselton based his whole disparagement of Sea of Faith on the United Kingdom organization. He either ignores or is not aware that the New Zealand Network has a very different outlook from its British counterpart. The Networks retain their independence, and only informally constitute a worldwide network of networks. They are also linked to other progressive organizations with similar outlooks, for example the Westar Institute in the United States.

In this Section my main concern is to examine Cupitt's relationship to the Networks that drew inspiration from his writings. I will dispel such invalid claims as the canards that it is a "movement within the Anglican Church," or that "most of the Sea of Faith Network are clergy." In fact, it is estimated that only about fifty Anglican clergy are members of the United Kingdom Network, the New Zealand has even fewer clergy-people amongst its ranks and the Australian Network is overwhelmingly comprised of "lay" people. Thus the majority of members of Sea of Faith Networks are *not* ordained ministers. I will outline the origins and development of the Sea of Faith Networks showing their different forms in the United Kingdom, New Zealand and Australia. I will compare some of the concerns of the principal writers within the Networks to Cupitt's own project, revealing divergences in thinking and showing how religious writing has progressed in an era *after* God. It will be my contention that the protean quality of the Sea of Faith literature is not only consistent with but an extension of Cupitt's writings. Indeed, it will be seen how the Sea of Faith Networks are now an unplanned fulfilment of one of Cupitt's major considerations, in that they function "like an art college . . . in which people are led to discover their own creative powers."[2]

George Pattison asserts that Cupitt's television series, *The Sea of Faith*, "was (and remains) an event in British religious life."[3] I will argue that this is too narrow an interpretation of a religious awakening that was (and remains) a *worldwide* phenomenon that has found a voice not only in Networks like Sea of Faith, but outside them as well. Sea of Faith is an international society, a sort of post-church, a fellowship of people who want to explore the changes that are taking place in religion. It will also become evident in chapter 7 that Cupitt has not been alone in his pioneering endeavours. Similar sentiments were expressed some decades before Cupitt by Lloyd Geering, whose ground-breaking works have only recently begun to be fully acknowledged and appreciated. The Networks are not dominated by "godless Anglican Vicars," or people who are "All at sea," or for whom their "Faith (is) at sea." Nor can it be anything but a gross slander to propose that the Sea of Faith is "a parasitic distortion of the church, and as such needs to be recognized as an heretical movement within it."[4] Rather the Networks are a response to cries from the human heart that new religious expressions of faith are needed. Indeed, more and more people are attempting to find a way through a postmodernity where the religious nostalgia promoted by the churches is being rejected and where the intimidating void leads many to nihilistic despair.

The United Kingdom Network

Commentators often assume and repeatedly assert that Cupitt was the founder of the United Kingdom Sea of Faith Network. This falls into the trap of either equating Cupitt's radical project with that of the Networks or making him responsible for everything promoted by the Networks and their members. On both counts this is wrong! The relationship between Cupitt and the Networks is much more fluid. To put the record straight, it needs to be said again that Cupitt did *not* found the Sea of Faith Network. It was begun by a group of people who were inspired by the television series bearing that name. Cupitt has never been on the Steering Committee of the Sea of Faith, and has never held any formal position in the Network. His major contributions have been to lecture at its annual conference and to provide a stimulus to new ways of religious writing.

His reluctance to be seen as the driving force behind the United Kingdom Network is based on three factors, all of which appear in his writings. First, it was *not his idea* but, as Pattison correctly indicates, "one of the [unforeseen] results" of *The Sea of Faith* television series and the accompanying book.[5] Second, since he was extremely reluctant to be involved in instituting some sort of religious sect, Cupitt initially remained very cautious — sympathetic to its intent, but wary of wholesale involvement. Third, his writing project requires that he remain independent of any constraints on his thought. He does not wish to be tied down to any particular program or school of thought, much less to be the spokesperson of any movement. Rather, he prefers to remain free to create his own religious writing. As he explains: "My own peculiar task seemed to demand that I should be and remain rather anomalous, marginal and unattached."[6] He certainly did not want to risk being seen as having founded his own fan club.

The Sea of Faith Network, then, began in the United Kingdom and grew out of the efforts of others who were already thinking along the same lines. Rather than functioning as the founding guru of the United Kingdom Network, Cupitt simply articulated the problems that many people faced in seeking to be "authentically religious in the contemporary (postmodern) cultural situation."[7] His writings and media presentation were effective because they resonated with those who had difficulty with supernatural language, yet still wished to retain a faith to live by. One of the themes that reverberated most profoundly was evoked by the scene from the television series in which Cupitt relates how at Christmas he was in church singing the carol, "It Came upon the Midnight Clear," and was struck by the words, "From angels bending near the earth, to touch their harps of gold." It was 1957, and he thought of the spaceship *Sputnik* orbiting the earth. He suddenly felt foolish, unable to reconcile the realist language of the song with living in the new space age. The old religious diction had become mythical.

It was exactly this emphasis on the metaphorical and symbolic nature of religious language that had prompted the Reverend Ronald Pearse, Anglican Rector of Thurcaston in Leicestershire, to write to Cupitt in 1984. Pearse found that he was not alone in his questioning of the Anglican tradition, and Cupitt put him in contact with another Anglican priest from the Leicester area who was exploring similar issues. Following *The Sea of Faith* television series they were joined by a third Anglican priest, and thus came to pass the historical connection between Leicester, Anglican clergy, and Sea of Faith.[8] It was hardly surprising that Anglican clergy should be the *first* to be involved, since (a) Cupitt himself was an Anglican priest, (b) his outlook in the 1980s was that of an Anglican apologist, and (c) the contemporary Anglican ethos permitted a great diversity of views. Moreover, as representatives of the Tradition that they now wished to reform in a non-realist way, the clergy would have most to gain (though to be sure, most to lose). The initial vision of these three priests was a Conference of like-minded persons, but it took four years to materialise. Pearse says that on two occasions Cupitt gave the excuse that he was unable to offer any help for two years. This delaying tactic stemmed from the three concerns mentioned above. Pearse does not reveal how it happened that the growing number of people who met to discuss radical theology in public-houses and at the University of Loughborough eventually decided to take matters into their own hands; but when they at last determined to organize a Conference Cupitt agreed to speak at it. He was willing to contribute, but not to assume a leadership role. Interestingly, one of his most practical (and extremely helpful) contributions was to provide a list of 143 names and addresses of people who had written positive responses to *The Sea of Faith* television series; and thus he afforded the organizers of the Conference an opportunity to invite those specifically interested in matters of shared concern.

The first Sea of Faith U.K. Conference, advertised as "an exploratory conference for radical Christians," took place in 1988 and reflected the initial Anglican clerical input. All three main speakers were male Anglican clergy — Dennis Nineham, Graham Shaw and Don Cupitt — and, according to Aileen La Tourette, the Conference was "too cold, cerebral, masculine, clerical" for some of the participants (especially women) and they never returned.[9] It was also, as the title of the Conference suggests, a specifically Christian gathering aimed at reforming the Church and very much influenced by Cupitt's writings. It is no coincidence that *Radicals and the Future of the Church* was published in the following year. A leaflet about the Conference included the following information:

> Public response to the work of Don Cupitt and other radical theologians indicates that there are many people in the churches (including priests and ministers) who are interested in the project of a completely non-supernaturalist interpretation of Christianity as a community faith, a way of life and a spiritual path.[10]

Admittedly, the initial thrust of the Sea of Faith was to reenvision the churches, especially the Anglican Church; but as the United Kingdom Network developed, its concerns and objectives diversified and expanded. It is to the credit of the "founding Fathers" of the United Kingdom Sea of Faith that they did not restrict their role to that of a pressure group for non-realism within the Church of England.[11] Be that as it may, the historical origins of the Network have left their mark. A tension still exists between those who view Sea of Faith as a group advocating church reform, and those who consider that its main role should be to aid people to create new forms of religious faith. This same tension remains unresolved in Cupitt's own writings though in *Life, Life* (2003) he has argued that Sea of Faith shouldn't beg for toleration from a Christian tradition that will never allow non-realism to be taken seriously. It is better simply to innovate, on the maxim that creative religious thinking is the only form that true religion can take. Accordingly, Sea of Faith should "do its own thing," whatever it may deem that to be.

It is often stated that Sea of Faith is a "movement,"[12] but this rests on a misunderstanding of a very important principle that evolved from the deliberations following the first Conference. It is reflected in the adoption of the word **Network**, a term that deters Sea of Faith from becoming what Cupitt most feared getting trapped in — a sect. Pearse notes that the group defined itself as a Network not long after the second Conference. Critical to this was the wording of a "Statement of Intent" adopted in 1989 that called for "exploring and promoting religious faith as a human creation."[13] Pearse sums up the lengthy debate concerning the word "promoting":

At the October 1989 meeting some would have been content to stop at the word "exploration," but others wanted to go further and include something which showed that we were not content to be simply an academic or other sort of talking shop. We did not find it easy to settle on a perfect word to express this. I remember suggesting "celebration," but that was not exactly right. In the end we settled for "promotion."[14]

It is important to note that this tension between those who view Sea of Faith as primarily a *milieu* in which to debate the latest in radical theology, and those for whom Sea of Faith is the promotion of *all* religion as a human creation, remains unresolved. It keeps resurfacing, as it did in an exchange on the Sea of Faith chat-line in which Correspondent 1 takes a proactive view of the Sea of Faith, whereas the respondent is content to have it a sort of religious debating society:

Correspondent 1: That God is a human creation surely follows from the understanding that all religion is a human creation. . . . Doesn't it? Unless we suppose God is so detached from humanity that he (*sic*) left it to create its religions without any divine assistance. Isn't our common ground in Sea of Faith that religion, like music, politics and lawn tennis is a human creation (I wouldn't object to invention myself)? And that the gods, spirits, devils and other-worldly entities of religion are likewise human constructs? If that's not our common purpose, I think we need a network which explores and promotes the idea that religion and its gods are a wholly human creation.

Respondent: Whatever coherence Sea of Faith has it is not at that level. We are "religion in the head" and for that reason, members need to look for avenues of religious expression elsewhere. I would be disappointed to discover Sea of Faith members for whom Sea of Faith activities make up their entire faith.

A further confusion brought out by Correspondent 1 concerns the question of just what is being promoted. Is it "religious faith as a human creation" *and* does that necessarily entail non-realism by implying that God is a human creation? Cupitt himself would agree that this is the case, but some members of Sea of Faith would argue by a different route that we cannot rule out the notion of an "unknowable X." For them, our existence is so hedged about by mystery that the only proper response is agnosticism.

The inclusion of the word Network was no doubt a very shrewd move, since it allowed Sea of Faith to remain ambivalent about what *exactly* it was. Indeed, Stephen Mitchell records that when at the 1990 Conference someone attempted to include in the description of Sea of Faith first that it was open to all — (whether of a church background or not), second that it was theologically "radical," and third that this implied "non-realism," all three propositions were rejected on the grounds that this would result in Sea of Faith being exclusive and divisive.[15] Likely enough the crux of the argument concerned the insistence on non-realism. As La Tourette recalls, an intense internal conflict arose, with delegates unwilling to sign on the dotted line to indicate that they were card-carrying non-realists.[16]

Underlying this disharmony, to use a Biblical image, was the difference between those who wished to follow Cupitt "to the letter," and those who sought to follow "the spirit" of what he was trying to do. It was extremely fortunate that Cupitt decided against direct involvement in the running of Sea of Faith; had he done so, he could have been caught up in an in-house feud that might have weakened the Network. Moreover, the election of La Tourette to the Chair of the Steering Committee meant that no one philosophical or theological viewpoint prevailed. As a lapsed Roman Catholic lay person who was employed in helping inmates of a prison to express themselves in writing, she was able to steer Sea of Faith away from the concerns of disaffected clerics. Indeed, she shifted the United Kingdom Network towards a balanced discussion of both intellectual *and* aesthetic understandings of religion.

However, it was not only this readiness to look beyond the membership of the churches that provided a spur to the Network. Just as Cupitt's *Sea of Faith* television series had provided the initial impetus, so a BBC television program *Heart of the Matter*, broadcast on Easter Day 1992, proved decisive. Although the program was aimed at discussing clergy who had doubts concerning various doctrines of faith, it so happened that the three clergy who were interviewed belonged to the Sea of Faith Network. Media and public attention turned to the Network, which within six months doubled its membership.[17] Thiselton contends that because Cupitt's focus had changed since the original TV series in 1984, those who now joined the Network were deceived.[18] This errs in equating Cupitt's writings with the Network — two things which, although linked, are hardly synonymous.

It was during these tempestuous years in the early 1990s, Mitchell recalls, that Cupitt was able to furnish the necessary articulation of radical philosophical and theological ideas. His numerous articles in the British press provided a valuable service for the Network, bridging (as he consistently has done in his books) the perceived gap between academia and the non-specialist. Yet while identifying himself with the Network, Cupitt resisted any and all claims that he was responsible for it or its ideas, insisting that it was "an independent, non-confessional and creedless society of people who were trying to imagine something new that religion might become in the future."[19]

Indeed, it was David Hart and the highly controversial Anthony Freeman who became the spokespeople of Sea of Faith. Freeman went so far as to admit that he had undergone a "conversion experience" to a non-realist understanding of God at a Sea of Faith U.K. Conference.[20] Unfortunately, the resulting media interest over the sacking of Freeman from his benefice only served to reinforce the initial stereotyping of the Network as inhabited by "atheist Vicars." Once again it was those within the Network who objected to being so classified.

The publication of *Surfing: Women on the Sea of Faith* was a very significant moment in the development of the Network. The idea of a book to be written by women lay members of the Network was conceived at the Sea of Faith U.K. Conference in 1994 in direct response to the media portrayal of the Sea of Faith as a group of dissident vicars. Its aim was to challenge this distortion. In an anthology of personal reflections on their own journeys of faith, fourteen women revealed themselves as representatives of a larger body of people grappling with much more diverse questions of belief. Indeed, as Ruth Robinson explains, the "difficulties of dissident clergy . . . [are] the merest tip of the iceberg. There are many of us out there from many different religious backgrounds and cultures for whom the issues are much wider."[21]

These wider issues, which can be identified from *Surfing*, encompass the following four major concerns:

1. The growing conservatism of the churches. Many parochial clergy are reluctant to discuss complex issues of faith. Even more alarming, they refuse to accept that the laity can cope with new ideas.

2. A new theology and new metaphors are needed to articulate what it means to be living in a godless universe. One contributor describes this as "the joy of Uncertainty," while another prefers "the mystery of the void."

3. A plea to extend the discussion beyond realism/non-realism to an engagement with how to create a more caring society, and involvement in social issues.

4. To discuss issues of personal suffering and create a faith or spirituality that connects with the struggles of ordinary people. Aileen La Tourette explores her own painful battle to come to terms with an abusive mother. Valerie Clark discusses what it means to have no belief in an after-life. Barbara Ratcliffe understands her experience of divorce from her husband as a metaphor for the spiritual journey that leads to separation from all controlling influences. Anthea Boulton examines how such an ordinary rural event as getting in the hay impacts the lives of villagers, and how the joy of the day is tempered by the realization that the eldest member of a family might not see another hay time.

These four concerns are still on the agenda of the Sea of Faith U.K. Network, and have all been discussed by Cupitt in his writings. Indeed, he has been pleased to learn how much his own radical project has been in tune with other people's thinking.

But *Surfing* also sounds some new notes that challenge both the Network and Cupitt. First, Marian Tomlinson questions whether the Network is actually needed, wondering whether a typical member is "some kind of religious fanatic who cannot kick the religious habit?" Describing it as an "escape lane" which will not last longer than a generation, she notes that its membership consists largely of elderly people who have long striven with orthodox theology only to find it inappropriate to their spiritual journey.[22] Those of the present generation who have not had to toil under the influence of Church Christianity will find other strategies for survival. This idea of the Network as a sort of sanctuary for the disaffected in the Church is echoed by Anne Horner, who decides that it is now time to leave her local church.[23] As I noted in chapter 4, it is an open question whether the Network can become "the church of the future." Valerie Clark takes an important further step by contemplating life *without* the Network and observes that "membership of Sea of Faith may, in time, prove to have been a very useful staging post in my life, just as many others have been before I may need to leave and come back, or even leave forever."[24]

Second, many of the writers express their gratitude to Cupitt's "darts [that] struck home" and prompted them to apply to a local Sea of Faith group or attend the annual Conference.[25] In an ironic twist, Wendy Worham takes Cupitt's radical agenda to its conclusion by announcing that "all true disciples of Cupitt are post-Cupitt; ultimately if people are to be truly radical they must break out of Cupitt's mould and think for themselves, because they will have realized that comprehending his message consists in rejecting prescribed accounts of how to live."[26] This is an important insight that accords fully with Cupitt's encouragement to others that they should "forget" and "leave behind" his writings, creatively making their own new forms of religion. Since Cupitt took the idea from Nietzsche's Zarathustra, who tells his disciples, "Go away: don't follow me, follow yourselves", Worham's words amount to a confirmation that by its very rejection Cupitt's Nietzschean project is being fulfilled!

Most commentators seem to dismiss the Sea of Faith Networks by making light of those who are sometimes referred to as the "theological heavyweights," a superficial form of criticism neatly summarised in this bit of doggerel by Penny Mawdsley:

> **Cupitt's** "Sea of Faith" dart
> **Pearses Freeman's** warm **Hart,**
> Hastening out through open **Dawes.**
> Travels on from English **Shaw,**
> Ups its **Geering** on the way. . . .
> Rejoicing in bold word play.[27]

In fact, however, the United Kingdom Network was (and is) fueled by many ordinary folk who seem to have been deprived any critical understanding of the reasons *why* it has survived for so long. Undoubtedly the "theological heavyweights" (who will be examined in the next chapter) have provided the necessary intellectual clout for academia to take radical Christianity and non-realism seriously, but without the support of ordinary members, they would no doubt have continued to be regarded as "ivory tower academics." Indeed, Moore's article, written from the perspective of an evangelical Anglican Christian (see chap. 4), is an indication that some of the churches in the United Kingdom are concerned about the influence of the Network upon their members.

It is in this context that a second book written by members of the Network once again dispels the notion that what Cupitt (and others) have pursued in the Academy is an isolated phenomenon. *This Is My Story: Voyages on the Sea of Faith* is a collection of writings by fourteen members of the Network, and its aim is to demonstrate the diversity of Sea of Faith members. The book shows how the Network has been able to provide a safe setting in which people can explore and debate contemporary issues about religion. The writers' denominational (or ex-denominational) affiliations — Anglican (4), Society of Friends (3), Roman Catholic (2), Church of Scotland (1), Salvation Army (1) [and Humanist (3)] — again refutes those who regard the Network as an Anglican special-interest group.

This Is My Story contains all of the four concerns identified in *Surfing*, and even explores the suggestion raised by Vivien Clarke that one day she might take leave of the Network. This is exactly what happened to one of those who attended the first Sea of Faith U.K. Conference (1988) and served as the founding Editor of the *Sea of Faith Magazine* — Clive Richards. It is a sign of the strength of the Network that it would include a contribution by someone who was no longer part of it! Describing himself as a "semi-detached member," Richards explains that his break with the Sea of Faith was due in part to "ideological discomfort" with its "Christian perspective."[28] Admitting that he "never really got much out of churchgoing," he targeted people within the Network who were labelled: "Non-church, ex-church, why-church?" His main complaint, however, is that he felt hampered by the membership's lack of energy in seeking to create new forms of religion. For Richards, the United Kingdom Network wasn't prepared to be radical enough and throw off its Christian heritage.

Richards' observation strikes at the heart of the dilemma enshrined in the Statement of Intent: just what is to be "promoted?" Richards had harboured the expectation of something more than rigorous debate — some sort of "moral vision" of religion that would help people create a more just society. Reflecting one of Hart's caveats concerning Cupitt, Richards insists that religion needs communitarian expression. It is worth noting that the United Kingdom Network is something of a boat without a captain, its members attempting to row in different directions, and some even jumping out! Indeed, many of the personal experiences of *This Is My Story* picture people who are, like Cupitt, continually "on the move." Thus Jude Bullock leaves the Roman Catholic priesthood and in 2002 he becomes an Assistant priest in the Church of England; John MacDonald Smith finds that campaigning for issues of "peace and justice" gives him more optimism than his priestly vocation ever did; Duncan Park resigns from the Salvation Army; David Paterson embraces multiculturalism; Derek Chorley seeks to reform his Roman Catholic tradition, and Patti Whaley finds peace in the meditative practices of Buddhism. Perhaps this collection of writings is no more than a reflection of the postmodern condition — one that has been described as "the interplay between the given and the novel," in which people freely move "in" and "out" sampling the rich variety of spiritualities that are available in their world. The Network is, for many, a temporary resting-place where they can linger and explore with others their own spiritual story. But in being so perceived, the Network all but forfeits the possibility of being the final destination. Here is another irony similar to that noted earlier: inherent in the Network's own postmodern philosophical outlook is the idea that people should continually re-create their own lives — even if that means stepping out beyond Sea of Faith. The Network is anxious about neither its power nor its perpetuation.

Indeed, it is noteworthy that in a paper presented at the Sea of Faith U.K. Conference in 1997, Cupitt succinctly summarised most of the issues that ordinary members (as reflected in *Surfing* and *This Is My Story*) were, and *still* are, deeply concerned about:

> . . . Sea of Faith is unfortunately not yet perceived as offering on its own account a constructive alternative and a hope for the religious future. Rather, we are seen only in negative terms, as a troublesome minority who dissent from an orthodoxy which is itself on the verge of extinction. And we are seen also as a dressing station or transit camp where refugees from the churches can briefly pause for refreshment, before they move on to sever their last remaining links with religion of any kind. . . . It seems to be the case that almost a third of our membership changes each year. Perhaps many of us are people whose spiritual journey is still continuing. We'll move on, and no doubt that will be right for us.[29]

It can be seen, then, that the United Kingdom Network reveals both a number of unresolved conflicts and an uncertainty as to the way forward. Cupitt himself is hesitant to provide a specific vision; rather by avoiding a prescriptive stance, he allows the thirty or so local groups, the annual Conference, and the Steering Committee to resemble the art college that creates its own future. As has become apparent in this section, it is both a strength and a weakness of the Sea of Faith Network in the United Kingdom that it is not constrained by Cupitt's own project. Its strength lies in its protean quality, though it perhaps fails to impart a strong sense of direction and belonging. In turning to the Network founded in New Zealand, we discover a group with a more practical and discernible focus.

The New Zealand Network

Three important historical factors helped launch the New Zealand Network: its Presbyterian roots, its early links to the Student Christian Movement, and the work of Lloyd Geering — whom some have called, "the Don Cupitt of New Zealand."

It is highly significant that both the United Kingdom and New Zealand Networks have a theologian of international standing amongst their ranks. It is a mutually beneficial arrangement when the principal theologian has access to well known professors and lecturers in the Academy who can serve as keynote speakers at annual conferences, and engage the debate at an academic level. At the same time, the theologian gains a friendly and necessary support group for himself in what might otherwise be a hostile environment. Moreover, it is a striking historical coincidence that Cupitt and Geering published very similar radical theologies (*Taking Leave of God* and *Faith's New Age*) in the same year (1980) while living on opposite sides of the world. It was Geering's recognition of an affinity between their thinking that prompted him to visit Cupitt in Cambridge in 1981. From this arose an occasional exchange of ideas, but it was not until a decade later in 1991 that Cupitt toured New Zealand at Geering's invitation to present a series of lectures. In the following year Geering visited the United Kingdom as a speaker at the Sea of Faith U.K. Conference. This obviously had a profound effect upon him for on his return, as Hugo Vitalis records,

> ... Geering lectured in New Zealand and generated interest in establishing a Network along similar lines as the British SOFN. Support for the establishment of local discussion groups was considerable. Similarly interest in a national conference was high and a conference was subsequently held in Hamilton, New Zealand, in August 1993. At this Hamilton conference the SOFN [New Zealand] was officially formed.[30]

Just as Cupitt had provided a list of respondents to his television series, so Geering supplied a list of over 150 people who had attended his lectures, and this was used to invite people to this first Sea of Faith Conference in New Zealand.

Although one cannot underestimate Geering's extraordinary pioneering work, establishing the New Zealand Network was possible (as was the case with Cupitt in the United Kingdom) *only because he was in tune theologically with what many local individuals and groups of radical/liberal Christians were already thinking and discussing*. This is indicated by the two main findings of Vitalis' study of the Network: first, it emerged in response to the declining credibility and relevance of the Christian churches; and second, most members of the Network have a non-realist understanding of God.[31]

Although Vitalis doesn't explore the connection between these two findings, I would suggest that they are linked. Indeed, Vitalis' conclusion that the Network provides a safe haven for exploring issues which can't be discussed in churches is surely connected to one of the results of his questionnaire, namely that sixty per cent agreed or strongly agreed that "God is a human creation which symbolises human values and provides a useful focus for religious faith."[32] If one begins to doubt both the existence of an objective God and the relevance of the churches, yet can still appreciate the value of religious faith, then where does one look for inspiration?

The religious questioning was in some measure fueled by the theologically liberal Student Christian Movement of the late 1940s and 1950s. This is substantiated by George Simmers, one of those involved in the beginnings of the New Zealand Network. For him both the initial appeal and the continued strength of Sea of Faith is due to people who grew up with the Student Christian Movement; indeed, a Sea of Faith Conference is like a reunion of the SCM from those days. The Student Christian Movement was, of course, inter-denominational, attracting those who wanted to explore issues of faith in an open way. Many New Zealand members also belonged to the Presbyterian Church, and were inspired by the liberalism of Geering, who was then Professor of Old Testament and Principal of the Presbyterian Theological Hall at Knox College in Dunedin.

Geering was especially well known in New Zealand because of his highly publicized "heresy trial" by the Presbyterian Church, which in 1967 charged him with two main offences. First it was stated, that he had quoted with some approval current European theological thinking, in particular a comment of the Scottish theologian R. Gregor Smith in his *Secular Christianity* that it would be of no relevance to Christian theology if the bones of Jesus were discovered in Palestine. His second offense was to assert that humans did not have immortal souls. The charges were brought against Geering by a Presbyterian layman and an evangelical minister. After a dramatic two-day televised trial, the Assembly judged that no doctrinal error had been proved, dismissed the charges, and declared the case closed.

Having successfully defended himself, Geering left Knox College in 1971 to become the first Professor of Religious Studies at the Victoria University of Wellington, an institution with no church links or responsibility for training ordinands. Along with his other duties, he undertook lectures and seminars in the University's "continuing education" program, and these became extremely popular. Three hundred would enroll for a day's seminar, and he was invited to present these lectures and seminars at a number of other centers around the country. For many this was the one place where they could find a disciplined, intellectual approach to the questioning and upheaval that was going on in their own experience, but which seemed to be totally neglected by the churches to which most of them still belonged. Among the writers to whom he drew attention was Don Cupitt.[33]

Thus, Geering's pioneering efforts were rewarded with the formation of radical Christian groups. Although Geering was now employed in a secular University he did not cut his ties with Presbyterianism. By remaining part of the Presbyterian Church, he provided a focus for other radicals within that denomination. Just as Cupitt's style of Anglicanism naturally attracted Anglicans to the Network in the United Kingdom, so Geering's radical Presbyterianism was a factor in setting up the Network in New Zealand. This is recognised by Vitalis:

> The evidence suggests that SOFN in New Zealand is, at least initially, a Presbyterian initiative. The large proportion of Presbyterians in the Network is partly explained by their high levels of attendance at Lloyd Geering's lectures and seminars, whereby they learned of the existence of the SOFN. The active role of Presbyterians in the establishment of SOFN is described in one informant's account of the founding of the religious group Ephesus in Wellington and its subsequent organization of the first SOFN conference.[34]

Although he mentions that the "Ephesus" group was instrumental in the initial organization of the Network, Vitalis fails to elaborate how together with another initiative from within the Presbyterian Church, it helped create a climate of radical questioning of faith. Beginning as the Research Group of the Presbyterian Church (which still continues as an inter-church group) its aim was to "find out the reality of spiritual understanding, beliefs and attitudes within the Presbyterian Church of New Zealand and New Zealand Society" and make it available to the Church. In 1989 the Research Group published three booklets in what it called its Ephesus Series, a related project which, recognizing a major contemporary shift in the spiritual search, sought new ways of understanding God and expressing faith in terms of New Zealand culture and experience. One of these booklets contained an essay by Ian Harris (then the Director of Communication for the Presbyterian Church) who had gathered a small group to pursue this project, and received some assistance from the

Church. When this support was soon withdrawn, Harris acted on his own to establish in 1990 a forum for open discussion — The Ephesus Group — on these issues. It attempted to follow the model of the early church at Ephesus, which had re-expressed the earlier Jewish-based faith in terms of Greek culture, in order to find ways of articulating the Christian faith in the contemporary culture of New Zealand. Thus, although many of its members had ceased attending church, it had a strong base in the Christian tradition. It was obviously very similar in its aims to what was to emerge as the Sea of Faith Network, but because of its specific focus on "the Christian faith," it is far from redundant, and still continues as a sort of parallel movement. Indeed, Ephesus and Sea of Faith groups often overlap, and Ian Harris became the first Chair of the Sea of Faith Network in New Zealand. The original Ephesus Group still meets twice a month in Wellington.

The second initiative was the creation at the inner-city Presbyterian Church of St. Andrew's, Wellington of the "St. Andrew's Trust for the Study of Religion and Society," whose aim was "to stimulate and inform the general public with new thoughts about religion." Geering, who was an Honorary Associate Minister at the Church, delivered numerous series of lunchtime lectures (subsequently published) that drew sizeable audiences. It was through his influence that Cupitt's visit in 1991 was sponsored by both the University of Wellington and the St. Andrew's Trust. In succeeding years, radical voices from around the world were invited to follow Cupitt to Wellington, and such eminent speakers as Charles Birch, John Shelby Spong, and Robert Funk afforded many in New Zealand the opportunity to hear the latest theological thinking.

It should be emphasised, however, that not only within the Presbyterian Church were alternative faith communities taking root. Groups of people within other churches as well as *outside* the church were exploring alternative ideas of faith. These included such groups as Galaxies, which focused on the spiritual needs of homosexuals, lesbians and bisexuals; the Kodesh community, which facilitated new ways of envisioning church; Peacemakers Trust, an interdenominational community; Te Wahi Ora, a retreat center staffed by women for women wanting to explore their spirituality; and the Tail of the Dragon, a group set up to explore postmodern and feminist theologies.

Ironically, perhaps, it was the decline of the churches that opened up a space in which these alternative faith communities — the sociologist Michael Hill describes them as, "religions of humanity" — could develop.

He so classifies any group that displays the following characteristics: (1) it is "individualistic," (2) it emphasizes "an idealized human personality," (3) it demonstrates an extreme degree of "tolerance," (4) it is "syncretistic," (5) it has a "monistic" world view in which spiritual power is diffuse and (6) "it emphasises a process whereby individuals are morally re-made or empowered." It is obviously beyond the scope of this book to explore how far each of these alternative faith communities exhibit these characteristics, but Hill's identification of Cupitt's theology as one that attracted enough people to form a "religion of humanity" is consistent with the thrust of the present argument — namely that the weakening of the Church gave birth to alternative faith communities. It was into this "space" that Sea of Faith (as one alternative faith community group) emerged as a "religion of humanity" which "could appeal to the experiences and values of modern individuals" in New Zealand.

The impact of the New Zealand Network was soon felt, for it was being described in 1994 as "the fastest growing group in Aotearoa."[35] It also differed from the United Kingdom Network in that it was less preoccupied with defending a non-realist position. As Vitalis' research has shown, it felt no need to keep on repeating these arguments because two-thirds of its members had already dispensed with an objective God. While still interested in the realist/nonrealist debate, the New Zealand Network began to broaden its focus, especially into such areas as ecological issues and how to create a spirituality that acknowledged that "the future of humankind is inextricably tied to the future of the earth."[36] Two important factors drove this expansion. First, it neatly mirrored the concerns of Geering, who in his writings in the 1990s (*Creating the New Ethic*, *Tomorrow's God*, and *The World to Come*) attempted to articulate a global religious eco-humanism. Second, it resonated with the concerns of New Zealand politicians and citizens who had been at the forefront of ecological protests, most notably as active opponents of French nuclear testing in the Pacific.[37] Thus, from its inception, the New Zealand Network was perhaps more focused in its approach to a practical application of what it understood by living in the knowledge that God is a symbol of our highest aspirations and human goals. As Geering has incisively put it,

> If we choose to speak of God, we shall be using this term to focus on all that we supremely value and on the goals which make human existence meaningful and worthwhile; and there is no thing and no place in which we do not encounter this

God. . . . This God is in the physical earth of which we are a tiny part. Even more, this God is to be found in all living creatures. Most of all, however, this God is rising to self-awareness in the (as yet) confused collective consciousness of the global human community. This is tomorrow's God, calling us from a world yet to be created. But, to create this world, this God has no hands but our hands, no voice but our voice, no mind but our mind, and no plan for the future except what we plan.[38]

The rapid rise of the Sea of Faith Network in New Zealand occurred because its concerns reflected those of ordinary New Zealanders who had become dissatisfied with official religious teaching (as reflected in the decline of the churches), yet did not want to abandon a religious attitude to life by becoming identified with the secular abandonment of religion, and now faced the impact of globalization.[39] Geering's comment that "the new religion will dispense with the natural/supernatural dichotomy [and] the natural world itself will be treated as sacred" represented a viable alternative to those who would dispense with religion altogether.[40] Thus the Network was and continues to be a safety-net preventing people from adopting the religiously-neutral stance of the State, offering them a *milieu* in which to explore and work out what it means to participate in a "religion of humanity" in the emerging global society. For Geering the main priority has steadily become "eco-consciousness," and the Network has similarly embraced such concerns. While this is obviously not the Network's only interest, I think that it is indicative of Geering's influence and guiding force, which are probably stronger than Cupitt's in the United Kingdom. This has provided the necessary impetus for what is now a vibrant and more unified Network than its older partner. Although recently Geering has begun to hand over the reins to younger members in full confidence that the Network is capable of exploring the ramifications of post-Christianity, it still bears the stamp of its maker.

In conclusion, the difference between the group Cupitt inspired and the New Zealand Network can be seen in the rather different "Statement of Identity" adopted at its first Conference. As I have shown, it was *not* necessary in the New Zealand context to focus exclusively on non-realism or "God as a human creation." Instead, the Conference Statement declared,

> The Sea of Faith Network is an association of people who have a common interest in the mode of non-dogmatic and human oriented religious thought and expression which

AFFIRMS the continuing importance of religious thought and practice as a vehicle for awe and wonder and for the cele-bration of key social and spiritual values;

DRAWS freely upon our spiritual heritage without being bound by it;

PROMOTES the quest for meaning and fulfillment as human activity;

PROVIDES encouragement, stimulation and support in fel-lowship with others engaged in the quest.[41]

This much broader approach has allowed the Network to connect to those both within and outside the churches who are seeking, to adopt Hill's "religion of humanity." As in the case of the United Kingdom Network, the original impetus came from those who were dissatisfied with existing church traditions, but now newer members, many of whom have never belonged to churches, are pushing the boundaries about what con-stitutes religious faith. This has been fueled especially by Geering's eco-logical concerns. The New Zealand Network is far removed from the non-realist debates that so preoccupy the United Kingdom Network, and in more recent times has downplayed its specifically Christian basis and promoted interest in other faiths (e.g. Buddhism) and in newer expres-sions of spirituality.

The Australian Network

The most recent of the Networks — Sea of Faith in Australia — is still very much in its infancy, having been conceived on Easter Day 1998 in Brisbane by Gregory Spearitt, Neville Buch, Alison Cotes and a few Unitarian Universalists. In the intervening years fourteen local groups have been established in centres throughout Australia. It has formulated its own Statement of Purpose — "to openly explore issues of religion, faith and meaning" — in an attempt to be inclusive of all religious points of view, both realist and non-realist. It has thus tried to avoid being seen as exclusively Christian-based and is much more open to exploring issues of belief in both the world's religions *and*, very importantly, in the diverse smorgasbord of therapeutic spiritualities that now inhabit the religious landscape. In seeking to establish itself, however, the Network faces dif-ferent challenges from those that confronted the United Kingdom and New Zealand Networks.

The challenges are twofold. First, the Australian Network has no immediate church base on which to draw. Apart from a few Unitarian

Universalists, Sea of Faith in Australia lacks historical ecclesiastical roots comparable to the Anglicanism or the Presbyterianism of the two other Networks. Second, it has, as yet, no local theological heavyweight from whom it can derive a measure of popular prestige and academic credibility. There is no Australian Cupitt or Geering to fuel the debate. These related issues raise crucial questions of how, and indeed whether, the Network is going to have an impact upon Australian society. Both the older Networks were able to target a substantial core religious population. Although the lack of a "theological heavyweight" means that the Network can develop in its own way, in order to gain popular respect and credibility in the eyes of the Academy, it will need a local theologian to represent it. Without doubt Cupitt's writings provide a springboard that enables debate to leap national and cultural boundaries, but in the absence of an authoritative Australian "voice," the Network is going to be (as is often said about Australia itself) looking over its shoulder and "paying lip-service elsewhere."[42]

The Network was given a boost in 2003 by the airing of an ABC Television *Compass* program that featured the New Zealand Network. Enough interest was aroused that the First National Sea of Faith Conference in Australia was held at Wollaston College in Perth in 2004 with keynote speakers Don Cupitt, Rachael Kohn and David Boulton. This was an extremely successful event with participants overcoming the tyranny of distance and travelling from all over Australia to attend the Conference. Of particular note was the paucity of clergy who were present; and its attendees were more youthful than those in the Networks in the United Kingdom and New Zealand. Thus Sea of Faith in Australia is quite progressive in that it is very much a lay-led movement having discarded the necessity to be dominated by clergy. Enough enthusiasm was generated by the event that it was agreed that a bi-annual Conference would be held. It appears that in the Third Millennium in Australia ordinary folk are shaking off ecclesiastical belonging and forging their own spiritual paths. Sea of Faith may be a necessary network that provides an appropriate forum in which people can discuss their spiritual quest.

Still, Sea of Faith in Australia will have to address the key issue of membership. Can people be drawn from the churches, other religions, humanists, the general public? As the churches contract and new religious movements proliferate, will potential adherents come to view Sea of Faith as an attractive alternative? Does its broad statement of intent suggest that it lacks coherence and purpose? Can non-realists and realists co-exist in such a community? It will be intriguing to see how the Network tackles these obstacles to its growth. For the moment it has generated good interest and its first National Conference may be seen as an important event in Australia's religious history.

Links with the Westar Institute

Very recently Sea of Faith has forged an alliance with another theologically progressive group — The Jesus Seminar/Westar Institute in the United States and its sister Institute (SnowStar) in Canada. Westar Institute was founded by Robert Funk in Santa Rosa, California in 1985 with the aim of bridging the gap between academic critical theology and popular Christianity. As he puts it, he wanted to teach the fourth "r" — religious literacy. The Seminar's first project, which lasted until 1999 or thereabouts, was a renewed quest for the historical Jesus, an attempt to separate historical fact from theological fictions in the writings of the first Christians. The Seminar's detailed investigations sought to distinguish the historical Jesus from the Christ proclaimed by the early Christian churches. The human person that emerged was very different from the divine figure preached by orthodox Christianity. Moreover, the definition of the New Testament was broadened to include such very early writings as the Saying Source (Q) and the Gospel of Thomas. The mythical matrix — Divine Son of God, miracle worker and apocalyptic prophet — was replaced by the portrait of an itinerant wisdom teacher who proclaimed the reign of unconditional love.

Once this project had been completed, Westar found itself engaging in a second agenda. How would this new understanding of Jesus affect the Christian faith? The radical findings of Biblical criticism have clearly altered the faith that the Christian Church has handed on for centuries. What was the faith of the future going to look like?

In 1999 Geering lectured before the Seminar, and the following year, members of Sea of Faith in the United Kingdom organised a British lecture tour for Funk. Cupitt joined the group when he was forced to change his publisher and Polebridge Press (part of Westar) came to his rescue. He has also spoken at several of Westar's semi-annual meetings. When the close affinity between Westar and Sea of Faith became apparent, a number of Sea of Faith members attended Westar's Conference in the Spring of 2001, entitled "The Once and Future Faith." The transcript of the conference, which was published under the same title, clearly shows the influence of Geering and Cupitt, for non-realism became part of the agenda and was debated by the Seminar.

But despite the similarities, clear differences between Westar and Sea of Faith remain. Westar is an educational project led by a group of scholars with many of its Fellows having a special interest in historical studies. Sea of Faith on the other hand is a relatively anarchic network of individuals who have a wide variety of theological interests. Many do not have an academic background. Like Westar, Sea of Faith eschews the adoption of any common creed or belief-system, but although it has its origins in reforming Christianity it has extended its brief beyond the confines of that religion. Like Cupitt who claims to be fifty per cent Christian, thirty per cent Buddhist and twenty per cent Jewish, Sea of Faith is far more eclectic and much more obviously post-Christian than Westar, though perhaps the latter's new agenda of looking for the faith of the future may in due course draw it in that direction.

Conclusion

After an initial steady growth since the establishment of the first one in the United Kingdom in 1988, the Sea of Faith Networks seem to have reached a plateau and are starting to look rather elderly in terms of their membership. Although worldwide the Networks boast a membership of only about two thousand five hundred, they have had a notable impact upon many more people. Some have taken leave of the Networks thankful for time spent at such a "transit camp," and are on their way to finding spiritual sustenance elsewhere. Others remain at the edges, uncertain whether Sea of Faith can be that church of the future — the post-church fellowship that wants to create new ways of being religious. That many "fellow-travellers and sympathetic outsiders" remain affiliated is shown in the Sea of Faith publication *Time and Tide* (2001), which includes (amongst others) contributions from the best-selling author Karen Armstrong, the Award-winning physicist Paul Davies, and Robert Ashby, Director of the British Humanist Association.

Cupitt himself has kept his distance from the Networks, preferring to encourage them to develop in their own particular ways. Yet his initial detachment has given way in recent years to a more affectionate and proactive promotion of their efforts. His whimsical comment that he now lectures only at Sea of Faith Conferences lest his health suffer from the attentions of a hostile crowd involves an acknowledgment that the

Networks are creating a relaxed and friendly environment in which true dialogue on religious matters can take place. Indeed, Cupitt considers that his "hands-off" approach to the Networks has been justified. Poor mental health in the mid-1990s led him to take early retirement in 1996; yet he managed to keep on writing, and says that it was a vindication of his policy of telling Sea of Faith to run itself and not become too dependent on him that it did flourish and grow at a time when he couldn't do much for it.

That deliberate policy has allowed the Networks to be a breeding ground for new experiments in religious writing and religious existence. In the next chapter I will examine some of religious writings of the theologians who have emerged from the Networks. In particular, I will show how their concerns compare and contrast with those of Cupitt himself.

Chapter 7

Cupitt and the Networks' writers

One or two members of Sea of Faith have written things . . . but it's not fashionable among the younger theologians, who are tending to go for neo-orthodoxy. They are ex-pupils of mine, but perhaps they are being prudent. They are tending to be cautious, steering clear of Sea of Faith. There is a paradox there, that although the Church is in rapid decline it still has certain "glittering prizes" to hand out — Bishoprics, Deaneries, Chairs of Theology — and people are willing to compete for them, regarding these as great prizes. In order to get into the top club you have to keep your nose clean, so there is a certain amount of keeping clean of noses. People are reluctant to take risks. I used to say myself to students: "Don't come out until you are professionally established at a sustainable level because they can be very ruthless in the way that they treat you." I didn't come out myself until I was forty-two.[1]

Cupitt's advice is intended for those who would follow him into publishing theological writings that are sympathetic to the Sea of Faith, and unambiguously warns that such people are likely to incur the wrath of many ecclesiastical bodies. For one who is ordained, it is akin to committing professional suicide and, as Cupitt himself discovered, guarantees being either censured or disregarded by the Academy. Still, despite Cupitt's warning to those who dare to "come out" in print, a steady stream of writers has stepped forward to follow Pascal in announcing that "the great god Pan is dead."

Most important amongst these writers are David Hart, Stephen Mitchell, Graham Shaw, Anthony Freeman and Lloyd Geering. The tolerably common assumption that these are carbon copies of Cupitt, peddling his latest offering to an innocent and gullible audience, grossly underestimates both the creative abilities of all these writers *and* the openness of ordinary folk to new ideas. Most commentators see non-realism as the theological doctrine that binds these writers to Cupitt, yet this distorts a complex picture by failing to recognize that "non-realism" can denote either a "broad" position in philosophy or a "narrow" theological stance. David Boulton correctly points out that there are at least three categories of non-realism: it is possible to be (1) both philosophically and theologically non-realist, (2) philosophically realist but theologically non-realist, *or* (3) rhetorically non-realist but theologically realist.[2]

This highly significant point is simply ignored by the most common detractors of Sea of Faith — Kalve, Thiselton and Moore — and recognised by only a few of the contributors to *God and Reality*, which purported to be a learned discussion of these matters. At issue is not a homogeneous theological/philosophical position, but a wide variety of views that have found a place within the Networks. Fully aware of this, of course, Cupitt teases his opponents, saying: "They want us to stand still so that we can be shot, and they find our variety and mobility very frustrating."[3] I will use Boulton's tripartite classification of non-realism as a useful way to examine the relation of other Networks theologians to Cupitt, and further include John Shelby Spong and Hugh Dawes, who are rhetorically non-realist but theologically realist. This third position is somewhat problematic, but it characterizes quite a few members of Sea of Faith.

Philosophically and theologically non-realist

Boulton identifies Hart and Mitchell, who follow Cupitt, as philosophically and theologically non-realist. To this I would add Geering and Freeman. It would be easy at this point to conclude that they are all simply Cupitt's fellow-travelers. However, this is to miss the great diversity within their writings, some of which takes them well beyond Cupitt. I will further divide these four theologians by categorizing Mitchell and Freeman as people whose essential aim is to reenvision the churches, while Geering and Hart, although likewise seeking to change the churches from within, are more adventurous in their call to escape the "Christian past" and embrace a "global future" and an encounter with "other religions." It is Hart and Geering — two "free spirits" who have extended Cupitt's original vision — that I shall examine first.

Sailing into new oceans

David Hart

David Hart is usually typecast as a "true Cupittian." This judgment is based on his first book, *Faith in Doubt: Non-Realism and Christian Belief*, in which he acknowledges a debt to Cupitt's ideas. Described by Thiselton as a "pioneer" of the United Kingdom Network, Hart has both the scholarly background and authorial skill that make him the natural heir to Cupitt. Combining academic rigour with practical application, *Faith in Doubt* could be described as a sequel to Cupitt's *The Sea of Faith* in its exploration of what it means to be a non-realist *within* the Christian church. If this had been where Hart terminated his writings, it would be fair to conclude that he was a true disciple who is loath to dissent from Cupitt. However, in the mid-1990s Cupitt's deteriorating health resulted in Hart finding himself at the helm of Sea of Faith, and he had no hesitation in sailing it into new oceans. In an important, but perhaps overlooked article, "On Not Quite Taking Leave of Don," Hart outlines "three caveats" to Cupitt's project:

1. It is "too cerebral" and lacking in "actual creativity."
2. It is too Christian-based and must engage more with the other major world religions.
3. It needs communitarian expression.[4]

Hart's reflections are indicative of the push to move beyond Cupitt. In his next book, *One Faith? Non-Realism and the World of Faiths,* he specifically tackles the second of these "caveats" arguing that a non-realist understanding of religious faith in five world religions "will increasingly enable believers to appreciate other traditions and take more time and trouble to 'cross over' into them."[5] Although Cupitt himself has entered into dialogue with Madhyamika Buddhism, and others have offered non-realist interpretations of Judaism, Hinduism, and Islam, this is the first attempt to use non-realist theory as a way into a postmodernist dialogue between adherents of different faiths.[6] Far from being an "academic" exercise, Hart answers his first caveat by showing that ordinary worshippers are often the first to recognize the dogmatic elements of their own faith and to find ways of resolving potential conflicts with those of other traditions. Although he identifies a non-realist strand within each world faith, his major concern is to show that adopting non-realism *philosophically* can lead to a both radical and expedient shift in thinking.

Essentially, Hart is promoting Sea of Faith's non-realist Statement of Intent, which describes "faith as a human creation." If the adherents of different religions can meet together and acknowledge that their faiths are equally the result of "the creative abilities of [their] own historical and very human imagination," then fruitful dialogue can take place.[7] Once people have adopted non-realism philosophically, inter-faith services such as Hart outlines in the book can be attempted. Whether that leads to theological non-realism, Hart is willing to allow each person to decide for him/herself. Starting with philosophical non-realism at least offers the chance to avoid the hostility engendered by those who begin with realist assumptions about the *exclusive* truth of their particular religious belief system. As he makes clear in a subsequent article, "non-realists believe that by removing the metaphysical 'charge' of truth-claims, and by emphasizing the telling and hearing of stories of the inter-connections between our gods, our spirits, and our human ideals, we can learn God together more meaningfully than before."[8]

The desired result of this philosophical non-realist approach to world religions is that more harmonious and tolerant communities can be established in multi-faith countries. This leads into Hart's third caveat: that Cupitt's project needs to find expression in communities that create "common meanings." Indeed, Hart proposes that the *further* step of adopting theological non-realism would have far-reaching effects for a global humanitarianism:

> We may even be able to come to worship together when we realize that God is not a reality external to our lives but is that burning desire within to create a more just and a more harmonious world for our children. Human(e) ideals personified in theological form enable us to bend our knees together to all that is loving and pure and to attempt to extirpate what would keep us from reaching our common goals. Non-realism as the polar opposite of fundamentalism enables us to value the goals not just of our like-minded group but of the traditions of our global village, to which we now have greater and easier access than at any time in the past.[9]

As I explained in chapter 1, Hart's vision of applying non-realism to creating more equitable societies is a major element in his *Linking Up*. Responding to his own caveats, he offers the Networks' members a positive approach to non-realism. Far more than simply opposing realism, it proposes a religious way of living that silences the critics for whom Sea of Faith is no more than a toothless debating society.

Lloyd Geering

Lloyd Geering too has taken the Networks into uncharted waters by promoting the idea that as the demands of culture change, so does religion. In *The World to Come*, he argues that "a faith for the future" must take into account the possible frightening scenarios that might befall the world, from thermonuclear holocaust to social and economic chaos. The religion of the future must work towards minimizing such threats.[10]

Geering's global religious eco-humanism has widened the scope of the Networks' agenda, and has persuaded even Cupitt himself to become more interested in a "large-scale vision." In 1994, after explaining that he and Geering both embrace non-realism philosophically and theologically, Cupitt admits that they differ in emphasis. Geering's canvas is global and historical, whereas Cupitt's is existential. Geering's concern is the emergence of a unified and fully globalized world and a global human consciousness; Cupitt is more interested in the individual struggle of getting oneself together and making sense of the human condition.[11]

Starting with *After All*, Cupitt attempts in his books to remedy this lack of "large-scale vision." In *After God*, for example, he rejects the criticism that he is uninterested in global issues, insisting that "in the long term [he] want[s] religion to become a unifying expressive activity through which we can simultaneously get ourselves together and build our common world."[12]

Still, it is fair to say that Geering, much more than Cupitt, tends to be concerned with the specifics of *exactly how* non-realism can be used to connect with the issues that face people day by day. His status as Special Lecturer for the St. Andrew's Trust for the Study of Religion and Society has meant that his booklet publications have targeted increasing religious literacy for the general public.[13] Like Cupitt, he aims at the successful metamorphosis of religion into secularity, so that the task of being religious is to be naturalized citizens of this world. Although Cupitt has lately become more focused on how people might create a better world, perhaps Geering has something of a head start in attempting to explore the possibilities of a global future in which we acknowledge that our world is exactly that: it is of our own making, and we have to supply its meaning.

Geering's *Christianity without God*, as its title suggests, is written without hiding behind the philosophical veil that often shrouds Cupitt's works. Consistent with his aim of making accessible complicated theological ideas, Geering argues that it is possible to conceive of Christianity without a supernatural understanding of God. Indeed, he proposes that the earliest Christianity was moving towards this rejection of theism, and only by the imposition of the (false) doctrines of the Incarnation and the Trinity did theism win the day. *Christianity without God* celebrates a Christian humanism that looks to the figure of the historical Jesus who shared the joys and sorrows of human life, and envisions a Kingdom that Geering describes as a new global and ecological culture that *must* be created by us. Geering thus combines his non-realism with the historical research of the Jesus Seminar in arguing for a non-theistic interpretation of the Christian story, a rendering that celebrates humanity and the potential for a new heaven and a new earth in this world. It is a bold project that once again broadens the parameters set by Cupitt.

Rebuilding the ship

Anthony Freeman

Anthony Freeman and Stephen Mitchell's concerns are perhaps closest to the original vision of Cupitt's *The Sea of Faith*, an attempt to reenvision Christianity from *within*. After being sacked by his Bishop for refusing to recant the ideas set forth in his controversial book, *God in Us: A Case for Christian Humanism*, Freeman has been elevated to something of a special status in the Network. He is, of course, not the first Anglican clergyman to be dismissed for expressing radical ideas. In the 1870s the Reverend Charles Voysey was deprived of his living as Vicar of Healaugh in the Diocese of York for denying the divinity of Jesus and the existence of Hell, while asserting that God's love was all-encompassing. In the early twentieth century Charles Gore, then Bishop of Worcester, forced the resignation of the Reverend C. H. Beeby for casting doubt on certain statements in the Creed. Likewise in 1911 Bishop Talbot of Winchester removed the Reverend J. M. Thompson from his post after publication of *Miracles in the New Testament*, in which he questioned the authenticity of Jesus's miraculous deeds.[14] These clergy were dismissed summarily without any proceedings, and without any proper hearings of their views or public debate. Voysey appealed to the Judicial Committee of the Privy Council, but his case was rejected. In contrast to the self-defense allowed Geering by the Presbyterian Church in New Zealand, Beeby, Thompson and Freeman were accorded no proper trial, appeal, or recompense.

In its account of Freeman's final service at St. Mark's Anglican Church in Stapleford, West Sussex, *The Times* reports his insistence that his removal from office had arisen despite his efforts to remain loyal to the Church, whose role in the spiritual life of England he views as important. And only a few days earlier the same newspaper had quoted his statement in the parish magazine that his ambition was to be permitted to continue as an Anglican priest, and the person he would most like to meet was a bishop willing to employ him! Indeed, Freeman's controversial little book (only 87 pages in its original form) is an attempt to explore the implications for himself *and his congregation* of what happens to the Christian faith when you substitute one understanding of "God" for another. What if, instead of the word "God" referring to a supernatural being, it designates the sum of all our values and ideals in life — like goodness, love, and freedom from the fear of death?

Freeman's radicalism centers on this redefinition of God. Far from being abandoned, the whole edifice of ecclesiastical belonging — liturgy, ethics and doctrine — is simply re-interpreted in the light of theological non-realism. Thus in his opening reference to the 1662 Prayer Book, comparing his former parish to members of the "Sealed Knot" re-enacting English Civil War battles, he is not calling for the abandonment of such language, but rather pointing to the realist, supernatural *understanding of God* which lies behind such language and its inappropriateness to postmodern people. This point was misunderstood by the national media who portrayed Freeman attacking those who addressed God using seventeenth-century language. In fact, he used the 1662 Prayer Book at his farewell service. He also dismisses the modern upgrading of language of *The Alternative Service Book* (1980), stating that "it still takes for granted that world-view which has God an absolute divine king intervening in earthly affairs."[15] The rest of the book is an exploration of Anglican belief without this supernatural understanding of God. The key issue is whether such an approach is permissible *within a parochial setting.* Hart and Cupitt had the relative security of university positions, whereas Freeman attempted to take theological non-realism into the parish. For his Bishop — the Right Reverend Dr. Eric Kemp — there *was* a difference between the public and private *persona*: priests may have doubts, but expressing them openly was not permitted.[16]

For Freeman the debate about theological non-realism is symptomatic of a deeper issue — the "openness" of the Church. Is it to be a "closed élite," or a "a mixed bag, a motley assortment of the good, the bad and the indifferent, all trying in their different ways to make something of their lives in the shadow of the Galilean?" For Freeman, an open Church, which traditionally the Church of England has been, "needs priests who can stand alongside their flocks in their questioning of received understandings of Christian teaching."[17]

Cupitt would whole-heartedly concur, but he now doubts whether the churches can ever be reenvisioned from within. Moreover, Cupitt was so incensed by the treatment meted out to Freeman by the Church authorities that he returned his priestly licence (to officiate) in protest. However, it is also fair to point out that Freeman's stance in *God in Us* echoes the Cupitt of 1984–1990 and is a far cry from his standpoint in the new millennium.

Stephen Mitchell

Despite his aggressive promotion of the Sea of Faith in television and media appearances, and his many years as Chair of the Steering

Committee of the Network in the United Kingdom, Stephen Mitchell has, however narrowly, escaped episcopal sanctions. Mitchell was also responsible for co-ordinating a protest letter from over seventy clergy in support of Freeman's being allowed to express his views and to remain within his parish. Accordingly, it is somewhat surprising to read in his main publication *Agenda for Faith* that he cannot agree with Freeman's theological position. This frank admission again reveals that different forms of non-realism are evident within the Networks. Mitchell's concern is that *God in Us* has "not gone far enough," and that Freeman is "relegating faith to the side lines."[18] Faith is more than replacing a supernatural understanding of God with a non-realist one and demythologizing the creeds.

For Mitchell, Freeman's emphasis on theological non-realism is not sufficiently contextualised by an account of what it means to belong to the church community and follow its practices. This has made Freeman an easy target for those like Bishop Richard Harries, who can assert that Freeman's position means that "everyone is locked into their own imaginings and communication is impossible. Individualism is taken to extremes and the Sea of Faith followers are simply solipsists."[19] Harries can counter Freeman by invoking Dr. Johnson's famous "common-sense" argument about kicking the "real" stone. For Harries, there is a "real" God (and a "real" Self) beyond all our interpretations. Mitchell agrees that Freeman's argument can be discredited in this way, but he counters that this is not what radical theologians (including Freeman) have intended to say. For Mitchell, radical theology as espoused by Cupitt is an end to all dualisms: God, the self, the mind, the body, etc. all co-arise in language:

> Holding such a view is *not* to say that there is no reality. It is to say that reality, experience and language arise inseparably together. Putting everything — truth, meaning, the self, even reality itself — into the language of human communities, and seeing these as aspects of our human relating and behavior, demands that the non-realist brings the ethical into the spiritual. Truth and knowledge are related to the goals of a community and the relationships within it.[20]

Mitchell thus shifts the emphasis away from the natural-supernatural distinction that preoccupies Freeman (and ironically reinforces Harries' argument) to the question of *how* the language of religious communities creates and re-creates meaning and value. Consequently, the story of "God" is not a private story of how an individual communicates with a supernatural source, but a *public* story about how the lives of people are valued within certain communities. Mitchell's *Agenda* is thus very pragmatic; it uses the stories and rituals of the Christian faith to "find the energy to engage with the hopes and aspirations of my friends and neighbours [and] to renew the traditions of the Christian church because they increase my feelings of solidarity with the rest of the world, in which solidarity I am created."[21]

Contrary to Freeman, it is Mitchell's argument that faith is more than the personification of ideals, and that religious communities are much more concerned with *how to live* (religious practices) than with the intellectual debate about the truth of doctrines or creeds. Perhaps in the spirit of the radical Christianity of William Blake, Mitchell asserts that Christian believers are those who use the language of faith not as indicative of supernatural truths, but by way of showing how Christ is identified in "the neighbour and the needy." Thus, Christian faith is the exploration within humanly created religious communities of what it means to be human.

As opposed to Freeman's overwhelming emphasis on contrasting the natural with the supernatural, Mitchell's total embrace of the postmodern "death of God and the self" broadens the scope of the meaning and importance of "faith." He is more successful than Freeman in showing how Cupitt's writings might help people to reenvision Christianity within a parochial setting. He stands in the tradition of *Radicals and the Future of the Church* and *What Is a Story?* defending a non-realist interpretation of the Christian story of "God" against both the liberal Christian (Harries) and the fundamentalist. It is mystifying that his writings have received scant attention outside the United Kingdom Network. Perhaps the ecclesiastical authorities are persuaded that they have already set an appropriate example in the dismissal of Freeman. It could also be that Mitchell, as Cupitt advises, is much more circumspect in his writings. While he obviously advocates theological non-realism, he also acknowledges that both realist and non-realist understandings of God are *secondary* to the human story that must be re-created afresh for each generation by the communities, and especially religious communities, in which people find themselves:

> To say that God is real and not unreal tells us nothing about the way the reality of God impinges upon our lives, nothing about the way the story of God came to be told, and nothing about the way that story is to be interpreted. Equally, to say that God is unreal and not real is to say nothing about the way the stories of the gods shape nations, communities, and people.

Rather gods, like all people, will be seen to be more like works of art, needing to be engaged with imaginatively, constantly interpreted and re-interpreted, and whose life and value is to be found in the flux of community life.[22]

Theologically non-realist, but philosophically realist

Graham Shaw

Boulton correctly identifies Graham Shaw as a philosophical realist and a theological non-realist. He had in fact espoused a non-realist understanding of God in his first book *The Cost of Authority*, but this was only in a closing paragraph that introduced the theme for his next book. Unfortunately, it became the focus for commentators who dismissed his thesis concerning the proper use of authority as an argument for atheism. As a philosophical realist, he is sympathetic to Iris Murdoch, repudiating post-structuralism and looking towards Wittgenstein rather than Derrida. Central to this "Neo-Platonist" position is the argument for the existence of transcendent values. For Shaw, as for many within the Networks, there exist permanent values that transcend those created by human beings *at this present time*. By his insistence on "God" as a word that symbolises transcendence, he attempts in *God in Our Hands* to transform Christianity from a religion of power to one of peace.[23] The life and teachings of Jesus, he proposes, clearly so direct us:

> For me the drama of the gospels . . . comes not from some model way of life, or exposition of timeless truth, but in the anguished affirmation of the highest human values in a world and a society which is either indifferent or hostile. The haunting transcendence in the gospels is not to be found in the tawdry stories of miracle and healing, but in the way in which, through his God, Jesus is able to transcend the cruel limitations of his immediate environment.[24]

Shaw links this notion of transcendent values to people's use of the word "God." Unlike the realist who equates transcendent values with belief in a transcendent God, Shaw argues that "God" is "a word of the creative imagination" which people use to transcend the values that are current in their world. In combining theological non-realism with philosophical realism, he offers hope to those who find Cupitt's ethical project too bleak, or who are convinced that there must be "something more" than the postmodern dependence on assertion and counter-assertion. The word "God" functions as "the possibility of the source of transcendence" which, according to Shaw, is how his parishioners make use of it:

The humbling experience of a parish clergyman is to see how people use their belief in God to transcend their immediate experience, in a way which enables them to retain and indeed reaffirm those fragile and vulnerable human values. We discover the dignity we share as human beings, not in sheltered lives which consign affliction to other people, but by opening our lives to the reality of others' affliction and by not trying to secure some privileged invulnerability for ourselves.[25]

Like Cupitt, Shaw retains a strong devotion to Jesus. His portrayal of Jesus as an advocate of a new "religion of peace" may have been instrumental in his move from the Anglican priesthood to the Society of Friends. In view of his involvement from the very beginning of the United Kingdom Network, it is significant that his divergence from Cupitt philosophically represents a strand of thinking that has been allowed to co-exist. He also represents a non-realist theological interpretation of the Christian story that may resonate with many fellow-Christians for whom it is an invitation "to enter a drama, in which we discover that we are as vulnerable as the values we wish to affirm."[26]

Rhetorically non-realist, but theologically realist

Hugh Dawes, John Spong

It might seem inappropriate for a non-realist Network to include those who are theological realists. However, if the emphasis is placed upon the statement that "religion is a human creation" that does not preclude an affirmation of the reality of God. Accordingly, one can hardly bar those like the Right Reverend John Shelby Spong who, on being asked by a lay person in his Diocese of Newark, New Jersey whether one can be a Christian without being a theist, answered thus:

If the theistic understanding of God exhausts the human experience of God, then the answer to the question of the EFM student from Vernon is clear. No, it is not possible to be a Christian without being a theist. But if, on the other hand, one can begin to envision God in some way other than in the theistic categories of the traditional religious past, then perhaps a doorway into a religious future can be created.[27]

The key point here is "the human experience of God" and how that can be expressed other than "in the theistic categories of the traditional past." Precisely this is the central question of Hugh Dawes' *Freeing the Faith*. He wants to "save God, a God which matters" for the world.[28] In much the same way as Spong does in his books, Dawes attempts to elucidate a more "open, provisional and contemporary faith," recognizing that much of traditional Christianity is now obsolete. Thus, he stands in the liberal church tradition, rather than adopting the radicalism of Cupitt. Whereas Cupitt seeks to live *after* God by repudiating realist theology, for Dawes the enemy is traditional Christianity, and his agenda is to "unmask the fallacies of the private language of conservative religion. It has got to call nonsense by its proper name. It has to find a way of speaking of the things of God which does not fly in the face of all we know and say about the world we live in, but which truly complements that knowledge and perception."[29]

Freeing the Faith is Dawes' liberal program for going on the offensive and articulating a contemporary understanding of God. It is highly significant that although many bibliographies describe his book as an example of the Sea of Faith Network literature, its content is rarely debated. This is due, I would assert, to its underlying theological realism. Throughout the book Dawes refers to "what people have named as God." This suggests a human response to something that is "real"; to use the language of non-realism, although a rhetorical step in the right direction, it can too easily promote the idea of a transcendent God beyond the god of human imagination and creativity.

Dawes advocates a Christianity that is open to a human understanding of what God represents to people as they search for meaning in their lives. Whether those perceptions of what is real correspond to "the ultimate purpose of life and the universe" remains unknown. Dawes is *not* denying that there is an Ultimate grounding to the Universe. Rather, he argues for a more open exploration of who or what that ultimate grounding might be than is currently found in most churches. He also emphasizes that it is better to seek a more human and this-worldly understanding of faith than to speculate on ultimate meaning.

Dawes' appropriation of non-realism (though he scarcely mentions the word) appears in the way that his Christianity is provisional, constantly changing and being re-created. By non-realism he means that faith is non-dogmatic, humanly created, centered on this world, and open to endless possibilities. He stands in the liberal (Anglican) tradition of David Jenkins, Maurice Wiles, Leslie Houlden, Dennis Nineham and others. For these writers the impulse to rethink faith comes chiefly from their awareness of historical change, rather than from philosophy. Thus, for example, despite Nineham's emphasis on historical (and cultural) relativism he is still a realist affirming "a unity in the experience of God and in God's

essential attributes, which appears to belie any thoroughgoing relativism."[30] They represent the reformist tradition in advocating a less dogmatic Christianity that can speak to "those in exile" as well as those
within the Church. Despite a close collegial association when Dawes was
Chaplain at Emmanuel College from 1982–1987, he is no "true follower"
of Cupitt.

For Dawes, then, "God" is real and the task of Christianity is to keep
the "rumour of God" alive by connecting with people's perception of that
reality.[31] This might not cut much ice with Cupitt, but it still strikes a
chord with some of those critical realists in the Networks for whom Sea
of Faith, rather than a conservative Church, is an opportunity to explore
a more open Christianity, one in which they can jettison "every religious
symbol," yet "cling to the reality to which those religious symbols point."[32]
As an apologist for open faith, Dawes provides them with an articulation
of that kind of Christianity. They are in a vulnerable position, not only
being ridiculed by the churches to which they belong, but also not quite
"kosher" within the Sea of Faith as the Networks expand their horizons
beyond the business of reforming Christianity. Indeed, the recent establishment of The Center for Progressive Christianity, with Spong and
Dawes actively involved, may attract people away from Sea of Faith to
this new movement. Spong, in particular, while sympathetic to Cupitt,
views Sea of Faith as rather to the left of his own theological position and
he seems happier imagining a more progressive Christianity than stepping
beyond this faith-system.

Conclusion

In this chapter I have examined the considerable diversity of views
held by the Networks' writers, all of whom are indebted to the pioneering
work of Cupitt, yet none of whom can be regarded as mere clones. It has
been my aim to show that Cupitt's radicalism has been taken up by a variety of scholars who present a wide range of opinion both in questions of
theological and philosophical non-realism, and in the matter of
Christianity's future as — or in the context of — a global religion. Cupitt
has been a catalyst to a far-reaching program of theological exploration
that has only just begun; for as Crowder notes, "Christian non-realisn,
therefore, is a much more complex phenomenon than many of its critics–and even some of its advocates–would have us believe."[33]

Conclusion

> In religion, as in many other areas of life, we have a very ancient, long-established culture of dependency. People reckon that they must have something out-there to lean on, however minimally. It can happen that a well-known philosopher like John Hick will go almost all the way with me in admitting the human and historically-evolved character of all religious language, in admitting that our experience is molded by our beliefs and so on. But he won't go all the way, because like so many others he clings fiercely to that tiny speck of objectivity, that feeling that there is, there must be, something Real out there to which all the symbolism refers, even though we cannot say anything about it. People cling fiercely, desperately to that last sliver of objectivity . . .[1]

As I have shown in this book, Cupitt has been trying to get people to take leave of "that last sliver of objectivity," insisting that *this* world is outsideless and that people are dependent on nothing greater than themselves. Everything, including God, ethics and religion, is a human creation.

It has been my concern not only to consider how a new ethics and religion might eventuate, but also to emphasize that Cupitt's search is increasingly a worldwide phenomenon that has been mirrored in the writings of other non-realists. Since Cowdell's study of Cupitt in 1988 people have shown more interest in exploring non-realist interpretations of God, ethics, and religion; and the Sea of Faith Networks now provide settings in which people can and *do* find an opportunity to discuss these issues. The growth of these Networks has been due not only to Cupitt, but also to the equally challenging writings of those who have been prepared to unleash their own creative powers and propel the discussion across new frontiers, most notably Shaw, Hart, Freeman, Mitchell and Geering.

It has become clear that the task of creating new ethics and new religion is a never-ending one. Cupitt's writings echo postmodernity's insistence that closure is a chimera. Just as since the nineteenth century art has learned to live by reinventing itself all the time, so we too have to live by improvisation. From an overview of Cupitt's own literary project and continual self-reinvention, we recognize that all his books are about the same thing: reinvention or rethinking. Thus any attempt to bring this study of Cupitt to a conclusion is fraught with difficulties. Cupitt is *still writing* and despite his retirement shows no sign of slowing his production of books. The best that I can do is to offer three brief ruminations that I believe point to the essential Cupitt, and to where he may be heading.

A latter-day Socrates?

Cupitt's advice to the United Kingdom Network to be a "latter-day Socrates," is a good description of his own writing project. Indeed, Maurice Wiles hits the nail on the head when he observes that Cupitt "continues to fulfil the valuable role of Socratic gadfly by making some telling points that provoke the rethinking of ideas one is inclined to take for granted."[2] Cupitt is one whose writings demand attention and cause lasting irritation. By nature errant and heretical, he encourages relentless questioning of accepted traditions. Yet, does he do more than question ad nauseam? Does it all result, as Cowdell wondered, in his having little constructive to say?[3]

It has been my aim to show that for all his love of being a "subtractor" (who, *mutatis mutandis*, acknowledges that his own texts must be deconstructed) Cupitt has much to offer in ethics, religion, and in the Sea of Faith Networks. He has advanced far beyond a mere reform of the Anglican Church. His early agenda encompassed all of Christianity, and recently he has become increasingly conscious of the need to be actively promoting a new global vision for the future. He issues both a warning and a challenge to those who seek to escape into the fantasy of the New Age or to download truth from their personal computer or decode it from the Bible. But he speaks powerfully to those post-Christians and post-theists who still wish to preserve the transformative potential of religion without God. His starting-point has always been "a democratic philosophy of life."

A democratic philosophy of life

Cupitt's ten-point: "A Democratic Philosophy of Life" is perhaps the nearest that he comes to presenting a creed for non-realism. While largely a sketch of postmodern philosophy, it neatly summarizes both the concerns that have dominated his lifetime journey and the way forward for religion in the third millennium:

- Until about two centuries ago human life was seen as being lived on a fixed stage, and as ruled by eternal norms of truth and value. (This old world-picture may nowadays be called "realism", "platonism" or "metaphysics").

- But now everything is contingent — that is, humanly postulated, mediated by language and historically evolving. There is nothing but the flux.

- There is no Eternal Order of Reason above us that fixes all meanings and truths and values. Language is unanchored.

- Modern society no longer has any overarching and authoritative myth. Modern people are "homeless" and feel threatened by nihilism.

- We no longer have any ready-made or "dogmatic" truth, nor have we access to any "certainties" or "absolutes" that exist independently of us.

- We are, and we have to be, democrats and pragmatists who must go along with a current consensus world view.

- Our firmest ground and starting-point is the vocabulary and world view of ordinary language and everyday life, as expressed, for example, in such typically modern media as the novel and the newspaper.

- The special vocabularies and world views of science and religion should be seen as extensions or supplements built out of the life-world, and checked back against it.

- Science furthers the purposes of life by differentiating the life-world, developing causal theories, establishing mathematical relationships and inventing technologies.

- Religion seeks to overcome nihilism, and give value to life. In religion we seek to develop shared meanings, purposes, narratives. Religion's last concern is with eternal happiness in the face of death.

Here in a nutshell is where Cupitt's writings have taken him. What is particularly revealing is that for Cupitt the realism versus non-realism debate is *now over*. There can be no turning back of the clock to the days of "realism," "platonism" or "metaphysics." Cupitt's agenda has begun to shift from total assault on realism to promoting a non-realist way of living. Indeed, he is confident enough to proclaim that "we are non-realists who have forgotten realism and therefore *no longer need to bother with the word non-realism either*."[4] We don't have to be continually in opposition to a philosophical/theological point of view that is untenable. It is time to push forward the business of reimagining and recreating *our* world, because non-realism "commands the high moral ground" and "asserts our complete appropriation of our world to ourselves and therefore our entire responsibility for our world. It stresses art, human creativity and the power of the utopian imagination."[5] It is this agenda, I believe, that Cupitt's future writings will more consciously advance.

Where to next?

To create a this-worldly and democratic religious humanism is the task that Cupitt has begun to set himself. His latest writings now ask, "Can it be done?" and "How is it to be done?" This book has identified Cupitt's central dilemma as the issue of whether this religious humanism can be created by reforming Christianity, or whether in view of the demise and irrelevance of the churches, contemporary culture has already largely appropriated the Kingdom values that Christianity has traditionally proclaimed. Indeed, in a discussion at the Sea of Faith U.K. Conference in 2000 Cupitt admits that he is faced with a paradox. As David Boulton explains,

> Don's answer was to present us with a paradox: secular society and the humanitarian movement, by emphasizing human rights, freedom of thought and speech, democracy and equality before the law, had done more to promote the ideals of the kingdom of heaven than the Church had ever done. But realization of the ideals of the kingdom was another matter. "We may be disappointed, just as Jews may be disappointed with the realization of the state of Israel and its failure to match up to their dreams and expectations". So does Don say postmodernity has delivered the kingdom, or just the prerequisites of the kingdom? Has the dream come true, or is it still no more than a dream? This argument will run![6]

To sum up, then, do people still need ecclesiastical anchors, or can they now create religion that provides for themselves and others? In my view this is the dominant question that will preoccupy Cupitt in the next few years. In fact, as my two Volumes on Cupitt have demonstrated, it is a question that has been gnawing away at him throughout his lifetime. In flirting with Buddhism and secularism, Cupitt has widened his horizons, and long since refuted Cowdell's assessment that he "is a rigorous apologist for prophetic monotheism, [and] for Christianity ranked first among the world religions."[7] Despite all this, however, he remains "fated to be one of the last ecclesiastical theologians," and he writes out of a primary engagement with Christianity. His long-standing devotion to the figure of Jesus and his recent links to the Jesus Seminar have reignited his desire to discover how a credible portrait of the historical Jesus can aid in constructing a Christian faith for the future. Although he has handed back his licence to officiate, he has neither given up his title of "the Reverend" nor resigned his ecclesiastical orders. Is he secretly hoping that the churches will survive? I think not! But what he does insist upon is the theme that has dominated this book: in spite of the demise or redundancy of the churches religion is *still* needed. It is this that makes him a kind of this-world prophet — one who proclaims the value of religion to provide meaningful individual and communal living:

> Religion is primarily not about supernatural belief, but about hope. It is our communal way of generating dreams of how we and our life and our world might be made better. We prepare ourselves for the dream, and we start to think about how we might actually start to make it all come true. My suggestion . . . has been that the so-called "decline of religion" is people's abandonment en masse of the kind of ecclesiastical religion that promised comfort and reassurance in the face of death. Instead, we should see religious thought and practice as imaginative and utopian. Religion is a communal way of reimagining and remaking the self and the world. It is what we are to live *by* and what we are to live *for*. At a time when political thought is very unadventurous, and when the world is becoming overwhelmingly dominated by technology, we need religion as much as ever. We need it as a human, value-creating *activity*.[8]

As Cupitt would conclude, so do I: Fare well — and that is two words, not one!

Notes

Introduction

1 Kettle, "When John Spong Met Don Cupitt," 23–28.

2 Cupitt, *The Revelation of Being*, 1.

3 Hastings, *A History of English Christianity 1920–1990*, 545.

4 This (in)famous maxim is attributed to Ivan Karamazov by the other characters in Fyodor Dostoyevsky's *The Brothers Karamazov*, 308–309. The novel is, of course, paradoxical in that Aloysha (the saint) confesses to not believing in God; whereas Ivan (the atheist) admits to believing in God. Karen Armstrong, links this paradox to Dostoyevsky's own internal struggle as "a child of belief and doubt" (*A History of God*, 412).

5 Hart, "On Not Quite Taking Leave of Don," 8. Hart appropriates the Cinderella image from Dennis Nineham ("A Partner for Cinderella," in *Explorations in Theology 1*, 134–44). Nineham explores Christopher Evans' suggestion that theology, as an academic discipline, always needs another discipline with which to "dance" (hence Cinderella), proposing sociology as a good partner.

6 See Caputo, *Against Ethics*, 260 n. 9.

7 Richard Holloway's theological position is somewhat problematic. He admits that "as far as the status of God is concerned, I find that the needle on my own dial trembles midway between non-realism (God is a human invention) and critical realism (there is a mystery out there, but we are inextricably involved in its interpretation . . .)." However, he adds, "I am not quite prepared to reduce the whole of religious experience to human projection." (See Holloway, *Doubts and Loves*, 28–29). Thus, I can legitimately claim him to be *still* a realist.

8 Hyman, *The Predicament of Postmodern Theology*, chap. 5.

9 Cowdell, *Atheist Priest?*, 27–28.

10 Cupitt, *The Time Being*, 60–61

11 Funk, "A Faith for the Future," in *The Once and Future Faith*, 1.

12 Clark, review of *Creation out of Nothing*, 559.

13 Bullock, "Twilight of the Idols," in *This Is My Story*, 46.

14 Cupitt, *The New Christian Ethics*, 97.

15 Cupitt, *The Long-Legged Fly*, 80.

Cupitt's five phases

1 Nietzsche, *Twilight of the Idols*, 80–81. For an insightful assessment of George Eliot's atheism see Wilson, *God's Funeral*, chap 7.

2 Gill, *Christian Ethics in Secular Worlds*, 20–21.

3 Cowdell, *Atheist Priest?*, 16.

4 See Cupitt, "A Final Comment," in *The Myth of God Incarnate*, 205.

5 See Robinson, *Where Three Ways Meet*, 24.

6 Cowdell, *Atheist Priest?*, 29, quoting *The World to Come*, 136f (his italics).

7 Cupitt, "The Ethics of This World and the Ethics of the World to Come," in *Explorations in Theology* 6, 107.

8 Cupitt, *The Long-Legged Fly*, 40–41.

9 Ibid., 61. Cupitt admits to probably misrepresenting both Lacan and Deleuze's positions but counters that he is just using them as symbols "standing for opposed tendencies of thought" (Ibid. 9).

10 Ibid., 115.

11 Cowdell, "The Recent Adventures of Don Cupitt," 35.

12 See especially Ruskin's Essay IV in *Unto This Last: Four Essays on the First Principles of Political Economy*.

13 Cowdell, "The Recent Adventures of Don Cupitt," 35.

14 Williams, *Revelation and Reconciliation*, 118.

15 Cowdell, "The Recent Adventures of Don Cupitt," 34.

16 Cupitt, *The New Christian Ethics*, 59.

17 Olds, "Don Cupitt's Ethics," 74

18 Cupitt, *The New Christian Ethics*, 173 n. 2.

19 Runzo, "Ethics and the Challenge of Theological Non-Realism," in *Ethics, Religion and the Good Society*, 78.

20 Wiiliams, *Revelation and Reconciliation*, 137.

21 Olds, "Don Cupitt's Ethics," 79, quoting Cupitt, *The New Christian Ethics*, 14 (his italics).

22 Ibid., 85 n. 17.

23 Cupitt, *The New Christian Ethics*, 129.

24 Cowdell, "All This, and God Too?" 270.

25 Schweiker, *Power, Value, and Conviction*, 10. Schweiker argues for the "moral passion" of antirealism while retaining realism (resulting in "hermeneutical realism") because he wishes to maintain that "God," as an objective Being, is the source of all value and is not a human creation. He thus becomes yet another "critical realist."

26 Gill, *Moral Communities*, 66. Gill's comments here are virtually word for word the same as in his *Christian Ethics in Secular Worlds*.

27 Edwards, *Tradition and Truth*, 90. For the same objection see Jones, review of *The New Christian Ethics*, 306–07.

28 Cupitt, *What Is a Story?* 154.

29 Cowdell, "All This, and God Too?" 268. Cowdell omits any reference to Durkheim and Weber.

30 Williams, *Revelation and Reconciliation*, 138–39.

31 Cupitt, *The New Christian Ethics*, 130.

32 Cupitt, "Unsystematic Ethics and Politics," in *Shadow of Spirit*, 151, 153.

33 Ibid., 153, 154.

34 Cupitt, *After All*, 107.

35 Cupitt, *The Revelation of Being*, 68 (his italics).

36 Cowdell, *Atheist Priest?*, 73.

37 Cupitt, *Solar Ethics*, 2.

38 Hastings, *The Shaping of Prophecy*, 19.

39 Cupitt, "Post-Christianity," in *Religion, Modernity and Postmodernity*, 230.

40 Ibid., 231 (his italics).

41 Cupitt, *The Last Philosophy*, 76–77.

42 Cupitt, *After All*, 95.

43 Richardson, *Georges Bataille*, 129. *Inner Experience* is the title of the first volume; and it was Jean-Paul Sartre who first promoted the anti-political shift of Bataille in a review of his work in 1943. For a disavowal of this, see Hollywood, "Beautiful as a Wasp," 221–22.

44 Richardson, *Georges Bataille*, 115.

45 Bataille, *Guilty*, 23, quoted in Richardson, *Georges Bataille*, 115.

46 Taylor, *Altarity*, 121. For "Virulent nihilism" see Land, *The Thirst for Annihilation*. Nick Land's book is not a standard textbook on Bataille, but rather an engagement with him. It is an extremely difficult read.

47 Taylor, *Altarity*, 127.

48 Ibid., 138. Derrida explores the ultimate "gifts" of life and death in *The Gift of Death*.

49 Land, *The Thirst for Annihilation*, 33.

50 Cupitt, *Solar Ethics*, 21.

51 Cupitt, *The Last Philosophy*, 81–82.

52 Margoliouth, *Thomas Traherne*, xl.

53 As cited in Wade, *Thomas Traherne*, 138.

54 Cupitt, *Solar Ethics*, 54.

55 Van de Wyer, *Spinoza in a Nutshell*, 13.

56 Olds, "Don Cupitt's Ethics," 76. As Olds points out, Cupitt's only discussion of Spinoza is found in *The Long-Legged Fly*, 45–46.

57 Olds, "Don Cupitt's Ethics," 76–77.

58 Cupitt, *Solar Ethics*, 36.

59 Berkeley, *Three Dialogues between Hylas and Philonous*, 113. Cupitt alludes to this image in *After All* (p. 119 n. 3) and then quotes it in full in *The New Religion of Life in Everyday Speech* (p. 101).

60 Cupitt, *After All*, 57. Cf. also Cupitt's *The Religion of Being*: "Now we begin . . . to diverge from Heidegger by saying that, fifty years later, it is no longer necessary to be obscure, nor to picture ourselves as being the captives of our own historical period . . . the time for Being is now. It is always the time of Being. Temporality is Being's *modus vivendi*, its manner of Be-ing. Being is always with us, and in us. It pours out change unchangingly, silently, effortlessly. Being is always Be-ing. The Fountain is never switched off" (p. 22).

61 Cupitt, "The Radical Christian World-View," 16 n. 7.

62 Cupitt, *The Revelation of Being*, 94. Cupitt is consistent in his insistence that the hierarchy of the Church ("big-hats" is obviously a reference to Bishops' miters) is simply there to control people and impose their power over others. He calls this "cosmic terrorism," and he reveals the personal cost of freeing himself from obedience to the received teachings of the Church (see *The Religion of Being*, 159ff).

63 Spong, *Why Christianity Must Change or Die*, 165.

64 Bultmann, *Jesus Christ and Mythology*, 14. Cupitt reiterates this point when he equates Kingdom theology with realized eschatology (see *Kingdom Come in Everyday Speech*, 97).

65 Cupitt, *Solar Ethics*, 16.

67 Cupitt, "Beyond Belief," 16 n. 1.

68 Hart, *Linking Up*, 111–12 quoting Foucault, *The History of Sexuality Vol. 1*, 9.

69 Cupitt, *Solar Ethics*, 17. Cf. this with Hart, *Linking Up*, 148.

70 Cuptt, "A Kingdom-Theology," 6. Cupitt here is addressing members of Sea of Faith and his use of "we" is justified. He often uses "we" in his books, thus causing some critics to berate him for his arrogance in assuming that everyone agrees with his viewpoint. This is not his intention, and George Myerson is nearest the mark in describing Cupitt's use of "we": "The 'we' is didactic humour, like a good lecture" ("The Philosopher's Stone," 132). Cupitt also is inconsistent with the term kingdom theology, sometimes hyphenating it kingdom-theology.

71 Cupitt, *Kingdom Come in Everyday Speech*, 62.

72 Ibid, 77. Cupitt fails to mention that California is also home to some of the largest realist churches in the world! For a good insight into the different versions of Christianity on offer in California see Ruthven, *The Divine Supermarket*, 171–202.

73 Wells, *Losing our Virtue*, 13.

Cupitt's ethics and his critics

1 Wells, *Losing Our Virtue*, 17.

2 Murdoch, *Metaphysics as a Guide to Morals*, 456. A. N. Wilson tries to put a different spin on Murdoch's estimation of Cupitt by saying that she called him "the Devil." But it is a bizarre incident having occurred over a very vinous lunch and has more to do with Wilson's mischief than anything else (see *Iris Murdoch*, 237–38).

3 Murdoch, *The Sovereignty of Good*, 51, 52.

4 Murdoch, *Metaphysics as a Guide to Morals*, 25.

5 Burns, "Iris Murdoch and the Nature of Good," 304.

6 Murdoch, *The Sovereignty of Good*, 93.

7 Hauerwas, *Wilderness Wanderings*, 161.

8 Burns, "Iris Murdoch and the Nature of Good," 307.

9 Ibid., 306.

10 Cupitt, *Life Lines*, 162.

11 Ibid., 162, 164.

12 Cupitt, *Kingdom Come*, 81.

13 MacIntyre, *After Virtue*, 278. The subsequent writings — *Whose Justice?* and *Three Rival Versions of Moral Enquiry* — expanded this earlier work.

14 Cupitt, *Solar Ethics*, 8.

15 MacIntyre, *After Virtue*, 118.

16 Ibid., 8.

17 Chapman, "Why the Enlightenment Project Doesn't Have to Fail," 379.

18 MacIntyre, *Whose Justice?*, 366.

19 Ibid., 367–68.

20 Murphy, Kallenberg, and Nation, eds, *Virtues and Practices in the Christian Tradition*, 19. For how *telos*, eudaimonia and virtue are inter-linked in Aristotle's model see ibid., 17–19.

21 Grenz, *The Moral Quest*, 194. Grenz's judgment is erroneous, since it is based on reading only MacIntyre's first book. Grenz also refuses to label MacIntyre's approach "Christian" because it relies on the philosophy of Aristotle rather than Scripture. Grenz prefers the specifically Biblical narrative program of Stanley Hauerwas to assist the Church in becoming a more peaceable kingdom.

22 MacIntyre, *Three Rival Versions of Moral Enquiry*, 179.

23 Cupitt, *The World to Come*, 135.

24 Cupitt, *The New Christian Ethics*, 162. Cupitt singles out MacIntyre as "attracting public attention" to the importance of moral tradition (see *Solar Ethics*, 7).

25 Cupitt, *The New Christian Ethics*, 137.

26 Wyschogrod, *Saints and Postmodernism*, 257.

27 MacIntyre, *After Virtue*, 11–12.

28 Vardy and Grosch, *The Puzzle of Ethics*, 49.

29 Russell, *The History of Western Philosophy*, 195.

30 Phillips, *Interventions in Ethics*, 59.

31 Ibid., 59.

32 Ibid., 60.

33 For a moving description of the reaction of those students at the University of Kent who served food to the Anglican delegates and were perplexed by their stance on homosexuality, see Holloway, *Doubts and Loves*, ix–xi.

34 See Boulton, "Sifting the 'Shock-Horror!' from the 'So What?'", 14.

35 Holloway, *Godless Morality*, 4.

36 Ibid., 20.

37 Ibid., 33.

38 Ibid., 148. This appropriation of Aristotle's idea of the mean is not documented, and the reader is simply directed in the bibliography to two of MacIntyre's books — *After Virtue* and *A Short History of Ethics*.

39 Holloway, *Godless Morality*, 95.

40 Murphy et al., *Virtues and Practices in the Christian Tradition*, 22.

41 Holloway, *Godless Morality*, 33.

42 Runzo, "Ethics and the Challenge of Theological Non-Realism," 74.

43 Ibid., 75.

44 Kaufman, *God–Mystery–Diversity*, 108.

45 Ibid., 99.

46 Runzo, "Ethics and the Challenge of Theological Non-Realism," 77.

47 Cupitt, *The Religion of Being*, 124.

48 Cupitt, *Philosophy's Own Religion*, 82–83, quoting Mark C. Taylor, *About Religion*, 165.

49 Ibid., 83.

50 Runzo, "Ethics and the Challenge of Theological Non-Realism," 78.

51 Rachael Kohn makes a similar charge asking how Cupitt knows whether some moralities are good or bad (see *The New Believers*, 143). For Cupitt moral world-views are expressed by societies/cultures in language and we (in the way that we use language) accept or reject them. None of us are morally-neutral.

52 Runzo, "Ethics and the Challenge of Theological Non-Realism," 81.

53 Ibid., 84, quoting Sallie McFague, *Models of God*, 152

54 Runzo, "Ethics and the Challenge of Theological Non-Realism," 85.

55 Ibid., 86.

56 Hebblethwaite, "A Critique of Don Cupitt's Christian Buddhism," in *Ethics and Religion in a Pluralistic Age*, 134–35.

57 Cupitt, *Kingdom Come*, 91–92.

58 Cupitt, *The Time Being*, 74.

59 Ibid., 78. Cupitt uses "Western culture," "Postmodernity," and "Late Capitalism" to mean the same thing.

60 Tanner, introduction to *Ecce Homo*, by Friedrich Nietzsche, vii.

61 Cupitt, *Kingdom Come*, 84. This is a variation of a description of Cupitt by a student that he was "a protestant-squared" and that he had attempted ". . . to produce a sort of protestant critique of protestantism. Result? Hyperbolic protestantism, which regards all dogma, all objectivity, and all desire for certainty as idolatrous" (Cupitt, "Friends, Faith and Humanism," 15).

62 Cupitt, *Kingdom Come*, 86.

63 Cupitt, *The Religion of Being*, 162–63.

64 Most vehemently by Dinah Livingstone in "A Mess of Postmodernism," 14–16. This article raised much debate at the Sea of Faith (U.K.) Conference XIII at the University of Leicester in July 2000.

65 Cowdell, *Atheist Priest?* 74.

66 Hart, "On Not Quite Taking Leave of Don," 9. Hart tries to redress this imbalance by exploring non-realism in the major "world religions" (see *One Faith?*). In Cupitt's defence, he would view his own project as aiming to inspire others to *express* themselves in new religious writing, and would welcome developments of his thinking. This theme is explored in more detail in chap. 5 of this book.

67 See Griffiths, "Cupitt: Serious Thinker or Practical Joker?" 19, and Livingstone, "A Mess of Postmodernism," 14–16.

68 Nicolson, "Real Evil Needs a Real God? Radical Theology in a Third World" 8. This was reprinted as "Real Evil Needs a Real God? Non-Realist Theology in a Third World," *The Heythrop Journal* 36 (1985): 140–52. All subsequent citations are to the paper presented at the Conference.

69 Nicolson, "Real Evil Needs a Real God?" 9.

70 Ibid., 9. Nicolson argued for a non-realist interpretation of Jesus as Saviour and liberator for black people in South Africa in *A Black Future?*

71 Nicolson, "Real Evil Needs a Real God?" 9.

72 See Cupitt, *After God*, chap. 14.

73 Knight, "One Small Cheer for Capitalism!" 23.

74 Cupitt, *The Revelation of Being*, 26.

75 Ibid., 30.

76 Cupitt, "The Radical Christian World-View," 10–11.

77 Cupitt, *Kingdom Come*, 86. For a full exposition of Cupitt's idea of life as a package deal of good and bad see his *Life, Life*.

78 Wyschogrod, *Saints and Postmodernism*, xxiv.

79 Ibid., xiv.

80 Caputo, *Against Ethics*, 7.

81 Ibid., 85.

82 Cupitt, *Solar Ethics*, 22 n. 1.

83 Ibid., 35.

84 Wyschogrod, *Saints and Postmodernism*, 147.

85 Ibid., 147.

86 Cupitt, *Kingdom Come*, 85.

Four ideas of the meaning of religion

1 Ward, "Theology and Postmodernism," 435.

2 Wyschogrod and Caputo, "Postmodernism and the Desire for God," 1.

3 Hart, "On Not Quite Taking Leave of Don," 6.

4 Lodge, *Paradise News*, 192. The character Bernard Walsh is probably based on Michael Goulder who declared himself an atheist and yet continued teaching New Testament Studies at Birmingham University.

5 Goulder and Hick, *Why Believe in God?*, 104–5.

6 Ibid., 110–11.

7 Mullen, "Serial Theology," 26.

8 Ibid., 28.

9 Transcript of *The Sea of Faith* BBC Production, 1984. Cupitt was Curate of Saint Philip's Anglican Church, Salford, from 1959 to 1962.

10 Cupitt, *Only Human*, 202.

11 Cupitt, "After Liberalism," in *The Weight of Glory*, 255.

12 Jenkins, review of *Radicals and the Future of the Church*, 60.

13 Clements, *Lovers of Discord*, 229.

14 Cupitt, *Radicals and the Future of the Church*, 143.

15 Ibid., 144–45.

16 Cupitt, *The Long-Legged Fly*, 102.

17 Wyschogrod and Caputo, "Postmodernism and the Desire for God," 1.

18 Cupitt, *After God*, 65.

19 Cupitt, "Religious and Non-Religious Humanism," 11–12.

20 Paul Lakeland, *Postmodernity*, 25.

21 Cupitt, *Rethinking Religion*, 11.

22 Ibid., 16.

23 Hampson, "On Being a Non-Christian Realist," in *God and Reality*, 99 n. 3.

24 Cupitt, "Post-Christianity," in *Religion, Modernity and Postmodernity*, 218.

25 Cupitt, *After All*, 5.

26 Cupitt, *Philosophy's Own Religion*, 131.

27 See Geering, *Fundamentalism*, 15. This small booklet is one of the best summaries of the rise of fundamentalism; and shows how Christianity has evolved via secular humanism into the Kingdom envisaged by Jesus.

28 Cupitt, *After All*, 116.

29 Cupitt, *After God*, 85.

30 Ibid., 128.

31 Ibid., 127.

32 Cupitt, "Post-Christianity," 219–20.

33 Ibid., 228.

34 Cupitt, "Spirituality, Old and New," 6.

35 Pattison, "Non Realism in Art and Religion," in *God and Reality*, 165.

36 Cupitt, *The Religion of Being*, 163.

37 Cupitt, "The Radical Christian World-View" 7. For Cowdell's reference to Cupitt still presiding at the altar see his *Is Jesus Unique?*, 413–14 n. 123.

38 Cupitt, *The Religion of Being*, 163.

39 Cupitt, *Kingdom Come in Everyday Speech*, 50.

40 Cupitt, "The Radical Christian World-View," 15–16.

41 Geering, *Fundamentalism*, 27

42 Ibid., 26–28.

43 Cupitt, *Reforming Christianity*, 128.

44 Ibid., 136.

45 Ibid., 134–35.

46 Cupitt, "Reforming Christianity," in *The Once and Future Faith*, 61.

Taking leave of the Church?

1 Goulder and Hick, *Why Believe in God?*, 28.

2 Hampson "On Being a Non-Christian Realist," in *God and Reality*, 85–99.

3 Hart, *Linking Up*, 61, quoting Karen Armstrong, *The Gospel According to Woman*, 302. For Mary Daly's own commentary on this "event" see Daly, *Outercourse*, 137–40.

4 Clack, "God and Language,'" in *The Nature of Religious Language*, 151.

5 Ibid., 155, quoting Carol Christ, *Womanspirit Rising*, 281.

6 Grant, "Almighty Gamble," 2, quoting David Boulton.

7 Goulder and Hick, *Why Believe in God?*, 29–30.

8 Hebblethwaite, *The Ocean of Truth*, 15–16.

9 White, *Don Cupitt*, 215

10 Ibid., 214, quoting Rowan Williams, "Religious Realism," 17.

11 Williams, foreword to *God and Reality*, viii.

12 Jenkins, "All Worked Out?" 9.

13 Harries, *The Real God*, 79.

14 Moore, "Rebuilding the Boat," 12, quoting Karl Barth, *Church Dogmatics* 1/1, 32.

15 Hampson "On Being a Non-Christian Realist," in *God and Reality*, 85–99.

16 Wallace, "On Finding a New Church," 6.

17 Padley, "An Unreasonable Distinction," 24–25.

18 Webster, "Why Are So Many Churches Intellect-Free Zones?" 16.

19 Borrowdale, *Distorted Images*, 6, quoting the research of J. Brown and R. Parker in *Christianity, Patriarchy and Abuse*, ed. J. Brown and C. Bohn, 3.

20 Larkin "Church Going," in *The Less Deceived*, 28.

21 Edwards, *Tradition and Truth*, 96.

22 Ibid., 286.

23 Cupitt, *Reforming Christianity*, 138.

24 Cupitt, *Radicals and the Future of the Church*, 7.

25 Ibid., 16.

26 Ibid., 29.

27 Ibid., 5.

28 Ibid., 97.

29 Ibid., 122.

30 Cupitt, *The New Christian Ethics*, 6.

31 Cupitt, *After God,* 127.

32 Gill, *Christian Ethics in Secular Worlds*, 21.

33 Hart, *Faith in Doubt*, 69–70.

34 See Ashworth, "Nonrealist Worship" 6; and Freeman, "Non-realism and the Life of the Church," in *God and Reality*, 31–33. Cupitt himself discusses Adoration, Confession, Thanksgiving and Supplication showing how these religious attitudes which traditionally were to be directed in one's prayer *only* towards an objective God are now widely disseminated into secular life, giving much of our experience a "religious flavour."(*Kingdom Come*, 37–39).

35 Cupitt, "All you really need is love," Face to Faith, *The Guardian*, December 1994.

36 Ashworth, "Nonrealist worship," 6.

37 I thank Ronald Pearse for his correspondence and for sending me these "Eucharistic Introductions, 1997." The reference to death-and-resurrection is an echo of Cupitt's understanding of Jesus' cry on the cross as he looks into the nihil (see *Creation out of Nothing*).

Unresolved tensions

1 Pearse, "Making Our Presence Felt in the Churches," 19.

2 Mitchell, *Agenda for Faith*, 39.

3 Freeman, "Non-realism and the Life of the Church," in *God and Reality*, 27.

4 Ibid., 37–38.

5 Freeman, *God in Us*, 72.

6 Ibid., 75.

7 Moore, "Rebuilding the Boat," 9.

8 Ibid., 10.

9 Ibid., 15.

10 Much of this section appeared in an earlier article, see Leaves, "On be(com)ing an atheist country."

11 Cupitt, "The Radical Christian World-View," 1. Cupitt's statistics are from *Church Times*, 14 May 1999. A year later, Cupitt quotes the *Sunday*

Times (London) reporting that a survey of 500 eighteen year olds finds that 77 per cent of them profess to have no religious beliefs ("Christianity after the Church," 1–2).

12 Moore, "Rebuilding the Boat," 5.

13 Gadamer, "Dialogues in Capri," in *Religion,* ed. Derrida and Vattimo, 205.

14 Cupitt., *The Revelation of Being,* 76.

15 Cupitt, "The Radical Christian World-View," 11–12.

16 Spearritt, review of *The New Religion of Life in Everyday Speech,* 7.

17 Cupitt, "A Democratic Philosophy of Life," online, Available: http://www.sofnorg.uk./cuplist.html.

18 Cupitt, *The Revelation of Being,* 13.

19 Cupitt, "The Radical Christian World-View," 1.

20 For a summary of how Cupitt's view of art had developed up to 1994 see Pickstone, "We Are Grateful to Don Cupitt," 10–17. However, Pickstone fails to mention the figure of the "creative artist" that appears first in *Taking Leave of God* (p. 2), preferring to locate this with Cupitt and *The Sea of Faith* in 1984.

21 Pattison, "Non-Realism in Art and Religion," in *God and Reality,* 160.

22 Cupitt, *The Long-Legged Fly,* 145.

23 Ibid., 146.

24 Ibid., 145.

25 Cupitt, *Radicals and the Future of the Church,* 26. Interestingly, Rothko's *Light Red over Black 1957* was chosen to adorn the cover of *God and Reality.*

26 Pattison, *Art, Modernity and Faith,* 117.

27 Cupitt, *After God,* 117.

28 Pickstone, "We Are Grateful to Don Cupitt," 15.

29 Cupitt, *After God,* 117. It should be noted that while van Gogh's paintings express the affirmation of life, van Gogh himself was a very tortured figure who, like Rothko, committed suicide.

30 Cupitt, *The Revelation of Being,* 89.

31 Cupitt, "Free Christianity," in *God and Reality,* 24–25.

32 Pickstone, "We Are Grateful to Don Cupitt," 10.

33 Nietzsche, *The Will to Power,* 452.

34 Pattison, *"Non-Realism in Art and Religion,"* in *God and Reality*, 164.

35 Ibid., 167.

36 Ibid., 170.

37 Ibid., 173.

38 Cupitt, *After God*, 124.

39 Cupitt, *The Religion of Being*, 2.

40 Cupitt, *Emptiness and Brightness*, 115.

41 Cupitt, *After God*, 124–27.

42 Cupitt, *Kingdom Come in Everyday Speech*, 42.

43 Cupitt, *Philosophy's Own Religion*, 162.

44 Cupitt, "Christianity

Cupitt, the origins and development of the Networks

1 Wallace, introduction to *This Is My Story*, 2.

2 Cupitt, "A Marginal Note," in *Five Years of Making Waves*, ed. David A. Hart, 25.

3 Pattison, "Editorial: *The Sea of Faith* — Ten Years After," 2.

4 Moore, "Rebuilding the Boat," 12. "Godless Anglican Vicars" is an appellation often used by the British press. "All at sea" or "Faith at sea" are slogans commonly used by those opposed to the Sea of Faith Networks to describe its members.

5 Pattison, "Editorial," 2.

6 Cupitt, "A Marginal Note," in *Five Years of Making Waves*, 25.

7 Pattison, "Editorial," 2.

8 I have attempted to find out the identities of these two other priests, but have been informed that they wish to remain anonymous.

9 La Tourette, "At Sea," in *Five Years of Making Waves*, 3.

10 Mitchell, "Creating An Identity," in *Five Years of Making Waves*, 12.

11 Within the *Sea of Faith (U.K.) Network* is a group called "Church-Members-in-Sea-*of*-Faith" which holds an annual gathering to discuss issues affecting those who are members of *any* church denomination.

12 For example, Kalve, "All at Sea?" 57–62; and Beeson, *Rebels and Reformers*, 171. Likewise, George D. Chryssides is unable to classify Sea of Faith as either a new religious movement or a sect. He compares the reaction it has received from some Protestants as akin to that which some Roman Catholics reserve for the Opus Dei: "No doubt there are more serious concerns about Opus Dei because of practices such as self-flagellation,

but many Protestants strongly disapprove of the Sea of Faith for theological reasons, since many of its members reject the notion of a transcendent God and are unable to accept Jesus Christ as fully divine" (*Exploring New Religions*, 22). If Chryssides classified Sea of Faith as a network, then his inappropriate comparison would evaporate.

13 It is surprising how many commentators misquote this Statement of Intent. Moore claims that it is "to explore and **create** religious faith as a human creation" ("Rebuilding the Boat," 3); whereas Crowder states that it is "to explore and promote religious **belief** as a human creation" (*God and Reality*, 3).

14 Pearse, "A Personal Perspective," in *Five Years of Making Waves*, 8.

15 Mitchell, "Creating an Identity," in *Five Years of Making Waves*, 12–13.

16 Tourette, "At Sea," in *Five Years of Making Waves*, 3.

17 Mitchell, "Creating an Identity," in *Five Years of Making Waves*, 15. Also in Hart, *Faith in Doubt*, xiv n. 2. For a good discussion of the *Heart of the Matter* by one of those "doubting clergy" see Mitchell, *Agenda for Faith*, 6–7.

18 Thiselton, *Interpreting God*, 82.

19 Cupitt, "Face to Face," *Guardian*, 2 October 1993, quoted in Mitchell, "Creating An Identity," in *Five Years of Making Waves*, 17.

20 Freeman, *God in Us*, 11.

21 Robinson, "Reconciling the World," in *Surfing*, ed. Green and Newton, 39.

22 Tomlinson, "Be Ready For Your Next Exit" in *Surfing*, 4–6.

23 Horner, "One Person's Experience," in *Surfing*, 29. John Pearson refers to the *Sea of Faith Network* as a "demob camp" ("No Safe Comforts," in *This Is My Story*, ed. Teresa Wallace, 11).

24 Clark, "Not Drowning, but Waving," in *Surfing*, 48–49.

25 Mawdsley, "Long-Time Passing," in *Surfing*, 1.

26 Worham, "Non-realist Faith?" in *Surfing*, 72.

27 Mawdsley, "Doggerel and Ditties," in *Surfing*, 38 (my bold).

28 Richards, "A Ghost at the Feast," in *This Is My Story*, 31.

29 Cupitt, "From Religious Doctrine to Religious Experience," 1.

30 A Non-Realist Alternative to Christian Realism", 2. I thank Hugo Vitalis for sending me a copy of his Master's thesis.

31 Ibid., ii.

32 Ibid., 77.

33 I thank George Simmers for his correspondence concerning the beginnings of the New Zealand Network.

34 Vitalis, "The Sea of Faith Network (NZ), 85. According to Vitalis' figures, in 1994 thirty-five percent of the New Zealand Network still belonged to the Presbyterian Church.

35 Adams and Salmon, *The Mouth of the Dragon*, 153.

36 Geering, *Tomorrow's God*, 7.

37 Most New Zealanders are still scarred by memories of the sinking of the anti-nuclear ship, *Rainbow Warrior*, by French agents in Auckland harbor in 1985.

38 Geering, *Tomorrow's God*, 235–36.

39 For an excellent overview of how New Zealand has changed from a "Christian" to a "secular" country; and the effect of globalization on the nation and religion, see Geering, *2100: A Faith Odyssey*.

40 Geering, *Does Society Need Religion?* 45.

41 Vitalis, "The Sea of Faith Network (NZ)," 2–3.

42 Australia is often perceived to exhibit a national characteristic of looking towards the United Kingdom for inspiration and intellectual stimulus. This obviously has historical roots and was one of the arguments debated in the 1999 referendum on the Republic. Pro-Republicans contended that being able to "stand on one's own" without reference to another nation would be a sign of Australian maturity.

Cupitt and the Networks' writers

1 Cupitt, interview with author.

2 Boulton, "Christians Awake!" 15.

3 Cupitt, "Free Christianity," in *God and Reality*, 24.

4 Hart, "On Not Quite Taking Leave of Don," 9.

5 Hart, *One Faith?* 4.

6 Reconstructionist Judaism has been identified by Rabbi Dan Cohn-Sherbok in his article, "Don Cupitt and Reconstructionist Judaism," 436–40. Dr. C. Ram Prasad presented a paper at the Sea of Faith U.K. Conference in 1999 on his understanding of non-realism in the Hindu school of Advaita Vedanta. The Iranian dissident, Abdul Karim Saroush, has interpreted Islamic texts in a non-realist way (see "An Islamic Sea of Faith?" 23–24).

7 Hart, *One Faith?* 147.

8 Hart, "Non-realism and the Universe of Faiths," in *God and Reality*, 49.

9 Ibid., 49.

10 For his "Scenarios of the Future" see Geering, *The World to Come*, 135–49. The final chapter of the book is entitled: "A Faith for the Future."

11 Cupitt, "Our Dual Agenda," 6.

12 Cupitt, *After God*, 127.

13 See, for example, *Images of the City* (1984); *Science, Religion and Technology* (1985); *Machines, Computers and People* (1986); *Encounters with Evil* (1986); *On Becoming Human* (1988); *Creating the New Ethic* (1991); *God and the New Physics* (1995); *New Idols for Old* (1997), *Fundamentalism: the challenge to the secular world* (2003).

14 See Clements, *Lovers of Discord*, 51ff.

15 Freeman, *God in Us*, 6.

16 "A Bishop's Difficult Move: Interview with Dr. Eric Kemp," *Times* (London), 5 August 1994, 14.

17 Freeman, "Non-realism and the Life of the Church," in *God and Reality*, 38.

18 Mitchell, *Agenda for Faith*, 8.

19 Mitchell, "All in the Mind?" in *God and Reality*, 51.

20 Ibid., 59.

21 Mitchell, *Agenda for Faith*, 39.

22 Mitchell, "All in the Mind?" 59–60.

23 Shaw, *God in Our Hands*, xvi.

24 Shaw, "The Vulnerability of Faith," in *God and Reality*, 68–69.

25 Ibid., 69.

26 Ibid., 69.

27 Spong, "Can One Be a Christian without Being a Theist?" 2. Spong presented a paper at the Sea of Faith U.K. Conference in 1995 on "Religion as a Human Creation?" David Kettle tries to argue that Spong shocked the Conference by admitting that he believed in a "realist" God. However, his critique of the Conference fails to grasp the diverse nature of the membership of Sea of Faith (see Kettle, "When John Spong Met Don Cupitt," 23–28). As I have indicated in this section, there are critical realists who are members of the Sea of Faith. Spong's speech at the Conference was extremely well received, and Spong and Cupitt are good friends who both

wish to reform the Church in a radical way. In an e-mail to me, Spong expressed the difference between himself and Cupitt: "...I am fond of ...Cupitt, but I still maintain that the word God is a human word that points to a reality that human words can never exhaust. The word God is a human construct. The reality the word points to is not. That is the distinction."

28 Dawes, *Freeing the Faith*, 121.

29 Dawes, "Liberal Theology in the Parish: A Lost Cause?" 123.

30 Cowdell, *Is Jesus Unique?* 216.

31 Dawes, *Freeing the Faith*, 119.

32 Spong, "Religion as a Human Creation?" 7.

33 Crowder, introduction to *God and Reality*, 10.

Conclusion

1 Cupitt, "Religion as a Human Creation?" quoted in Kettle, "When John Spong Met Don Cupitt," 23–24.

2 Wiles, review of *Mysticism after Modernity*, 392.

3 Cowdell, *Atheist Priest?* 79–81.

4 Cupitt, *Philosophy's Own Religion*, 122 (my italics).

5 Ibid., 125.

6 Boulton, "Reflections," 4.

7 Cowdell, *Atheist Priest?* 84.

8 Cupitt, "Christianity after the Church," 11.

Bibliography

Books

Allison, David B., ed. *The New Nietzsche*. Cambridge, Massachusetts: MIT Press, 1985.

Altizer, Thomas J. J., Max A. Myers, Carl A. Raschke, Robert P. Scharlemann, Mark C. Taylor, and Charles E. Winquist. *Deconstruction and Theology*. New York: Crossroad Publishing, 1982.

Anderson, Walter T., ed. *The Truth about the Truth: De-Confusing and Re-Constructing the Postmodern World*. New York: Penguin Putnam Books, 1995.

Armstrong, Karen. *A History of God*. London: Mandarin, 1994.

———. Don Cupitt, Arthur J. Dewey, Robert W. Funk, et al. *The Once and Future Faith*. Santa Rosa, California: Polebridge Press, 2001.

Basho, Matsuo. *The Narrow Road to the Deep North and Other Travel Sketches*. London: Penguin, 1966.

Bataille, Georges. *Blue of Noon*. Translated by Harry Mathews. London: Marion Boyars, 1986.

———. *Theory of Religion*. Translated by Robert Hurley. New York: Zone Books, 1

Beeson, Trevor. *Rebels and Reformers: Christian Renewal in the Twentieth Century*. London: SCM Press, 1999.

Berkeley, George. *Three Dialogues between Hylas and Philonous*. Edited by Colin M. Turbayne. New York: Bobbs Merrill Company, 1954.

Bowker, John. *Licensed Insanities: Religions and Belief in God in the Contemporary World*. London: Darton, Longman and Todd, 1987.

Braithwaite, R. B. *An Empiricist's View of the Nature of Religious Belief*. Cambridge: Cambridge University Press, 1955.

Brown, David. *Continental Philosophy and Modern Theology: An Engagement*. Oxford: Blackwell, 1987.

Bultmann, Rudolf. *Jesus Christ and Mythology*. New York: Charles Scribner's Sons, 1958.

Cabanne, Pierre. *Van Gogh*. London: Thames and Hudson, 1963.

Campbell, Lorne. *Rogier Van Der Weyden*. London: Harper and Row, 1980.

Caputo, John D. *The Mystical Element in Heidegger's Thought*. Athens, Ohio: Ohio University Press, 1978.

———. *Deconstruction in a Nutshell: A Conversation with Jacques Derrida.* New York: Fordham University Press, 1997.

———. *The Prayers and Tears of Jacques Derrida: Religion without Religion.* Bloomington and Indianapolis: Indiana University Press, 1997.

Carnley, Peter F. *The Structure of Resurrection Belief.* Oxford: Oxford University Press, 1987.

Clements, Keith W. *Lovers of Discord: Twentieth Century Theological Controversies in England.* London: SPCK, 1988.

Cottingham, John. *Descartes.* Oxford: Blackwell, 1986.

Cowdell, Scott. *Atheist Priest?: Don Cupitt and Christianity.* London: SCM Press, 1988.

———. *Is Jesus Unique?: A Study of Recent Christology.* New Jersey: Paulist Press, 1996.

———. *A God for this World.* London: Mowbray, 2000.

Crowder, Colin, ed. *God and Reality: Essays on Christian Non-Realism.* London: Mowbray, 1997.

Cupitt, Don. *Christ and the Hiddenness of God.* London: Lutterworth Press, 1971. 2nd ed. London: SCM Press, 1985.

———. *Crisis of Moral Authority.* London: Lutterworth Press, 1972.

———. *The Leap of Reason.* London: Sheldon Press, 1976. 2nd ed. London: SCM Press, 1985.

———. *Taking Leave of God.* London: SCM Press, 1980.

———. *The World to Come.* London: SCM Press, 1982. Xpress Reprints, London: SCM Press, 1993.

———. *The Sea of Faith.* London: BBC, 1984. 2nd ed. London: SCM Press, 1994.

———. *Only Human.* London: SCM Press, 1985.

———. *Life Lines.* London: SCM Press, 1986.

———. *The Long-Legged Fly: The Theology of Longing and Desire.* London: SCM Press, 1987. Xpress Reprints, London: SCM Press, 1995.

———. *The New Christian Ethics.* London: SCM Press, 1988. Xpress Reprints, London: SCM Press, 1996.

———. *Radicals and the Future of the Church.* London: SCM Press, 1989. Xpress Reprints, London: SCM, 1996.

———. *Creation out of Nothing.* London: SCM Press, 1990.

———. *What Is a Story?* London: SCM Press, 1991.

———. *The Time Being.* London: SCM Press, 1992.

———. *Rethinking Religion.* Wellington: St. Andrew's Trust for the Study of Religion and Society, 1992.

———. *After All: Religion without Alienation.* London: SCM Press, 1994.

———. *The Last Philosophy.* London: SCM Press, 1995.

———. *Solar Ethics.* London: SCM Press, 1995.

———. *After God: The Future of Religion.* London: Weidenfeld and Nicolson, 1997.

———. *Mysticism after Modernity.* Oxford: Blackwell, 1998.

———. *The Religion of Being.* London: SCM Press, 1998.

———. *The Revelation of Being.* London: SCM Press, 1998.

———. *The New Religion of Life in Everyday Speech.* London: SCM Press, 1999.

_____. *The Meaning of It All in Everyday Speech*. London: SCM Press, 1999.

_____. *Kingdom Come in Everyday Speech*. London: SCM Press, 2000.

_____. *Philosophy's Own Religion*. London: SCM Press, 2000.

_____. *Reforming Christianity*. Santa Rosa, California: Polebridge Press, 2001.

_____. *Emptiness and Brightness*. Santa Rosa, California: Polebridge Press, 2001.

_____. *Is Nothing Sacred? The Non-Realist Philosophy of Religion: Selected Essays*. New York: Fordham University Press, 2002.

Dawes, Hugh. *Freeing the Faith: A Credible Christianity for Today*. London: SPCK, 1992.

Dawkins, Richard. *River Out of Eden: A Darwinian View of Life*. London: Phoenix, 1995.

Deleuze, Gilles. *Nietzsche and Philosophy*. Translated by Hugh Tomlinson. New York: Columbia University Press, 1983.

Derrida, Jacques. *Writing and Difference*. Translated by Alan Bass. Chicago: The University of Chicago Press, 1978.

Derrida, Jacques and Gianni Vattimo, eds. *Religion*. Cambridge: Polity Press, 1998.

Edwards, David L. *Tradition and Truth: The Challenge of England's Radical Theologians 1962–1989*. London: Hodder and Stoughton, 1989.

Farias, Victor. *Heidegger and Nazism*. Philadelphia: Temple University Press, 1989.

Feyerabend, Paul. *Against Method: An Outline of an Anarchistic Theory of Knowledge*. London: N.L.B., 1975.

Freeman, Anthony. *God in Us: A Case for Christian Humanism*. London: SCM Press, 1993.

Garvin, Harry R., ed. *Romanticism, Modernism, Postmodernism*. Lewisburg: Bucknell University Press, 1980.

Geering, Lloyd. *God in the New World*. London: Hodder and Stoughton, 1968.

_____. *Faith's New Age: A Perspective on Contemporary Religious Change*. London: Collins, 1980.

_____. *Creating The New Ethic*. Wellington: St. Andrew's Trust for the Study of Religion and Society, 1991.

_____. *Tomorrow's God: How We Create Our Worlds*. Wellington: Bridget Williams Books, 1994.

_____. *Does Society Need Religion?* Wellington: St. Andrew's Trust for the Study of Religion and Society, 1998.

_____. *The World to Come: From Christian Past to Global Future*. Santa Rosa, California: Polebridge Press, 1999.

_____. *Christianity without God*. Santa Rosa, California: Polebridge Press, 2002.

Gill, Carolyn B., ed. *Bataille: Writing the Sacred*. London: Routledge, 1994.

Gillespie, Michael Allen. *Nihilism before Nietzsche*. Chicago: The University of Chicago Press, 1995.

Goodchild, Philip. *Gilles Deleuze and the Question of Philosophy*. Madison: Farleigh Dickenson University Press, 1996.

Goulder, Michael, and John H. Hick. *Why Believe in God?* London: SCM Press, 1983.

Grenz, Stanley J. *A Primer on Postmodernism*. Grand Rapids, Michigan: Eerdmans, 1996.

Guignon, Charles, ed. *The Cambridge Companion to Heidegger*. Cambridge: Cambridge University Press, 1993.

Hamburger, Michael, trans. *The Poems of Paul Celan*. London: Anvil Press, 1988.

Hare, David. *Racing Demon*. Rev. ed. London: Faber and Faber, 1991.

Harries, Richard. *The Real God: A Response to Anthony Freeman's God in Us*. London: Mowbray, 1994.

Harris, Ian. *Creating God, Re-Creating Christ: Re-imagining the Christian Way in a Secular World*. Wellington: St. Andrew's Trust for the Study of Religion and Society, 1999.

Hart, David A. *Faith in Doubt: Non-Realism and Christian Belief*. London: Mowbray, 1993.

———. *One Faith?: Non-Realism and the World of Faiths*. London: Mowbray, 1995.

———. *Linking Up: Christianity and Sexuality*. Hertfordshire: Arthur James, 1997.

———. ed. *Five Years of Making Waves*. Loughborough: Sea of Faith Network U.K., 1994.

Hart, Kevin. *The Trespass of the Sign: Deconstruction, Theology and Philosophy*. Cambridge: Cambridge University Press, 1989.

Hastings, Adrian. *A History of English Christianity: 1920–1990*. 3rd ed. London: SCM Press, 1991

———. *The Shaping of Prophecy: Passion, Perception and Practicality*. London: Chapman, 1995.

Hayman, Ronald. *Nietzsche: A Critical Life*. London: Weidenfeld and Nicolson, 1980.

Hebblethwaite, Brian. *The Ocean of Truth: A Defence of Objective Theism*. Cambridge: Cambridge University Press, 1988.

———. *Ethics and Religion in a Pluralistic Age: Collected Essays*. Edinburgh: T and T Clark, 1997.

Heidegger, Martin. *Basic Writings*. Edited by David F. Krell. London: Routledge and Kegan Paul, 1978.

———. *An Introduction to Metaphysics*. Translated by Ralph Manheim. New Haven: Yale University Press, 1987.

———. *Being and Time*. Translated by John Macquarrie and Edward Robinson. Oxford: Blackwell, 1967.

Hick, John. *Disputed Questions in Theology and the Philosophy of Religion*. New Haven, CT: Yale University Press, 1993.

———, ed. *The Myth of God Incarnate*. London: SCM Press, 1977.

Holloway, Richard. *Dancing on the Edge*. London: Fount, 1997.

———. *Godless Morality: Keeping Religion Out of Ethics*. Edinburgh: Canongate, 1999.

———. *Doubts and Loves: What is Left of Christianity?* Edinburgh: Canongate, 2001.

House, Vaden D. *Without God or His Doubles: Realism, Relativism and Rorty*. New York: E. J. Brill, 1994.

Hume, David. *Dialogues and the Natural History*. Oxford: Oxford University Press (World's Classics), 1993.

Huntington, C. W. Jr. *The Emptiness of Emptiness*. Honolulu: University of Hawaii Press, 1989.

Hyman, Gavin. *The Predicament of Postmodern Theology: Radical Orthodoxy or Nihilist Textualism?* Louisville: Westminster John Knox Press, 2001.

James, Eric. *A Life of Bishop John A. T. Robinson: Scholar, Pastor, Prophet*. London: Collins, 1987.

Jencks, Charles. *What is Post-Modernism?* London: Academy Editions, 1989.

Jenkins, David, and Rebecca Jenkins. *Free to Believe*. London: BBC Books, 1991.

Kaufman, Gordon D. *God — Mystery — Diversity: Christian Theology in a Pluralistic World*. Minneapolis: Fortress Press, 1996.

Kaufmann, Walter. *Nietzsche: Philosopher, Psychologist, Antichrist*. 3rd ed. Princeton: Princeton University Press, 1968.

Kearney, Richard. *Dialogues with Contemporary Continental Thinkers: The Phenomenological Heritage*. Manchester: Manchester University Press, 1984.

Kerr, Fergus. *Theology after Wittgenstein*. Oxford: Blackwell, 1986.

Koelb, Clayton, ed. *Nietzsche as Postmodernist: Essays Pro and Contra*. New York: The State University of New York Press, 1990.

Krell, David F., ed. *Martin Heidegger — Basic Writings*. Rev. ed. San Francisco: HarperSanFrancisco, 1993

Lakeland, Paul. *Postmodernity: Christian Identity in a Fragmented Age*. Minneapolis: Fortress Press, 1997.

Land, Nick. *The Thirst for Annihilation: Georges Bataille and Virulent Nihilism*. London: Routledge, 1992.

Lawson, Hilary. *Closure: a story of everything*. London and New York: Routledge, 2001.

Lecercle, Jean-Jacques. *Philosophy through the Looking Glass*. La Salle, Illinois: Open Court, 1985.

Lindbeck, George A. *The Nature of Doctrine: Religion and Theology in a Postliberal Age*. Philadelphia: The Westminster Press, 1984.

Macquarrie, John. *Heidegger and Christianity*. New York: Continuum Publishing, 1994.

Madison, Gary B., ed. *Working Through Derrida*. Illinois: Northwestern University Press, 1993.

Magnus, Bernd and Kathleen M. Higgins, eds. *The Cambridge Companion to Nietzsche*. Cambridge: Cambridge University Press, 1996.

Malcolm, Norman. *Ludwig Wittgenstein: A Memoir*. Oxford: Oxford University Press, 1966.

———. *Wittgenstein: A Religious Point of View?* Edited by Peter Winch. London: Routledge, 1993.

Mansel, Henry L. *The Limits of Religious Thought Examined*. 1859. Reprint, New York: AMS, 1973.

Mantle, Jonathan. *Archbishop: A Portrait of Robert Runcie*. London: HarperCollins, 1991.

MacDonald Smith, John. *On Doing without God*. Bicester: Emissary Publishing, 1993.

Megill, Allan. *Prophets of Extremity: Nietzsche, Heidegger, Foucault: Derrida*. Berkeley, California: University of California Press, 1985.

Miles, T. R. *Religion and the Scientific Outlook*. London: Macmillan Press, 1969.

———. *Religious Experience*. London: Macmillan Press, 1972.

———. *Speaking of God: Theism, Atheism and the Magnus Image*. York: Sessions of York, 1998.

Milbank, John. *Theology and Social Theory: Beyond Secular Reason*. Oxford: Blackwell, 1990.

Milbank, John, Catherine Pickstock, and Graham Ward, eds. *Radical Orthodoxy: A New Theology*. London: Routledge, 1999.

Monk, Ray. *Ludwig Wittgenstein: The Duty of Genius*. London: Vintage Books, 1991.

Moore, Gareth. *Believing in God: A Philosophical Essay*. Edinburgh: T and T Clark, 1988.

Murdoch, Iris. *Metaphysics as a Guide to Morals*. London: Chatto and Windus, 1992.

———. *The Sovereignty of Good*. London: Routledge and Kegan Paul, 1970.

Murphy, John P. *Pragmatism: from Pierce to Davidson*. Boulder: Westview Press, 1990.

Nietzsche, Friedrich. *The Will to Power*. Translated by R J. Hollingdale and Walter Kaufmann. London: Weidenfeld and Nicolson, 1968.

———. *Thus Spoke Zarathustra: A Book for Everyone and No One*. Translated by R. J. Hollingdale. 1961. Reprint with new introduction, London: Penguin, 1969.

———. *Twilight of the Idols and the Anti-Christ*. Translated by R. J. Hollingdale. 1968. Reprint with a new introduction by Michael Tanner, London: Penguin, 1990.

———. *Ecce Homo: How One Becomes What One Is*. Translated by R. J. Hollingdale. 1979. Reprint with a new introduction by Michael Tanner, London: Penguin, 1992.

Nineham, Dennis E. *Explorations in Theology 1*. London: SCM Press, 1977.

Nishitani Keiji. *Religion and Nothingness*. Translated by Jan Van Bragt. Berkeley and Los Angeles: University of California Press, 1982.

Ott, Hugo. *Martin Heidegger: A Political Life*. Translated by Allan Blunden. London: Fontana Press, 1994.

Pattison, George. *Art, Modernity and Faith: Restoring the Image*. 2nd ed. London: SCM Press, 1998.

———. *Kierkegaard and the Crisis of Faith*. London: SPCK, 1997.

———. *Agnosis: Theology in the Void*. London: Macmillan, 1996.

Patton, Paul, ed. *Deleuze: A Critical Reader*. Oxford: Blackwell, 1996.

Pears, David. *The False Prison: A Study of the Development of Wittgenstein's Philosophy*. Vol. 1. Oxford: Clarendon Press, 1987.

Perloff, Marjorie. *Wittgenstein's Ladder: Poetic Language and the Strangeness of the Ordinary*. Chicago: The University of Chicago Press, 1996.

Phillips, D. Z. *Religion without Explanation*. Oxford: Blackwell, 1976.

————. *Interventions in Ethics*. New York: State University of New York Press, 1992.

————. *Wittgenstein and Religion*. London: Macmillan Press, 1993.

————. *Faith after Foundationalism: Plantinga—Rorty—Lindbeck—Berger: Critiques and Alternatives*. Colorado: Westview Press, 1995.

Plato. *The Republic*. Rev. 2nd ed. Translated by Desmond Lee. London: Penguin, 1974.

Rapaport, Herman. *Heidegger and Derrida: Reflections on Time and Language*. Lincoln: University of Nebraska Press, 1989.

Richardson, Michael. *Georges Bataille*. London: Routledge, 1994.

Robinson, John A. T. *Where Three Ways Meet*. Edited by Eric James. London: SCM Press, 1987.

Rorty, Richard. *Contingency, Irony and Solidarity*. Cambridge: Cambridge University Press, 1989.

Rosen, Stanley. *The Question of Being: A Reversal of Heidegger*. New Haven: Yale University Press, 1993.

Runzo, Joseph, ed. *Is God Real?* New York: St. Martin's Press, 1993.

Sallis, John, ed. *Reading Heidegger: Commemorations*. Bloomington and Indianapolis: Indiana University Press, 1993.

Schacht, Richard. *Making Sense of Nietzsche: Reflections Timely and Untimely*. Urbana and Chicago: University of Illinois Press, 1995.

Scharlemann, Charles E. *Theology at the End of the Century*. Charlottesville: University Press of Virginia, 1990.

Schrift, Alan D. *Nietzsche and the Question of Interpretation: Between Hermeneutics and Deconstruction*. New York: Routledge, 1990.

————. *Nietzsche's French Legacy: Genealogy of Poststructuralism*. New York: Routledge, 1995.

Schutte, Ofelia. *Beyond Nihilism: Nietzsche without Masks*. Chicago: The University of Chicago Press, 1984.

Schweitzer, Albert. *My Life and Thought*. 2nd ed. Translated by C. T. Campion. London: Allen and Unwin, 1958.

Sedgwick, Peter R. *Nietzsche: A Critical Reader*. Oxford: Blackwell, 1995.

Shaw, Graham. *The Cost of Authority*. London: SCM Press, 1983.

————. *God in our Hands*. London: SCM Press, 1987.

Silverman, Hugh. J., ed. *Continental Philosophy 11: Derrida and Deconstruction*. London: Routledge, 1989.

Sluga, Hans, and David G. Stern, eds. *The Cambridge Companion to Wittgenstein*. Cambridge: Cambridge University Press, 1996.

Smith, Wilfred Cantwell. *The Meaning and End of Religion: A New Approach to the Religious Traditions of Mankind*. New York: Mentor, 1964.

Solomon, Robert C., and Kathleen M. Higgins, eds. *Reading Nietzsche*. New York: Oxford University Press, 1988.

Soskice, Janet Martin. *Metaphor and Religious Language*. Oxford: Clarendon Press, 1985.

Spong, John. S. *Why Christianity Must Change or Die: A Bishop Speaks to Believers in Exile*. San Francisco: HarperSanFrancisco, 1998.

Spong, John S. *Here I Stand: My Struggle for a Christianity of Integrity, Love and Equality*. San Francisco: HarperSanFrancisco, 2000.

Spong, John S. *A New Christianity For A New World*. San Francisco: HarperSanFrancisco, 2001.

Stambaugh, Jean. *Impermanence is Buddha Nature: Dogen's Understanding of Temporality*. Honolulu: University of Hawaii, 1990.

Sturrock, John, ed. *Structuralism and Since*. Oxford: Oxford University Press, 1979.

Tanner, Michael. *Nietzsche*. Oxford: OPUS, 1994.

Taylor, Mark C. *Altarity*. Chicago: The University of Chicago Press, 1987.

———. *About Religion: Economies of Faith in Virtual Culture*. Chicago: The University of Chicago Press, 1999.

Thiselton, Anthony C. *Interpreting God and the Postmodern Self: On Meaning, Manipulation and Promise*. Scottish Journal of Theology: Current Issues in Theology. Edinburgh: T and T Clark, 1995.

Thiel, John E. *Nonfoundationalism*. Minneapolis: Fortress Press, 1994.

Vardy, Peter. *The Puzzle of God*. London: Fount, 1995.

Ward, Graham. *Theology and Contemporary Critical Theory*. London: Macmillan Press, 1996.

———, ed. *The Postmodern God: A Theological Reader*. Oxford: Blackwell, 1997.

Ward, Keith. *Holding Fast to God: A Reply to Don Cupitt*. London: SPCK, 1982.

———. *The Turn of the Tide: Christian Belief in Britain Today*. London: BBC Publications, 1986.

Warnock, Mary. *Imagination and Time*. Oxford: Blackwell, 1994.

White, Stephen Ross. *Don Cupitt and the Future of Christian Doctrine*. London: SCM Press, 1994.

Williams, Stephen N. *Revelation and Reconciliation: A Window on Modernity*. Cambridge: Cambridge University Press, 1995.

Wilson, A. N. *God's Funeral*. London: Abacus, 2000.

Wittgenstein, Ludwig. *Tractatus Logico-Philosophicus*. Translated by D. F. Pears and B. F. McGuiness. London: Routledge and Kegan Paul, 1961.

———. *On Certainty*. Translated by Denis Paul and G. E. M. Anscombe. New York: Harper and Row, 1969.

———. *Philosophical Investigations*. Translated by G. E. M. Anscombe. Oxford: Blackwell, 1974.

———. *Culture and Value*. Translated by Peter Winch. Oxford: Blackwell, 1980.

Wolin, Richard, ed. *The Heidegger Controversy: A Critical Reader*. Cambridge, Massachusetts: MIT Press, 1993.

Wright, Dale S. *Philosophical Meditations on Zen Buddhism*. Cambridge: Cambridge University Press, 1998.

Wyer, Robert Van De. *Spinoza in a Nutshell*. London: Hodder and Stoughton, 1998.

Wyschogrod, Edith. *Saints and Postmodernism: Revisioning Moral Philosophy*. Chicago: The University of Chicago Press, 1990.

————. *An Ethics of Remembering: History, Heterology and the Nameless Others*. Chicago: The University of Chicago Press, 1998.

Zeitlin, Irving M. *Nietzsche: A Re-Examination*. Cambridge: Polity Press, 1994.

Articles

Adams, Daniel. "Towards a Theological Understanding of Postmodernism." *Cross Currents* 47, no. 4 (winter 1997). Online. Available: http:// www.aril.org/adams.html. 7 September 1999.

Altizer, Thomas. "Why So Conservative?" Paper presented at Sea of Faith U.K. Conference X, University of Leicester, 1997. Online. Available: http://www.sofn.org.uk/altiz97.html. 24 November 1999.

Brinkman, B. R. "'Outsidelessness' and 'High Noon.'" *The Heythrop Journal* 35, no. 1 (1994): 53–58.

Brummer, Vincent. "Has the Theism-Atheism Debate a Future?" *Theology* 97 (November/December 1994): 426–32.

Cairns, Adrian. "Inconclusions — for the Time Being." *Sea of Faith U.K. Magazine*, no. 33 (summer 1998): 10–11.

Chapman, Mark. D. "Why the Enlightenment Project Doesn't Have to Fail." *The Heythrop Journal* 39, no. 4 (1998): 379–93.

Cheetham, David. "Postmodern Freedom and Religion." *Theology* 103, (January/February 2000): 29–36.

Clack, Beverley. "God and Language: A Feminist Perspective On the Meaning of 'God.'" In *The Nature of Religious Language: A Colloquium*, edited by Stanley E. Porter, 148–158. Sheffield: Sheffield Academic Press, 1996.

Clark, Stephen R. L. Review of *Creation out of Nothing*, by Don Cupitt. *Religious Studies* 27, no. 1 (1991): 559–61.

————. "Cupitt and Divine Imagining." *Modern Theology* 5, no. 1 (1998): 45–60.

Cowdell, Scott. "The Recent Adventures of Don Cupitt." *St. Mark's Review*, no. 134 (winter 1988): 32–35.

————. "Radical Theology, Postmodernity and Christian Life in the Void." *The Heythrop Journal* 32 (1991): 62–71.

————. "All This, and God Too? Postmodern Alternatives to Don Cupitt." *The Heythrop Journal* 33 (1992): 267–82.

Crewdson, Joan. "Faith at Sea? A Critique of Don Cupitt's *After All: Religion Without Alienation*." *Modern Believing* 36, no. 3 (1995): 28–33.

Crowder, Colin. Review of *Atheist Priest?: Don Cupitt and Christianity*, by Scott Cowdell. *Modern Theology* 6, no. 3 (1990): 301–3.

Cupitt, Don. "Mansel's Theory of Regulative Truth." *Journal of Theological Studies* 18 (April 1967): 104–126.

———— "How We Make Moral Decisions" *Theology* 76 (May 1973): 239–50.

————. "God and Morality." *Theology* 76 (July 1973): 356–64.

————. "On the Finality of Christ." In *The Leap of Reason*, 119–31. London: Sheldon Press 1976.

_____. "On Christian Existence in a Pluralist Society." In *The Leap of Reason*, 132–42. London: Sheldon Press, 1976.

_____. "Critical Christian Ethics." In *Explorations in Theology* 6, 87–97. London: SCM Press, 1979.

_____. "The Ethics of This World and the Ethics of the World to Come." In *Explorations in Theology* 6, 98–109. London: SCM Press, 1976.

_____. "Religion and Critical Thinking 2." *Theology* 86 (September, 1983): 328–35.

_____. "*The Sea of Faith*: the Backwash." *The Listener*, 1 November 1984, 24.

_____. "The Anglican Gorbachev." Review of *Robert* Runcie, by Adrian Hastings. *New Statesman and Society*, 25 January 1991, 35–36.

_____. "Dear God." *New Statesman and Society*, 20 December, 1991, 13–14.

_____. "After Liberalism." In *The Weight of Glory: A Vision and Practice for Christian Faith: The Future of Liberal Theology*, edited by D. W. Hardy and P. H. Sedgwick, 251–56. Edinburgh: T and T Clark, 1991.

_____. "Unsystematic Ethics and Politics." In *Shadow of Spirit: Postmodernism and Religion*, edited by Philippa Berry and Andrew Wernick, 149–55. London: Routledge, 1992.

_____. "Nature and Culture." In *Humanity, Environment and God*, edited by Neil Spurway, 33–45. Oxford: Blackwell, 1993.

_____. "Learning to Live with One Foot in the Grave." *The Guardian*, December 1993. Online. Available: http://www.sofn.org.uk/ofigrave.html. 4 September 1999.

_____. Review of *Kierkegaard and Modern Continental Philosophy: An Introduction*, by Michael Weston. *Religious Studies* 30, no. 4 (1994): 529–30.

_____. "All You Really Need Is Love." *The Guardian*, December 1994. Online. Available: http: www.sofn.org.uk/aynil.html. 4 September 1999.

_____. "Matters Eternal," *Financial Times*, 22/23 June 1996. Online. Available: http://www.sofn.org.uk/purity.html. 2 March 2000.

_____. "Friends, Faith and Humanism." *Sea of Faith (U.K.) Magazine*, no. 29 (summer 1997): 15–16.

_____. "My Postmodern Witch." *Modern Believing* 39, 4 (1998), 5–10.

_____. "Post-Christianity." In *Religion, Modernity and Postmodernity*, edited by Paul Heelas, 218–32. Oxford: Blackwell, 1998.

_____. "Magnus the Mastermind." *Sea of Faith (U.K.) Magazine*, no. 33 (summer 1998): 9.

_____. "A Democratic Philosophy of Life." Online. Available: http://www.sofn.org.uk.cuplist.html. 12 May 1999.

_____. "Religious and Non-Religious Humanism." Paper presented at the Sea of Faith U.K. Conference 1V, University of Leicester, 1991. Reprinted in *New Humanist* 106, no. 3 (September 1991): 11–12.

_____. "A Kingdom-Theology." Paper presented at the Sea of Faith Conference, New Zealand, 1994. Online. Available: http://www.geocities.com /Athens/Marble/1826/dckingdm.html. 29 March 2000.

———. "Our Dual Agenda." Paper presented at the Sea of Faith U.K. Conference V11, University of Leicester, 1994. Online. Available: http://www.sofn.org.uk/dcdual.html. 12 February 2000.

———. "World Religion." Paper presented at the Sea of Faith U.K. Conference 1X, University of Leicester, 1996.

———. "From Religious Doctrine to Religious Experience." Paper presented at the Sea of Faith U.K. Conference X, University of Leicester, 1997.

———. "Spirituality, Old and New." Paper presented at the Sea of Faith U.K. Conference X1, University of Sheffield, 1998.

———. "The Radical Christian World-View." Paper presented at the Sea of Faith U.K. Conference X11, University of Leicester, 1999.

——— "Saturday night fervour." *The Guardian* ("Face to Faith" series), April 3, 1999.

———. "Christianity after the Church." Paper presented at the Sea of Faith U.K. Conference X111, University of Leicester, 2000.

——— "Beyond Belief." Paper presented at the Sea of Faith in Australia Conference, Brisbane, October 2000.

——— "Fear of ideas: The decline of Anglicanism." *The Guardian* ("Face to Faith" series), Saturday July 7, 2001.

———. "Comparative Religions." *The Guardian* ("Face to Faith" series), Saturday 27th October, 2001.

———. "The Simpsons in search of Jesus." *The Guardian* ("Face to Faith" series), February 24, 2001.

———. "An Apologia for my thinking." Paper presented at the multi-faith centre at the University of Derby, 11th May 2002.

Dyson, Anthony. Review of *The New Christian Ethics*, by Don Cupitt. *Theology* 92 (September 1989): 538–39.

Evans, Stephen C. "Realism and Anti-Realism in Kierkegaard's Concluding Unscientific Postscript." In *The Cambridge Companion to Kierkegaard*, edited by Alistair Hannay and Gordon D. Marino, 154–76. Cambridge: Cambridge University Press, 1998.

Gaskin, J. C. A. "Absolute Relativism." *The Expository Times* 104 (October 1992 — September 1993): 191.

Griffiths, Leslie. "Cupitt: Serious Thinker or Practical Joker?" *Sea of Faith (U.K.) Magazine*, no. 38 (autumn 1999): 19.

Hampson, Daphne. Review of *The Religion of Being*, by Don Cupitt. *Theology* 102 (March/April, 1999): 131–32.

Hart, David A. "On Not Quite Taking Leave of Don." *Modern Believing* 35, no. 4 (1994): 6–9.

———. Review of *Solar Ethics*, by Don Cupitt. Online. Available: http://www.sofn.org.uk/solar.html. 20 August 1999.

Hart, Kevin. "Nietzsche, Derrida and Deconstructing the True Gospel." *Zadok Perspectives*, no. 60 (autumn 1998): 8–11.

Hey, John. Review of *Solar Ethics*, by Don Cupitt. *Theology* 99 (September/October 1996): 394.

Hollywood, Amy. "'Beautiful as a Wasp': Angela of Foligno and Georges Bataille." *Harvard Theological Review* 92 no. 2 (April 1999): 219–36.

Hyman, Gavin. "Towards a New Religious Dialogue: Buddhism and Postmodern Theology." *The Heythrop Journal* 39, no. 4 (October 1998): 394–413.

———. 'D. Z. Phillips: The Elusive Philosopher.' *Theology*, 102 (July/August 1999): 271–78.

James, Eric. Review of *Taking Leave of God*, by Don Cupitt. *The Times*, 10 February 1981, 10.

Jenkins, David. Review of *Radicals and the Future of the Church*, by Don Cupitt. *Theology* 94 (January/February 1991): 60–61.

Jones, Richard. Review of *The New Christian Ethics*, by Don Cupitt. *The Expository Times* 100 (October 1988–September 1989): 306–7.

Leaves, Nigel. "Be(com)ing an atheist country? Pastoral and theological implications from an Australian perspective *after* Don Cupitt." *Colloquium: The Australian and New Zealand Theological Review*, Volume 31 No. 1 (May 1999), 21–30.

Mark, James. Review of *Taking Leave of God*, by Don Cupitt. *Theology* 84 (May 1981): 211–13.

Mullen, Peter. "Serial Theology." *Theology* 86 (January 1983): 25–29.

Myerson, George. "The Philosopher's Stone: A Response to Don Cupitt." *History of the Human Sciences* 11, no. 3 (1998): 131–36.

Nineham, Dennis. "In Praise of Solar Living." Review of *After God*, by Don Cupitt. *Times Literary Supplement*, 26 December 1997, 5.

Nolan, Steve. Review of *The Religion of Being*, by Don Cupitt. *Reviews on Religion and Theology* 4, no. 4 (1998): 51–54.

Olds, Mason. "Don Cupitt's Ethics." *Religious Humanism* 28, no.2 (spring 1994): 73–85.

Paterson, Torquil. "Why I Resigned." Unpublished Paper.

Pattison, George. "Editorial: *The Sea of Faith* — Ten Years After." *Modern Believing* 35, no. 4 (1994): 2–5.

Pearse, Ronald. "How Myth Could Enrich the Spirit," *The Times* (London), 23 February 1985.

Phillips, D. Z. "Theological Castles and the Elusiveness of Philosophy — A Reply." *Theology* 102 (November/December1999): 436–41.

Pickstone, Charles. "We Are Grateful to Don Cupitt: Don Cupitt on Art." *Modern Believing* 35, no. 4 (1994): 10–17.

Runzo, Joseph. "Ethics and the Challenge of Theological Non-Realism." In *Ethics, Religion, and the Good Society*, edited by Joseph Runzo, 72–91. Kentucky: Westminster/John Knox Press, 1992.

Russell, Brian. "With Respect to Don Cupitt." *Theology* 88 (January 1985): 5–11.

Schacht, Richard. "After Transcendence: The Death of God and the Future of Religion." In *Religion without Transcendence?* edited by D. Phillips and Timothy Tessin, 73–92. London: Macmillan Press, 1997.

Shakespeare, Steven. "The New Romantics: A Critique of Radical Orthodoxy." *Theology* 103 (May/June 2000): 163–77.

Sheehan, Thomas. "Heidegger and the Nazis." *The New York Review of Books*, 16 June 1988, 38–47.

———. "A Normal Nazi." *The New York Review of Books*, 14 January 1993, 30–35.

Spearritt, Gregory. "Christianity: From Modernism to Postmodernism." *Colloquium* 24, no. 2 (1992): 67–81.

———. "Don Cupitt: Christian Buddhist?" *Journal of Religious Studies* 31 (1995): 359–73.

———. Review of *The New Religion of Life in Everyday Speech*, by Don Cupitt. *Sea of Faith in Australia Bulletin*, May 1999, 7.

Sutherland, Stewart. "En route for the Ineffable." *The Times Literary Supplement*, 28th May, 1982, 574.

Tarbox J. Jr., Everett. "The A/Theology of Don Cupitt: A Theological Option in Our Post-Modern Age." *Religious Humanism* 35, no. 2 (spring 1991): 72–82.

———. "Beyond Postmodern: Don Cupitt's Theology of Expressionism." *Religious Humanism* 28, no. 2 (spring 1994): 55–72.

Turner, Denys. "De-Centring Theology." *Modern Theology* 2, no. 2 (1986): 125–43.

Ward, Graham. Review of *The Last Philosophy*, by Don Cupitt. *Theology* 98 (November/December 1995): 477–78.

———. "Theology and Postmodernism." *Theology* 100 (November/December 1997): 435–40.

Wiles, Maurice. Review of *Mysticism after Modernity*, by Don Cupitt. *Theology* 101 (September/October 1998): 392–93.

Wilson, Kenneth. Review of *The Revelation of Being*, by Don Cupitt. *Reviews in Religion and Theology* 3, no. 3 (1999): 328–30.

Williams, Rowan. "Religious Realism: On Not Quite Agreeing with Don Cupitt." *Modern Theology* 1, no. 1 (1984): 3–24.

Wyschogrod, Edith, and Caputo, John D. "Postmodernism and the Desire for God: An E-Mail Exchange." *Cross Currents* 48, no. 3 (fall 1998). Online. Available: http://www.crosscurrents.org/caputo.html. 7 September 1999.

Yam, Philip. "Exploiting Zero-Point Energy." *Scientific American* 277, no. 6 (1997): 82–85.

York, Anne. "Wittgenstein's Later Mysticism." *Theology* 100 (September/October 1997): 352–63.

Dissertation and Radio Talks/Interviews

Cupitt, Don. "Faith in Future." Lent Talk, BBC Radio 4, April 2000.

Cupitt, Don. Interview by Rachael Kohn. *Post-Millennial Prophets: The Spirit of Things*. ABC Radio, 16 May 1999.

Vitalis, Hugo. "The Sea of Faith Network (NZ): A Non-Realist Alternative to Christian Realism." Master's Thesis: Victoria University, Wellington, New Zealand, 1994.

Index

194   **Index**